Praise for Leonard Sax's
The Collapse of Parenting

"One of the premier experts on parenting, Dr. Leonard Sax brilliantly articulates the problems parents experience with their children, then gives solutions. *The Collapse of Parenting* is academic but practical, simple but deep. If you have time to read only one book this year, *read this one*."

—MEG MEEKER, MD, BESTSELLING AUTHOR OF *STRONG FATHERS, STRONG DAUGHTERS* AND *STRONG MOTHERS, STRONG SONS*

"The family unit is in unprecedented decline and under assault from a wide variety of cultural forces. With years of experience and research working directly with parents and children, Dr. Leonard Sax provides an important glimpse into parenting in modern times, where it's gone wrong, and how to fix it. Being a parent has never been more important and Dr. Sax explains how to avoid parenting pitfalls and raise your children well."

—DR. BILL BENNETT,
FORMER UNITED STATES SECRETARY OF EDUCATION

"If you're going to read one book on parenting this year, make it *The Collapse of Parenting* by Leonard Sax. What makes a good nonfiction instructional book is an author who has extensive real-world experience in the subject matter and who has the ability to write clearly. Leonard Sax has both. . . . This is quite simply a good book that is easily read and will provide sound advice for giving our children the best chance to succeed in life."

—*NEW YORK JOURNAL OF BOOKS*

"Based on years of extensive clinical practice and interviews with students and parents internationally, Sax presents a sobering and alarming picture of the collapse of parenting in this country. But he does not leave the reader without hope; he offers simple, if not easy solutions, giving parents an accessible guide to help them regain their rightful roles."

—DR. NANCY KEHOE, ASSISTANT CLINICAL PROFESSOR OF
PSYCHOLOGY AT HARVARD MEDICAL SCHOOL, AND AUTHOR OF
WRESTLING WITH OUR INNER ANGELS: FAITH, MENTAL ILLNESS
AND THE JOURNEY TO WHOLENESS

"It is time for us to get real as a society. Dr. Leonard Sax has issued both a warning and an encouragement for parents to take up their proper roles in leading their children to a truly mature adulthood. His book is a highly readable and well-informed challenge for us."

—DR. TIMOTHY WRIGHT, HEADMASTER, SHORE SCHOOL,
SYDNEY, AUSTRALIA

"There are many 'holy' trinities, but in educational terms, one of them is definitely the relationship between parents, children, and schools. I certainly will be recommending this book to the parents of my school. It does not preach; it cajoles, encourages, guides, and helps. It allows one to stand back and step back on one of the most important aspects of life—looking after our youngsters."

—ANDREW HUNTER, HEADMASTER,
MERCHISTON CASTLE SCHOOL, SCOTLAND

"A comprehensive breakdown of where parents have gone awry and how they can get back on track to teach virtue and character to their children. . . . Sax provides a series of easy-to-follow solutions that help bring parents and children back to the same page, working toward a healthier, more respectful, and conscientious attitude. . . . With the author's solid advice, parents have a good shot at achieving these goals."

—*KIRKUS*

"*The Collapse of Parenting* is one of the best books I've ever read on the subject of raising children. It's not written from a religious perspective, but it's chock-full of information every parent should have."

—*NATIONAL CATHOLIC REGISTER*

"[Sax's] guidelines are clear and well-supported."

—*BOOKLIST*

"*The Collapse of Parenting* may sound like a lone voice in the world of American parenting these days, but it's a desperately needed one. . . . If you're going to read a single parenting book this year, please make it this one."

—*TREEHUGGER.COM*

"Dear Dr. Sax, thank you so much for your brilliant book. Two days ago I was on the phone with a friend. She was distraught because that morning she and her husband asked their ten-year-old son to shovel [the snow off] the walk. From the couch not ten feet away, he texted to her, 'I think it is rude that you ask me to shovel the walk when all you do is slouch around.' I asked her where her son could have learned to say such a thing. She was at a loss. Later that day I heard an interview with you on NPR and I immediately downloaded an audio version of your book. Listening to it was like having all my parenting instincts affirmed. I kept saying, 'Yes! Yes!

Yes!' I know your book is a tough sell in this town that is rife with permissive parenting, but I am recommending it to everyone I know. I will use your book as a shield when people ask me why we don't have a PS4 or a Gameboy, why our kids (nine and ten) don't have a Facebook account, etcetera. I hope your book marks a sea change in parenting. It's high time."

—VIVIENNE PALMER, BOULDER, COLORADO

"Dear Dr. Sax, I want to thank you so much for validating with experience and research what has always seemed like common-sense parenting to me and my husband. I know we are not perfect parents, but we are those parents about whom people whisper one minute and then tell us the next, 'You don't understand how lucky you are that you have such good kids.' They never connect the dots between our authoritative parenting, of which they disapprove, and the resultant respectfulness of our children, of which they are envious. Incidentally, we have six children, three biological and three adopted, so their respectfulness can't be pinned on biology. We aren't perfect parents. Our kids aren't perfect kids. But they are good kids, and we have been parenting, to the best of our abilities in the manner you prescribe for eighteen years now. Thank you for helping me to feel a little less alone as I navigate parenthood in this culture of disrespect. May *The Collapse of Parenting* reach a vast audience and help effect true cultural change."

—ELAINE BOURRET, SUBURBAN DETROIT, MICHIGAN

"I just wanted you to know that this is one of the best books about TEACHING that I have ever read. I LOVED IT! Perhaps it is confirmation bias on my part, but you expressed everything I have learned about good teaching over the past twenty-six years. I have recommended your book to all of my colleagues and during my recent parent interviews I had your book sitting at the table and recommended it to all the parents with whom I met. I am not a parent, but you can bet that your book has made me a better teacher. "

—ANDREA VAN SLYKE, TORONTO, CANADA

"Dear Dr. Sax, It is unusual for me to read a book in one sitting, especially a book on parenting, but I could not put down *The Collapse of Parenting*. Please know this book will be talked about, studied, recommended (maybe as a requirement of attendance!), and referenced in newsletters for many years to come. Brilliant! Thank you for writing it."

—LLEANNA MCREYNOLDS, HEAD OF SCHOOL,
RAINTREE MONTESSORI SCHOOL, LAWRENCE, KANSAS

"In *The Collapse of Parenting*, Leonard Sax identifies and addresses children's social, educational, and behavioral issues and connects these factors back to the home. The emphasis of this book is not putting blame on parents. The focus is on explaining how this situation developed, and suggesting what can be done about it. This book is the first book I have come across that makes sense of what caused the shift in education, why current efforts aren't achieving desired outcomes, and what the family unit has to do with all of it."

—SUSAN DEIERLEIN, PhD, LAPEER COUNTY, MICHIGAN

"Whenever parents ask me for the 'secret' to raising my three hard-working, thoughtful, polite boys, I tell them, 'No secret!' and then I hand them a copy of *The Collapse of Parenting*. I am the manager of a homeschooling co-op that serves over 35 families, and I can tell you that this eye-opening book has singlehandedly changed the way most of our parents are raising their children. We've seen only positive changes as a result!

—HINA KHAN-MUKHTAR, SAN RAMON, CALIFORNIA

"As a school principal, I have observed firsthand the 'culture of disrespect' which Dr. Sax describes so accurately in his book. While designed primarily as a guide for parents, the book provides concrete examples that school leaders and teachers can use to encourage character building in children. Clear, insightful research and practical solutions make it an excellent resource for any school or classroom."

—SARAH BLAIR, PRINCIPAL,
PINE CREEK COLONY SCHOOL, AUSTIN, MANITOBA

The Collapse of Parenting

Also by Leonard Sax:

Girls on the Edge

Boys Adrift

Why Gender Matters

The Collapse of Parenting

How We Hurt Our Kids When
We Treat Them Like Grown-Ups

Leonard Sax, M.D., Ph.D.

BASIC BOOKS
New York

Hardcover first published in 2016 by Basic Books
Paperback first published in 2017 by Basic Books,
an imprint of Perseus Books, LLC,
a subsidiary of Hachette Book Group, Inc.

Books published by Basic Books are available at special discounts for
bulk purchases in the United States by corporations, institutions, and
other organizations. For more information, please contact the Special Markets
Department at Perseus Books, 2300 Chestnut Street,
Suite 200, Philadelphia, PA 19103, or call (800) 810-4145, ext. 5000,
or e-mail special.markets@perseusbooks.com.

Book design by Cynthia Young

The Library of Congress has catalogued the hardcover as follows:
Sax, Leonard.
The collapse of parenting : how we hurt our kids when we treat
them like grown-ups / Leonard Sax.
Description: New York: Basic Books, 2015
Includes bibliographical references and index.
Identifiers: LCCN 2015036659 |
ISBN 978-0-465-04897-7 (hardcover : alk. paper) |
ISBN 978-0-465-07384-9 (e-book)
Subjects: Parenting. | Parent and child. | Children and adults.
LCC HQ755.8.S298 2015 | DDC 306.874—dc23
LC record available at http://lccn.loc.gov/2015036659

ISBN: 978-0-465-09428-8 (paperback)

LSC - C
10 9 8 7 6 5

Dedicated to my wife, Katie,
and my daughter, Sarah

Contents

PART ONE
Problems

Introduction:
Parents Adrift

I knew what I wanted to say. But I didn't say it.

Al and Mary McMaster* have two daughters, Tara and Margo. Mom brought 14-year-old Tara in to see me. Mom was concerned about an irritated rash at both corners of Tara's mouth. "I've tried some over-the-counter creams, but nothing has worked," mom said. "What do you think it is?"

After examining the rash, I answered, "This rash sometimes can be a sign of vitamin deficiency. I see this rash frequently in people who aren't eating cruciferous vegetables, such as broccoli, Brussels sprouts, cabbage, and cauliflower, or green leafy vegetables such as spinach and kale. How good is Tara at eating those vegetables?"

Tara snorted. Mom sighed. "Her father and I eat very healthy," mom said. "But Tara refuses to eat most vegetables. To be honest,

*All names have been changed, except where noted.

3

right now pretty much the only things she will eat are French fries—"

"*McDonald's* French fries," Tara interrupted.

"McDonald's French fries, pizza, chicken nuggets, and potato chips," mom finished. "That's pretty much it right now, except for frozen desserts like Italian ices and ice cream."

"How about broccoli or cauliflower? Or spinach?" I asked.

"She just won't eat those things," Mary said.

She would if she were hungry enough, I thought to myself. But I didn't say it.

Jim and Tammy Bardus have one child, Kimberly, 8 years old. After carefully researching the local public schools, Jim and Tammy were concerned about what they considered an overemphasis on basic skills, such as reading and writing, and the elimination of what the public schools now call "enrichment" programs, art and music in particular. Those programs had been cut because of shortfalls in the district's budget. So Jim and Tammy decided to enroll Kimberly in a private school, even though it wouldn't be easy for them financially.

Tammy took Kimberly to visit four different schools. Tammy and Jim both liked school X: the atmosphere was warm and nurturing, the teachers were enthusiastic, and the long-term outcomes of the students were well documented. But Kimberly liked school Y. On her visit to school Y, Kimberly had clicked with the student escort, a 9-year-old named Madison. Madison and Kimberly discovered that they both liked the Ramona and Beezus books by Beverly Cleary, and they both liked American Girl dolls. But the parents were concerned about the dilapidated condition of the school, the lack of enthusiasm on the part of the teachers and administrators, and the school's refusal to disclose where graduates of the school (a K–8 school) went to high school. Tammy and Jim advised their daughter to attend school X. But Kimberly insisted on school Y. And that's the school where she is now enrolled.

When I asked Tammy why she and her husband allowed their 8-year-old daughter to have the final say, Tammy answered, "I think good parenting means letting kids decide. That's how kids learn, right? If I make all the decisions for her, how will she ever learn to decide on her own? And if I force her to go to a school that wasn't her first choice, what can I say if she complains about the school later?"

Forty years ago, most parents who sent their kids to private schools didn't ask their child which school the child preferred. Forty years ago, the parents made that decision, often overruling their child's preference. Even 30 years ago, when I graduated from medical school, it would have been unusual for parents to let an 8-year-old have the final say in the choice of school. Today it is common.

I'm not suggesting that the 1970s or the 1980s were better than our own era. Every era has its shortcomings. But I don't think we are facing up to ours.

My friend Janet Phillips and her late husband, Bill Phillips, (their true names) raised four sons. When the boys were in high school, Janet and Bill became concerned about stories they were hearing about kids drinking. Then they saw it for themselves: high school kids who were clearly drunk but who were nevertheless getting behind the wheel of a car. What to do?

Bill bought a Breathalyzer. The next time there was a party at their house, Bill saw a boy who appeared to be drunk. Bill told the boy, "Come with me." He handed the boy the Breathalyzer and told him to blow into the device. Sure enough, the boy was drunk. Janet called the boy's parents and asked them to take their intoxicated son home. To the surprise of both Bill and Janet, the boy's parents were offended by the phone call. The boy's mother did take her son home, without a word of thanks to either Janet or Bill.

Other parents did not receive Janet and Bill's Breathalyzer strategy enthusiastically either. One parent, Ms. Stoltz, gave Janet a piece of her mind. "Kids these days are going to drink, whether you like it or not," Ms. Stoltz said. "I think our job is to teach them to drink responsibly."

"At 15 years of age?" Janet asked.

"At whatever age. I'd rather have them drink in my own home than hide their drinking from me."

Several days later, Janet happened to be standing just a few feet away when Ms. Stoltz picked up her youngest son, about 12 years old, from school. The boy climbed into the back seat of the car. Ms. Stoltz turned around and asked him, "How was your day?"

Her son said to her, "Turn around. Shut up. Drive."

Ms. Stoltz glanced at Janet and drove away without saying a word.

As near as Janet can recall, she and her husband actually used the Breathalyzer only twice. But they always kept it in full view, where every kid could see it, whenever any of their teenage sons had a party. Their home became known as the home where "those crazy parents will use a Breathalyzer on you." And that had consequences.

Some of the consequences were predictable, and some perhaps were not. The four sons were popular, so their house was a favorite hangout—*early* in the evening. Then, around 9:30 p.m., a certain contingent would leave to go to other parties where alcohol would be freely available. But other kids would stay.

And sometimes still other kids would arrive. That's what was unexpected. Not all teenage kids like to get drunk. Some do not. But in contemporary American culture, it's hard for a teen to "just say no" without looking uncool. An excuse is helpful. A girl or boy could say, when offered a drink, "Hey, I'd love to, but I'm on my way to the Phillips' house and you know their crazy dad—he's the one with the Breathalyzer." And that provides a respectable excuse not to drink.

Here's what's weird. We parents are spending more and more time and money on parenting, but when you look at the results, things are getting worse, not better. American kids are now much more likely to be diagnosed with ADHD or bipolar disorder or other psychiatric disorders than they were 25 years ago (I will present that evidence in Chapter 3), and they are heavier and less fit than they were 25 years ago (Chapter 2). Long-term outcome studies suggest that American kids are now less resilient and more fragile than they used to be. In Chapter 5, I will explain what I mean by "more fragile" and I will present the evidence supporting that claim as well.

What's going on?

Here's my diagnosis. Over the past three decades, there has been a massive transfer of authority from parents to kids. Along with that transfer of authority has come a change in the valuation of kids' opinions and preferences. In many families, what kids think and what kids like and what kids want now matters as much, or more, than what their parents think and like and want. "Let kids decide" has become a mantra of good parenting. As I will show, these well-intentioned changes have been profoundly harmful to kids.

The first half of this book poses the problems. The second half provides the solutions. I think I have figured out where we have gone wrong and how to fix it. My prescription is based primarily on what I have seen in the office over the past quarter century, but also draws on what I have learned from my conversations with parents, teachers, and kids both within and outside the United States.

You may be wondering, *Who is this Leonard Sax guy and what makes him the expert?* It's a fair question. I am a family physician, board certified in family medicine, currently in practice in Chester County, Pennsylvania. I also have a PhD in psychology. I grew up in the suburbs of Cleveland, Ohio, where I attended public schools from kindergarten through grade 12. I earned my undergraduate degree in biology at MIT in Cambridge, Massachusetts. I earned both my MD and my PhD at the University of Pennsylvania. After doing a three-year residency in family medicine, I practiced for 19 years in the Maryland suburbs of Washington, DC. I then relocated to Pennsylvania. My primary sources for this book are the more than 90,000 office visits I have conducted in my role as a practicing physician between 1989 and today. I have seen children, teenagers, and their parents, from a wide variety of backgrounds and circumstances. I have seen, from the intimate yet objective perspective of the family physician, the profound changes in American life over the past quarter century. I have witnessed firsthand the collapse of parenting.

In 2001, I began visiting schools and communities—first across the United States and then in Australia, Canada, England,

Germany, Italy, Mexico, New Zealand, Scotland, Spain, and Switzerland—meeting with teachers and parents, talking with children and teenagers, and comparing notes with professors.[1] I published three books for parents, sharing what I was learning: *Why Gender Matters* (2005), *Boys Adrift* (2007), and *Girls on the Edge* (2010). The success of those books led to more invitations to visit schools and communities. From July 2008 through June 2013, I took an extended leave from medical practice in order to devote myself full-time to these visits. I have now visited more than 380 venues across North America and around the world, meeting with students, teachers, and/or parents face-to-face.

In my earlier books I focused on gender issues, which I still think are important. What a girl needs in order to become a successful and fulfilled woman may sometimes differ from what a boy needs in order to become a successful and fulfilled man. But the issues I explore in this book transcend gender differences.

In this book, I will share with you what I have learned about the collapse of parenting over the past 30 years. Like any competent physician, I will first review the evidence. Then I will explain my diagnosis and I will prescribe a treatment. The treatment will be something—three things, in fact—that you can do starting today, in your home, without spending any money, that will improve the odds of a good outcome for your child.

And I will share success stories. We will hear more about Janet Phillips and her four sons and other families like hers: families who have achieved good outcomes, despite the odds. These stories, supplemented by recent scholarly research, will provide the basis for the three things you must do if you're going to raise a healthy child in the modern world—healthy not only physically but also emotionally and of good character, honest and conscientious. It's still possible to raise a healthy child. It is not easy, but it can be done.

Some aspects of the collapse of parenting are just as problematic in England and Australia as they are in the United States. In every country I have visited, I have found parents who are unsure about their role. They ask, "Should I be my child's most trusted confidante? My child's best friend? But if I am my son's best friend, how can I tell him that he is not allowed to play violent video games?" Dr. Timothy Wright is headmaster of Shore, a private school I visited in Sydney, Australia. He recently told me how a parent asked him to counsel her son about the appropriate use of video games: which games are OK to play, which games are not, and how much time he should spend playing. Gently but firmly, Dr. Wright refused. He explained that the job of guiding and governing a boy's use of video games is the job of the parent, not the job of a school administrator.

So some aspects of this problem are found worldwide. But other aspects of the collapse of parenting are peculiar to North America and especially to the United States. Chief among these is the culture of disrespect.

I

The Culture of Disrespect

What is childhood for?

Let's define *childhood* as the interval between weaning and sexual maturity. In most species, the object of the game is to zip through childhood as quickly as possible in order to start reproducing as soon as possible. Baby rabbits can be weaned at 2 months of age or sooner.[1] Four months later, when the bunnies are 6 months old, they are ready to start making babies of their own.[2] So the interval between weaning and sexual maturity in rabbits is about 4 months. Rabbits live to be 4 years or older, so they typically spend less than one-tenth of their lives in childhood.[3]

Horses next. Foals are usually weaned from the mare around 6 months of age. Most fillies reach sexual maturity—are capable of becoming pregnant—by 18 months. So horses have a "childhood," or juvenile period, of about 12 months. But the 18-month-old horse is not full-grown. When biologists or veterinarians talk about *adolescence*, they are referring to the interval between the onset of sexual maturity and the achievement of completely mature, adult status. Horses are full-grown by 4 years of age. That means a horse is an adolescent for about 2½ years: the difference between 18 months and 4 years.[4] The 6-month-old bunny, by contrast, is already a full-grown adult. There's no such thing as a teenage rabbit.

The average lifespan of a horse is 25 to 33 years.[5] So a horse spends about 4 percent of its life in childhood and up to 10 percent of its life in adolescence.

Most human babies are weaned from the breast by 1 year of age, often earlier.[6] The age of menarche—the age at which girls can become pregnant—now averages around 12 years.[7] Most boys nowadays are sexually mature around 13 years of age. In humans, then, childhood now lasts about 11 years for girls and 12 years for boys. Two centuries ago, girls reached sexual maturity around 16 years of age; the age of menarche is still around 15 or 16 for girls living in hunter-gatherer communities under primitive conditions.[8] Life expectancy for humans in developed countries has increased substantially over the past two centuries. In 1820, life expectancy in the United States was 39 years. So, two centuries ago, a girl was a child until 16 years of age but had a total life expectancy of only 39 years.[9] Today, the average life expectancy at birth in the United States is 78 years, but childhood has *shortened*—although the proportion of life that humans spend in childhood, at roughly 15 percent, is still longer than for any other species.[10] And that doesn't include adolescence.

Adolescence, as I said, is the time between the onset of sexual maturity—the ability to bear or father a child—and the achievement of full maturity. We can think about maturity not only in terms of physical development but also brain development and in terms of mental and emotional maturity. Girls reach full maturity in terms of brain development by about 22 years of age; boys not until about 25 years.[11] If we define an adult woman as a female over 22 and an adult man as a male over 25, then *adolescence* lasts roughly 10 years for girls (from age 12 to age 22) and 12 years for boys (from ages 13 to 25).[12] No matter how you calculate the exact intervals, both childhood and adolescence are longer in humans than in any other mammal, both in absolute duration and in proportion to the lifespan.[13]

What's the point? Why are we humans so different from other animals?

The answer is *culture*. When anthropologists use the term "culture," they are referring to the collection of practices and customs which are characteristic of individuals in one community but which are not shared by individuals of the same species who live in another community. They also mean that the differences between the two communities are not genetically programmed. Children and adolescents learn these customs and practices either by watching the adults or by receiving active instruction from the adults.[14]

Biologists and anthropologists are still arguing about whether any animals other than humans truly exhibit "culture":[15] consistent variations that distinguish one community from the next, that are sustained across generations, and that do not appear to be genetically programmed. There is now fairly good evidence that chimpanzees in the wild do have culture, defined this way. Chimpanzees in the Kibale rainforest of Uganda often use sticks to get food, while those in the Budongo rainforest rarely use sticks, although sticks are just as readily available in the Budongo as in the Kibale. The Budongo chimps prefer to use their fingers. These differences between the two neighboring groups of wild chimpanzees occupying similar habitats appear to be learned, not innate.[16] The two groups have different table manners, if you like.[17]

Using sticks to get food, instead of eating with your fingers, is a relatively small difference. In our species, cultural variation explodes to a degree which has no analogue in any other animal. Imagine a child raised in Kyoto, Japan. Contrast that child with one raised in Appenzell, Switzerland. The two children speak different languages. They observe different rules of behavior, both with their same-age peers and with their parents. They eat different foods, and they eat them differently (using chopsticks versus a fork, knife, and spoon). The Swiss child may learn about the making of the local Appenzeller cheese and, by age 12, might be able to perform some of the tasks of the cheese maker. The Japanese child raised in Kyoto knows nothing of cheese manufacture but may know something about the protocol of tea ceremony.

These differences are not genetically programmed. They are specific to the culture. Suppose the Japanese child and the Swiss child were switched at birth, with the Swiss child raised in Kyoto and the Japanese child raised in Appenzell. The experience of adoptive parents teaches us that the Japanese child will speak *Schwyzertüütsch* (Swiss German) as flawlessly, and will master that culture with the same ease, as any other child raised in Appenzell; likewise, the Swiss child raised in Kyoto will speak Japanese as well, and be as culturally proficient, as any child born and raised in Kyoto.

Scholars generally agree that the purpose of our species' prolonged childhood and adolescence is *enculturation*:[18] the process of acquiring all the skills and knowledge and mastering all the customs and behaviors required for competency in the culture in which you live. It takes years to master the details of Japanese language, culture, and behavior; the same is true of Swiss language, culture, and behavior. If you or I were to move to Kyoto or to Appenzell as adults, we might struggle for the rest of our lives to master the intricacies of the language, the local arts, the local *culture*. We would likely always feel like outsiders, even if we did manage to master at least the language after 20 years or so.

But we are adults. The adult brain is harder to change in any fundamental way, compared with the brain of the child or the adolescent. There has been much buzz in recent years about "neuroplasticity," the ability of the adult human brain to change.[19] It's true that the adult human brain is not fixed in concrete. But it's also true that the adult human brain is much harder to alter than that of the child or the adolescent. Once a young woman is 22 years of age, once a young man is 25, it becomes harder to master fully a new language, a new culture, a new life.[20]

What does it mean to learn a culture? It's more than learning a particular trade or profession, or a language, or a cuisine. It means learning how people get along with one another in that culture.

Three decades ago a pastor named Robert Fulghum wrote a short book titled *All I Really Need to Know I Learned in Kindergarten*, which sold more than 15 million copies. Here's an excerpt:

Share everything.
Play fair.
Don't hit people.
Put things back where you found them.

Clean up your own mess.

Don't take things that aren't yours.

Say you're sorry when you hurt somebody.

Wash your hands before you eat.

Flush.

Live a balanced life—learn some and think some and draw and
   paint and sing and dance and play and work every day some.

When you go out into the world, watch out for traffic, hold
   hands, and stick together.[21]

You might think that these rules are universal and/or innate,
but they are neither. The son of a samurai, raised in Japan circa
1700, would not have been taught "Don't hit anyone"; nor would
he have been taught "Say you're sorry when you hurt somebody."
Let's contrast Fulghum's book above with some lines from *Hagakure: The Book of the Samurai*, written by Yamamoto Tsunetomo
in the early 1700s:

The arts bring ruin to the body. In all cases, the person who
   practices an art is an artist, not a samurai, and one should have
   the intention of being called a samurai.

Common sense will not accomplish great things.

All of man's work is a bloody business.

The way of avoiding shame . . . is simply in death.

When there is a choice of either dying or not dying, it is better to
   die. . . . The Way of the Samurai is found in death.

A real man does not think of victory or defeat. He plunges
   recklessly towards an irrational death.

If you are slain in battle, you should be resolved to have your
   corpse facing the enemy.

> [The best way] of bringing up the child of a samurai: from the time
> of infancy one should encourage bravery.[22]

Each culture constructs its rules of right behavior differently. I'm not saying our way is right and the Japanese samurai was wrong. I am saying that *no child is born knowing the rules*. Every child must be taught.

We used to do a much better job of teaching the rules specific to our culture. Thirty years ago, kindergarten and first grade in American schools were all about "socialization," as it was then called: teaching Fulghum's Rules and more. Beginning in the mid-1980s, many American schools and school districts decided that the first priority of early elementary education should not be socialization but rather should be literacy and numeracy. There was great concern in the United States at that time because Japanese students had pulled ahead of American students on some measures of academic achievement.[23] The unspoken assumption seems to have been that kids would learn the basic rules of good behavior—the most important part of enculturation—in some other way: either from their families at home or from the larger culture.[24] At the time, throughout the 1980s and 1990s—and in many districts, even today—school administrators prided themselves on introducing "rigor" into elementary education. I was living in Montgomery County, Maryland, when the local superintendent garnered national praise for making kindergarten "academically rigorous," cutting down on "fluff," such as duck-duck-goose, field trips, and singing in rounds, and requiring instead that kindergarten teachers spend more time teaching phonics.[25]

The change in the early elementary curriculum and the consequent neglect of teaching socialization places a greater burden than ever before on the American parent. But just when kids need parents more than ever to teach them the whole package of what it means to be a good person in this particular culture, the authority of parents to do that job has been undermined. We now live in a culture in which kids value the opinion of same-age peers more than they value the opinion of their parents, a culture in which the authority of parents has declined not only in the eyes of children but also in the eyes of parents themselves.

Parents today suffer from *role confusion*. "Role confusion" is a plausible translation of *Statusunsicherheit*, a term used by German sociologist Norbert Elias to describe the transfer of authority from parents to children.[26] Elias observed that in the second half of the 20th century, Western Europeans became less comfortable with any sort of power differential in social relations. Elias noted that before World War I, power differentials were sharply defined in multiple domains: between aristocrats and the lower classes, between men and women, between managers and employees, and between parents and children. Throughout the 20th century, and especially in the decades after 1945, people in Western Europe—and in North America too, I might add— became uncomfortable with all such power differentials. With regard to the power differential between men and women: in the name of social justice, women acquired equal rights, though at a varied tempo from one region to the next (women in Appenzell, Switzerland, did not gain the right to vote on local issues until 1991). Regarding the power differential between managers and employees: in recent decades, many companies have abandoned the old-fashioned hierarchical management system in favor of "giving employees a voice." With regard to the former deference of the lower classes to the upper classes: the aristocracy has nearly vanished, at least in the traditional master-and-servant *Downton Abbey* sense of the term. And with regard to parents and children: the authority of parents, and, even more significantly, the *importance* of parents, in the lives of their children has declined substantially.[27]

More than 50 years ago, Johns Hopkins sociologist James Coleman asked American teenagers this question: *"Let's say that you had always wanted to belong to a particular club in school, and then finally you were asked to join. But then you found out that your parents didn't approve of the group."* Would you still join? In that era, the majority of American teenagers responded No. They would not join the club if their parents did not approve.[28] In that era, for most kids, the opinion of parents mattered more than the good regard of same-age peers.

Not so today. I posed an updated version of Professor Coleman's question to hundreds of children and teenagers at dozens of venues across the United States between 2009 and 2015. I asked them, "If all your friends joined a particular social media site, and they all wanted you to join, but one of your parents did not approve, would you still join the site?" The most common response to the question was neither Yes or No, but laughter. The notion that kids would bother to consult their parents about joining a social media site was so implausible that it was funny. *My parents don't even know what ask.fm is. They would probably think it was some kind of radio station! So why would I ask them if I should join? If all my friends are joining that site, then **of course** I am going to join.*

In American culture today, same-age peers matter more than parents. And parents are reluctant to change the rules—to insist, for example, that time with parents and family is more important than time with same-age peers—because parents are suffering from the "role confusion" described by Elias. They are unsure what authority they ought to have and how to exercise it. As a result, it's much harder for American parents to teach Fulghum's Rules to their kids. And the older the child, the more true that is. In one study, the attitude of American teenagers toward their parents was described as "ingratitude seasoned with contempt."[29]

As Canadian psychologist Dr. Gordon Neufeld has observed: in most cultures in most times and at most places, the job of enculturing the child is not primarily the job of the mother and father. The entire culture takes part: schools, the community, and even popular stories all are in synch in inculcating the basic rules, the fabric of the culture.[30] In our time, the schools have retreated from normative instruction about right and wrong in order to focus on academics. It's less controversial to concentrate on phonics than to teach Fulghum's Rules or any other absolute notions of good behavior. It's easier for teachers and school administrators to suggest that a child has Attention Deficit / Hyperactivity Disorder and /or Oppositional-Defiant Disorder and might benefit from medication than to exhort parents to work harder at the task of teaching social skills to their child. The end result, as I have already said, is that parents today shoulder a greater burden than parents in previous generations but have fewer resources to do their job.

Before we go any further in our discussion of the loss of parental authority, I have to make sure you and I are on the same page with regard to what I mean by "parental authority." I have learned that when I speak to parents, many confuse "parental authority" with "parental discipline." They think that parental

authority is all about enforcing discipline. In fact, parental authority is primarily about a *scale of value*. Strong parental authority
means that parents matter more than same-age peers. In contemporary American culture, peers matter more than parents.

For most of the history of the human race, children have
learned culture from the adults. That's why childhood and adolescence have to last so long in our species. But in the United
States today, kids no longer learn culture from the grown-ups.
American kids today have their own culture, a culture of disrespect, which they learn from their peers and which they teach to
their peers.

When I speak about the culture of disrespect, I am referring
not only to the "ingratitude seasoned with contempt" already
noted, which is now the characteristic attitude of many American
kids toward their *parents*; I mean also that American kids now
commonly show disrespect *toward one another* and that they live
in a culture in which such disrespect is considered the norm. Five
decades ago, the Beatles' single "I Want to Hold Your Hand" was
a worldwide hit. In 2006, Akon released a single titled "I Wanna
F*** You." (The clean version, titled "I Wanna Love You," was
broadcast on radio, but the original version with the foul language
was the one which reached #1 in the United States.)

T-shirts. Here are some of the slogans I have seen American
kids wearing on T-shirts recently:

DO I LOOK LIKE I CARE?

OUT OF YOUR LEAGUE

IS THAT ALL YOU GOT?

YOU LOOK LIKE I NEED ANOTHER DRINK

Or its variant:
BUY ME ANOTHER DRINK, YOU'RE STILL UGLY

I'M NOT SHY, I JUST DON'T LIKE YOU

YOU LOOKED BETTER ON FACEBOOK

These T-shirts are not intended primarily for display to adults (men over 25, women over 22). These T-shirts are meant to be seen by same-age peers. The slogans on these T-shirts epitomize disrespect *for one another*.

It's not just hip-hop and T-shirts. It's everywhere. Even the Disney Channel actively promotes the culture of disrespect and undermines the importance of parents. Consider the most popular shows on the Disney Channel, such as *Jessie*, a sitcom in which the parents are almost always absent (and irrelevant), while the three kids are more competent than the bungling butler and the ditsy nanny. Or *Liv and Maddie*, in which the pathetic mom—who happens to be a school psychologist—is regularly put to shame both by her girly-girl daughter and by her tomboy daughter (both played by the same actress). Or *Dog with a Blog*, in which the father is a psychologist—another psychologist!—who knows nothing about the behavior of children, a peculiarity that leads to much well-deserved mocking of the father by his children. The father's cluelessness is a recurrent laugh line in the show. The talking dog is more insightful than the father.

You don't have to look far to see how American culture has changed in this regard. The most popular TV shows of the 1960s through the 1980s consistently depicted the parent as the reliable and trusted guide of the child. That was true of *The Andy Griffith Show* in the 1960s; it was true of *Family Ties* in the 1980s. But it's not true today. Looking through the list of the 150 most popular

TV shows on American television right now, I did not find one that depicts a parent as consistently reliable and trustworthy.[31]

It's tough to be a parent in a culture that constantly undermines parental authority. Two generations ago, American parents and teachers had much greater authority. In that era, American parents and teachers taught right and wrong in no uncertain terms. *Do unto others as you would have them do unto you. Love your neighbor as yourself.* Those were commands, not suggestions.

Today, most American parents and teachers no longer act with such authority. They do not command. Instead they *ask*, "How would you feel if someone did that to you?" The command has been replaced by a question. American parents and teachers struggle to respond when the student replies, "If someone did that to me, I'd kick him in the nuts." Even when students produce the canned answer they know the grown-ups want to hear, they are merely regurgitating. They have digested nothing. No real communication across the generations—the most important feature of enculturation—has occurred.

What does it mean to assert your authority as a parent? It doesn't necessarily mean being a tough disciplinarian. Among other things, it means ensuring that the parent-child relationship takes priority over the relationships between the child and her or his same-age peers. Not just for toddlers, but for teenagers as well. It means that parents are doing their job—fulfilling their biological role, if you like—of teaching the child how to behave both within and outside of the family unit. Recall that the purpose of a prolonged childhood in our species seems to be, first and foremost, for the child to learn the grown-up culture from the grown-ups. When parents lose their authority—when same-age peers matter more than parents—then kids are no longer interested in learning the culture of the parents. They want to learn the kiddie culture, the teen culture. Throughout this book we will see just how harmful that is.

The benefits of parental authority are substantial. When parents matter more than peers, they can teach right and wrong in a meaningful way. They can prioritize attachments within the family over attachments with same-age peers. They can foster better relationships between their child and other adults. They can help their child develop a more robust and more authentic sense of self, grounded not in how many "likes" a photo gets on Instagram or Facebook but in the child's truest nature. They can *educate desire*, instilling a longing for higher and better things, in music, in the arts, and in one's own character.

*W*hy did this change occur—and why here in the United States to a greater degree than in Western Europe? To answer that question, I begin with the insights of Norbert Elias mentioned above. Throughout the 20th century, the legitimacy of almost every kind of authority became suspect throughout Western Europe and North America. Politically, we might summarize the second half of the 20th century as the empowerment of the previously disenfranchised: People of color were empowered. Women were empowered. Employees (at least in theory and in lip service) were empowered. And children were empowered. Nobody stopped to say, "Yes, it is right that adults should have equal rights in their relations with one another. It is right that women and people of color should have equal rights relative to white males. But what is true for adults in their relations with other adults may not be true for parents in their relations with children."[32] Empower everybody! Why not?

My answer is: because the first job of the parent is to teach culture to the child. And authoritative teaching requires authority.

As I have mentioned, some aspects of this problem are global. Others are more pronounced here in the United States. How come? Part of my answer has to do with how we Americans regard the idea of "progress." In the United States, "progress" is generally seen as a good thing. American history, as I have seen it taught in many American schools K–12, has a smooth upward trajectory, albeit with a few hiccups in the past half century or so (e.g., Vietnam). We used to be a coastal collection of British colonies; now we are a mighty nation of 50 states spanning a continent, plus Alaska and Hawaii. Our institutions used to be racist; we now affirm equal rights for all under the law. Two centuries ago, our nation was not wealthy; now we are rich. In the lexicon of American advertising, "new" is practically a synonym for "improved."

This notion pervades not only our history and our advertising but even our architecture. It is more common in the United States than elsewhere for developers to tear down old buildings to put up new ones. In defense of the developers, the new buildings are usually bigger and occasionally even better than the old buildings. When people in Europe think about old buildings, they think: Cologne Cathedral. When people in the United States think about old buildings, they think: asbestos.

In my experience, the assumption that "new" usually means "better" is much less evident in countries such as Switzerland and Scotland. With regard to architecture, in Zurich and Lucerne (Switzerland) and Edinburgh and Stirling (Scotland), the grandest buildings are the medieval cathedrals, castles, and towers, which are maintained and celebrated by locals of all ages, including children and teenagers. With regard to history, all Europeans share a memory of World Wars I and II. Even in neutral Switzerland, most people can tell stories of relatives who died in those wars. The notion of history as a smooth trajectory of progress was actually popular across Europe from the 1870s right through the summer of 1914.[33] But you don't find it in Europe today. And when I turn on a television in Stirling or Lucerne, even the style of the advertising is different: it's less common to find an advertisement promoting a product whose principal claim is that it is "new."

Celebration of the new over the old easily translates into celebration of the young over the old, of young people over old people. The cult of youth, the celebration of youth for youth's sake, is more pervasive in the United States than in any other country I have visited. In American cities, I often see billboards promoting plastic surgeons who promise to make you look younger. I have rarely seen such billboards in the United Kingdom or Germany or Switzerland.

When the culture values youth over maturity, the authority of parents is undermined. Young people easily overestimate the importance of youth culture and underestimate the culture of earlier generations. "Why should we have to read Shakespeare?" is a common refrain I hear from American students. "He is *so* totally irrelevant to, like, *everything*."

The ambivalent European attitude toward progress is nicely summarized by the late 20th-century philosopher Nicolás Gómez-Dávila, educated in France, who wrote: "Two hundred years ago, it was reasonable to trust in the future without being utterly stupid. Who can believe now in today's prophecies, seeing as we are yesterday's splendid future? . . . 'Progress' means, in the final analysis, taking away from man what ennobles him in order to sell him cheaply what debases him."[34]

There is also greater cultural ballast in Western Europe and the United Kingdom than in the United States. When I met with Scottish students and their families in Edinburgh, Perthshire, and Stirling, I found many boys and some girls who were proud to wear the traditional clothes worn by their parents and grandparents. Kilts are passed down from one generation to the next, not as museum pieces but as clothing to be worn whenever the occasion arises. And occasions for wearing a kilt arise often. Boys in Scotland are happy to give an impromptu lecture on the characteristics of a proper Scottish kilt and how to distinguish the genuine article from the cheap imported frauds sold to tourists.

It would be unusual to find an American girl or boy who is proud to wear her or his grandparent's clothes.

But as far as concerns our job as parents, it doesn't really matter why the culture changed or why the culture of disrespect is more pronounced here in the United States compared with other developed countries. We need to understand *what to do about it*, which is the focus of this book.

The issue isn't always that parents are unwilling to assert their authority. Sometimes they believe that they are helping their children by stepping back and letting their kids decide. Here's an example of what *not* to do—in other words, an example of how many American parents now behave.

Megan and Jim, both forty-something parents, had planned a four-day ski vacation between Christmas and New Year's. Their 12-year-old daughter, Courtney, politely declined to join them. "You know I'm not crazy about skiing," she said. "I'll just stay at

Arden's house for those four days. Her parents said it's OK. They have a spare guest room and everything." So her parents went on the ski vacation by themselves, and Courtney spent four days at the home of her best friend. "I didn't mind. In fact, I was pleased that Courtney could be so independent," Megan told me.

But Megan is mistaken. Courtney isn't independent. No 12-year-old truly is. Instead, Courtney has transferred her natural dependence from her parents, where it should be, to her same-age peers, where it shouldn't be. Courtney's top priorities now lie in pleasing her friends, being liked by her friends, being accepted by same-age peers. Her parents have become an afterthought, a means to other ends.[35]

You can see how good parents who love their kids can fall into this trap. You love your child. It's natural to want to please someone you love. If your daughter doesn't want to join you and your spouse on a ski vacation, it feels harsh to say, "Nevertheless, despite your protests, you are going to come with us." But that's what you must say. Why? Because having fun together is one foundation of authoritative parenting in the modern world. Because if most of the good times come when kids are having fun with other kids, then it's no wonder that kids don't want to spend more time with adults. Because your kids won't value time with you above time with same-age peers if they rarely spend any time with you doing fun stuff. That's part of what it means to exercise parental authority.

I just mentioned Dr. Neufeld, a Canadian psychologist who recently retired from active practice after 40 years of working with children and adolescents. Over the past four decades, he observed firsthand a fundamental change in the ways in which kids across North America form and prioritize attachments. Forty years ago, kids' primary attachment was to their parents. Today, for most kids in the United States and Canada, kids' primary attachment is to other kids. "For the first time in history," Neufeld observes, "young people are turning for instruction, modeling, and guidance not to mothers, fathers, teachers, and other responsible adults but to people whom nature never intended to place in a parenting role—their own peers. . . . Children are being brought up by immature persons who cannot possibly guide them to maturity. They are being brought up by each other."[36] Today, most North American kids care more about the good regard of their peers than they care about the good regard of their parents.

Neufeld describes a girl, Cynthia, who "had become rude, secretive, and sometimes hostile" toward her parents while remaining "happy and charming" when around her friends. "She was obsessive about her privacy and insistent that her life was none of her parents' business. Her mother and father found it difficult to speak with her without being made to feel intrusive. Their previously loving daughter appeared to be less and less comfortable in their company. . . . It was impossible to sustain any conversation with her."

I personally have found this scenario common with kids from elementary through high school, not only in my medical practice but in my meetings with parents all across the United States. How best to understand it?

Neufeld asks,

Imagine that your spouse or lover suddenly begins to act strangely: won't look you in the eye, rejects physical contact, speaks to you irritably in monosyllables, shuns your approaches, and avoids your company. Then imagine that you go to your friends for advice. Would they say to you, "Have you tried a time-out? Have you imposed limits and made clear what your expectations are?" It would be obvious to everyone that, in the context of adult interaction, you're dealing not with a *behavior* problem but a *relationship* problem. And probably the first suspicion to arise would be that your partner was having an affair.[37]

Neufeld observes that the primary problem in Cynthia's relationship with her parents is that she has come to value her attachment to her peers more than her attachment to her parents. Once this happens, any attempt by parents to set limits on a child's interactions with peers—for example, no texting or phone calls after 9 p.m.—can prompt sulking or a tantrum. Parents need to recognize such tantrums or sulking as symptoms of a shift in the child's primary attachment from parents to their peers.

Too often, parents today allow their desire to please their child to govern their parenting. If your relationship with your child is governed by your own desire to be loved by him or her, the odds are good that you will not achieve even that objective.

Something hardwired is going on here. The child expects to look up to the parent, to be instructed by the parent, indeed to be commanded by the parent. If the parent instead serves the child, then that relationship falls out of its natural balance. You may not earn your child's love at all—and the more you try, the more pathetically unsuccessful you may be. I have seen precisely this dynamic play out at least a hundred times in my own medical practice over the past quarter century. The parent who puts the child's wishes first may earn only the child's contempt, not their love.

But if you are not primarily concerned about winning your child's love and affection and focus instead on your duties as a parent—teaching your child right from wrong and communicating what it means to be a responsible man or woman, a gentleman or a lady, within the constraints of the culture you are trying to inculcate and to share—then you may find that your child loves and respects you. When you're not looking for it.

I recently visited multiple schools across Scotland, meeting with students, talking with parents, and leading workshops for teachers at each. To get to Scotland, I flew from Philadelphia to London-Heathrow, then connected on a smaller plane to Edinburgh. I arrived well ahead of time for the long flight across the Atlantic on a big Airbus A330. Waiting at the gate in Terminal A at the Philadelphia International Airport, I watched an American family: a mother, father, teenage daughter, and two younger sons.

"Where are my doughnuts?" one of the boys asked. He looked to be about 8 years old.

"Sweetie, I thought we should save those for the plane," his mom said.

"Where are my doughnuts? I want them right now!" he said more loudly.

"Honey, you just had dessert. Let's wait till—"

"I WANT THEM RIGHT NOW!!" he shouted at the top of his lungs. His mom looked guiltily around, as though the TSA might arrest her. Without another word, she fished in her bag and handed over the entire box of doughnuts.

The voice of the gate attendant came over the public address system. "In a few minutes, we will begin boarding US Airways Flight 728 to London's Heathrow airport. We board by zone number. You will find your zone number on your boarding ticket. Please have your passport open to the photo page . . . "

The teenage daughter was texting on her cell phone. "Trish, it's time to put the cell phone away. We need to get ready to board," the mom said. Her daughter ignored her. "Trish?"

"Mom, would you please SHUT UP. Can't you see that I'm BUSY."

"Trish? We need to get ready to board? The plane?" The mom's words sounded like questions. Her daughter continued to ignore her. Mom glanced at me. I felt uneasy and walked away.

I could sense the mom's discomfort. I was uncomfortable too. But the kids were in their element, living in a different culture. Mom had not *encultured* her kids into her own culture. Instead she was trying to adapt to the children's culture, the culture of disrespect, which they had learned from their peers. And while these kids might have been enjoying themselves at the moment, after a fashion, eating the doughnuts and texting, their parents' failure to enculture and instruct them rightly means that these kids will be ill-equipped to withstand the challenges of later adolescence and adulthood.

Sometimes you have to wait before you eat the doughnuts. Sometimes you don't get to eat the doughnuts at all. That's life.

2

Why Are So Many Kids Overweight?

American kids are heavier today than they used to be. The trend started in the 1970s and continued steadily through 2000. Since the mid-2000s, the trend has tapered. But the shape of childhood has changed.

In the early 1970s, only 4 percent of American children age 5 to 11 were obese. In 2008, 19.6 percent of American children in that age range were obese. The proportion of obese kids more than quadrupled—from 4 percent to 19.6 percent—in less than four decades. There was a similar quadrupling in the rate of obesity among American adolescents age 12 to 19, from 4.6 percent in 1970 to 18.4 percent in 2010.[1] And we're talking *obese*, not merely overweight.[2]

There was a recent flurry of news reports about new data allegedly showing that this 40-year trend is over and may even have reversed. "Obesity Rate for Young Children Plummets" was a typical headline in American media.[3] A columnist for the *New York Times* crowed that the new data were "fantastic news" and that the report proved the effectiveness of Michelle Obama's Play60 program, which encouraged kids to exercise at least 60 minutes every day.[4]

Wait a second. What did the new data actually show? There was no improvement at all in obesity rates for any age group of Americans, with the sole exception of children 2 to 5 years of age. The rate of obesity among those very young children has dropped so that they are now about as likely to be obese as 2- to 5-year-old children were in 2000.

The enthusiasm in the *New York Times* and elsewhere was based on the reasonable guess that if 3-year-olds today are less likely to be obese compared with 3-year-olds 5 years ago, then 5 years from now, when those 3-year-olds have grown to be 8-year-olds, maybe we will see a lower rate of obesity among 8-year-olds, and so forth. But that guess is only a guess. The historical record suggests otherwise. The data for the United States suggests that obesity rates among 3-year-olds underpredict obesity rates among older children, as shown in the figure on the facing page.

Don't get me wrong. The decline in obesity among children ages 2 to 5 is good news. But it's premature to celebrate. Even if our wishes come true and we do see a comparable decline among all age groups in the coming decade, with the rates of obesity reverting back to the rates seen in the year 2000 across the board, that's not good enough. If you want to roll the clock back to when obesity wasn't a huge problem for American kids, you have to go back more than 40 years, to 1971.

Fitness is not the same thing as slenderness, and lack of fitness is not the same thing as obesity. Yes, fat kids tend to be less physically fit than slender kids. But there are plenty of slender kids in the United States who are out of shape: they can't run a

Prevalence of obesity among American children and teenagers.

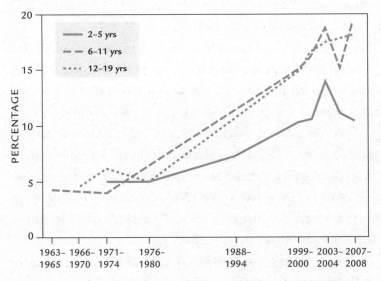

Source: Centers for Disease Control and Prevention.

quarter-mile without huffing and puffing. Over the past decade, as I just observed, rates of *obesity* have been pretty stable for American kids 6 to 18 years of age. But over the same decade, the *fitness* of American kids has declined significantly, even though the average kid hasn't gotten any fatter. In 2014, researchers at the Centers for Disease Control and Prevention (CDC) released the results of a study that compared the physical fitness of 12- to 15-year-olds in 2012 with their counterparts back in 1999 and 2000. They found that the average fitness of both girls and boys declined significantly over that time span. The proportion of kids who met the minimum standard for physical fitness, based on how much they were able to exercise, decreased from 52.4 percent in 1999 and 2000 to 42.2 percent in 2012. And this decrease in fitness occurred despite the fact that the kids in 2012 were not significantly fatter than the kids in 1999 and 2000. The kids in 2012 were just less capable of exercise.[5]

Race, ethnicity, and household income played no role in the CDC findings. Affluent kids were in no better shape than low-income kids. White kids were not in better or worse shape than Black or Hispanic kids. American kids are just becoming less fit, regardless. "This is not good news," said Janet Fulton, a lead investigator at the CDC. Dr. Gordon Blackburn, a cardiologist at the Cleveland Clinic, echoed her comments. "Thirty years ago, we would not have expected to see 12-year-olds with symptoms of cardiac disease," Dr. Blackburn said. "Now we've had to start a pediatric preventive cardiology clinic."[6]

A mom and dad brought their 11-year-old son into the Urgent Care facility where I was working. The boy had been running around on the playground with his friends when he felt chest tightness and shortness of breath. We did a thorough evaluation, including an EKG and chest X-ray. (The boy put his iPad aside so that I could do my exam.) Everything was normal. I concluded that the cause of his chest tightness and shortness of breath was "deconditioning," which is a fancy word for "out of shape."[7]

I see this a lot.

Similar trends have been reported across the developed world. Researchers have documented a rise in the rates of overweight and obesity in recent decades in Australia, Canada, Finland, Germany, the Netherlands, Spain, Sweden, Switzerland, and the United Kingdom. The magnitude varies from one country to the next. For example, in the Netherlands, only 1 boy in 1,000 was obese in 1980; that increased to 11 boys in 1,000 by 1997. Technically, that signifies an elevenfold increase in the rate of obesity among boys in the Netherlands between 1980 and 1997, but the actual prevalence of obesity among Dutch boys in 1997 was below the rate of obesity among boys in the United States in 1980. (The rate of obesity for girls in the Netherlands increased from 5 in 1,000 to 19 in 1,000 over the same time period.) So the trends are similar across developed nations, but the absolute magnitude of the problem varies significantly.[8] Separately from overweight, a decline in fitness in recent decades has been documented in children outside the United States, just as it has here.[9]

What happened over the past four decades? In 1971, it was rare to find a child or teenager who was obese or couldn't run a quarter-mile without gasping for breath. By 2000, it was common. In the years since 2000, the average American kid hasn't gotten any fatter, but she or he is now less likely to be physically fit. How come?

Researchers now generally agree on three factors that have driven the rise in obesity and overweight and the decline in fitness among children. Those three factors are:

1. What kids *eat*
2. What kids *do*
3. How much kids *sleep*

Other factors—such as endocrine disruptors, intestinal bacteria, consumption of genetically modified wheat, and antibiotics— may play a role, but there is less consensus regarding those other factors.[10] Let's talk about factors 1, 2, and 3, so you can see the pivotal role played by parental authority—or more precisely, by the abdication of parental authority and by parents' role confusion—in each of those factors.

What Kids *Eat*

Healthy foods have given way to less healthy foods and beverages in the diet of the average American kid. Pizza, French fries, potato chips, ice cream, and soda have displaced fruit, vegetables, and milk. This change has not occurred in every American household, but it has occurred in many.

When parents are unequivocally in charge, then the parents decide what is for supper, and their kids either eat what is offered or they go hungry. That was the norm in American families as recently as the 1970s, but today it is the exception. In the 1970s, it was common for parents to say, "No dessert until you eat your broccoli," and "No snacking between meals." Some American parents still insist on such rules, but they are now the minority. Per capita consumption of soda nearly tripled for teenage boys in the United States between 1978 and 1994.[11] Between 1977 and 1995, the percentage of meals which Americans ate at fast-food restaurants increased by 200 percent.[12] Some American schools even tried to raise money by installing vending machines selling Coke, Pepsi, Pop-Tarts, and Doritos. Federal regulations that took effect in 2014 are supposed to prohibit the sale of junk food and sugary drinks in schools.[13]

And speaking of school: In the 2009–2010 school year, the National School Lunch Program spent $458 million on pizza, $241 million on chicken nuggets, and $104 million on hamburgers.[14] Michelle Obama was a cheerleader for the federal statute that took effect in 2010 that mandated a phase-in of healthier meals in American schools—not just for kids who get their lunches for free through the National School Lunch Program, but for all kids who eat in public schools, including kids who pay for their lunch. The bill was named The Healthy, Hunger-Free Kids Act. It required schools to offer healthier foods at lunch and to remove some of the less healthy options. Four years later, in 2014, a pundit joked that the new law had resulted in "healthy, hunger-free trash cans," because much of the healthy food was being rejected by kids, and was ending up in the trash.[15] In October 2014, the National School Boards Association reported that 84 percent of American school districts reported an increase in wasted food after the law took effect, and 76 percent saw a decrease in student participation in the lunch program.[16]

Michelle Obama publicly expressed her dissatisfaction with reports that much of the healthy food mandated by the new law was being trashed. She alleged that administrators in some school districts "just sit back and say, 'Oh, the kids like junk food so let's just give them junk food.'" She asserted that if more districts put more effort into marketing the new meals to kids, then the meals would be more popular.[17]

With all due respect, I think the First Lady was mistaken to put the blame on a supposed lack of enthusiasm by district administrators. American children today grow up in a culture in which their desires are paramount; in which school lessons are often presented as entertainment; in which university professors are graded by students based in part on how much fun their classes are. In such a culture, it is unreasonable to expect kids to accept broccoli and Brussels sprouts without protest when they are accustomed to pizza and French fries. In districts serving affluent neighborhoods, many kids have started bringing in their own brown-bag lunches rather than buying the healthier lunches mandated by the new law.[18] Especially in more affluent neighborhoods where kids have many options, **it is unrealistic to expect that simply *offering* kids**

healthy choices will consistently and reliably lead to kids *making* healthier choices.

Parents, especially affluent parents, now commonly carry bags of snacks in the car on the way to and from school. Heaven forbid that the children should experience even a moment of hunger. "I don't want them to get hypoglycemic," one parent told me as I watched her lug a cooler of refrigerated snacks into the car for the 30-minute trip to her children's private school. I didn't criticize. Better that the kids should eat carrot sticks from home than that they should stop at Burger King for a cheeseburger and fries.

New evidence suggests that allowing kids to have on-demand access to food may be one factor promoting obesity, independent of the total number of calories consumed. *Ad lib* feeding throughout the day appears to disrupt circadian rhythms, interfering with normal metabolism and disturbing the balance of hormones that regulate appetite. Recent studies with laboratory animals have found that animals with *ad lib* access to food become fatter than animals with only scheduled access to food, even when the total calories consumed are kept the same in the two groups. Restricting the amount of time when food is available to 9 or 12 hours out of 24—without restricting calories—improves health and brings weight back to normal. "Time-restricted eating didn't just prevent but also reversed obesity," said Dr. Satchidananda Panda, author of one of the studies cited here.[19]

Anyhow, since when did a few minutes of hunger become unacceptable? When kids have the final say, then parents must make every effort to ensure that kids are not uncomfortable. Not even for 5 minutes. Hunger—even just on the car ride home from school—is now intolerable. Kids who have never been hungry will grow up to be heavier; yet psychologically they are likely to be more fragile. They haven't learned to master their own needs.

When parents begin to cede control to their kids, food choices often are the first thing to slide. *No dessert until you eat your broccoli* morphs into *How about if you eat three bites of broccoli, and then you can have dessert?* As I described earlier, the command has melted into a request or a question, capped with a bribe. Recently I was at a restaurant where I watched a well-dressed father pleading with his daughter, who looked to be about 5 years old. "Honey, could you please do me a favor? Could you please just try a bite of your green peas?" Kids take such appeals literally. If this girl does condescend to eat a bite of her green peas, she is likely to believe that she has done her father a favor and that he now owes her a favor in return.

What Kids *Do*

American kids today are substantially less active compared with their counterparts 30 or 40 years ago. The most common leisure activity of American kids in 1965 was outdoor play. American kids today are more likely to be sitting in front of a TV or computer screen. In 1965, according to one study, the typical American spent 92 minutes a day watching TV, which works out to about 10½ hours a week.[20] Even more importantly, in 1965, more than 80 percent of American households with a TV had just one TV set, which meant that the parents and children were watching TV together.[21] There were only three nationally broadcast television channels in 1965: ABC, CBS, and NBC. Cable television did not exist: there was no Disney Channel, or Nickelodeon, not even MTV. In the late 1960s and early 1970s, daytime television meant soap operas such as *As the World Turns*, *Love Is a Many Splendored Thing*, and *General Hospital*. Not the sort of thing that kids want to watch. According to the latest nationwide survey, the average 9-year-old American child now spends more than 50 hours per week in front of an electronic screen, which includes TV, computer screens, and cell phones. The average American teenager now spends more than 70 hours per week in front of a screen.[22]

When I was growing up in Ohio in the 1960s and 1970s, most of the kids on my block—and definitely all the boys—spent their free time outdoors. We came inside for meals, but that was pretty much it. Our backyard was so worn down from our baseball games that 3 years after the last of us had moved away, you could still see where the pitcher's mound and the bases had been.

Not long ago, a mother I know told her 11-year-old son, "It's such a beautiful day. Why don't you play outside?" He answered, in all seriousness, "But where would I plug in my Xbox?"

American children have less free time for play than they used to, and the play is more likely to be organized and supervised by grown-ups.[23] But the biggest change is simply that many American kids today would prefer to "play" with an electronic device rather than go outside to play hopscotch or dodgeball or jump rope. Many school districts have even banned some traditional American games, such as dodgeball, because of liability considerations, and because of the belief that such games promote bullying, and because of the concern that such games might lower a child's self-esteem.[24]

Turn off the screens. Get your kids outdoors. Go outside and play with them. If your children are within walking distance of their school and you live in a safe neighborhood, why not ask them to walk to school? In 1969, 41 percent of American kids

either walked or rode their bikes to school. By 2001, that proportion had dropped to 13 percent.[25] If there is a grocery store within
a mile of your home, then take a daily or every-other-day walk to
the store with your child and carry a bag home.

How Much Kids *Sleep*

In the past 15 years, researchers have recognized that getting less
sleep at night appears to lead to overweight and obesity. This effect appears to be more pronounced for children and teenagers
than it is for adults.[26]

I started reading the research on the relationship between sleep
deprivation and obesity about 10 years ago. At first the idea that
sleeping *less* would cause you to *gain* weight didn't make any sense
to me. If you are sleeping less, then presumably you are more active because you are doing something. You aren't sleeping. And almost any activity burns more calories than sleeping does. But it
turns out that if kids or grown-ups are sleep-deprived, the hormones that regulate appetite get messed up, which confuses our
brains in all kinds of bad ways. Your brain starts to say, *I'm so tired,
I **deserve** some potato chips / ice cream / candy / cookies / cake / and
I need them right **NOW**.*

It's bad.[27]

American kids are not getting the sleep they need. And there
has been a significant decline over the past two decades in the
amount of sleep kids are getting.[28] Here's the expert consensus on
the amount of sleep children should have:[29]

- Preschool and kindergarten, age 2 to 5 years: at least 11
  hours a day

- Elementary and middle school, 6 to 12 years of age: at least 10 hours a day
- Teenagers, 13 to 18 years: at least 9 hours a day

How does that compare to the amount of sleep that American kids are actually getting? At age 10, the average American kid is getting 9.1 hours of sleep a night; at age 15, 7.3 hours of sleep; at age 17, just 6.9 hours of sleep.[30] In every age group from 6 to 18, the average American kid is sleep deprived; and the older the child, the more sleep deprived she or he is likely to be. American kids today are getting significantly less sleep compared with American kids 20 years ago. British kids today, on the other hand, are actually getting slightly *more* sleep compared with British kids 20 years ago.[31]

How come? The presence of devices in the bedroom may be one factor contributing to sleep deprivation among American kids. If a child or teenager has a TV in the bedroom, or a mobile phone, or a video-game console, or a computer with Internet access in the bedroom, then there's a temptation to use those devices rather than sleep. There is now good evidence that screens in the bedroom interfere with sleep.[32]

In 2013, the American Academy of Pediatrics (AAP) released new recommendations for the use of media by children and teenagers, the first major rewrite of the guidelines since 2001.[33] Among other recommendations, the pediatricians advised that there be *no screens in the bedroom*: no TVs, no mobile phones, no computers or tablets. They didn't say that kids should not use those devices. They said that those devices should not be in the bedroom. The bedroom should be for sleeping.

The AAP recommendations struck me as reasonable and sensible. I have been saying much the same thing myself for years. So I was bothered by the scornful response that the AAP guidelines received in American media. The Associated Press began its nationally syndicated article on the new guidelines with the ironic hashtag "#goodluckwiththat."[34] Another major media outlet branded the new AAP guidelines as "an exercise in futility" and predicted that the new guidelines would be "ignored."[35]

I started leading workshops for children and teenagers back in 2001. My workshops for students are neither sermons nor didactic presentations, but conversations. I ask questions and I call on those who have their hands raised. Then I ask other kids to respond to their peers' comments. One question I have asked regularly since 2001 is, "What's your favorite thing to do in your spare time, when you are by yourself with no one watching?" From 2001 through about 2010, I heard lots of different answers. But since about 2011, one answer has become predominant among American kids, especially affluent kids. That answer is: Sleep. Affluent American kids are now so busy trying to do so much that the majority of them now appear to be sleep-deprived—so much so that their favorite leisure-time activity is not music or art or sport or reading, but sleep.

That's sad.

You can already see several ways in which the culture of disrespect might result in more fat kids. When kids don't respect parental authority, they are less likely to eat their vegetables. They are less likely to do chores, and more likely to play video games. They are less likely to go to sleep when they should, and more likely to stay up late in front of a screen. But there is also some intriguing evidence that appears to support a direct link: the child who is most disrespectful is also the child who is most likely to become fat.

In the past two decades, quite a few studies have reported just that finding: namely, that children and teenagers who are defiant, disrespectful, and just plain bratty are more likely to *become* overweight or obese, compared with kids who are better behaved.[36] It turns out to be a big effect. In one study, researchers found that kids who were chronically defiant and disrespectful were about three times more likely to become obese, compared to kids who were better behaved. And the slimmer the child, the bigger the effect. Slender kids who were persistently defiant and disrespectful were more than *five* times as likely to become obese, compared with equally slender kids who were better behaved.[37]

It makes sense. If kids are being defiant or disrespectful and refusing to eat their vegetables, some American parents will let them have pizza and French fries for supper. Those parents won't say, "No dessert until you eat your vegetables." Those parents may find it easier to give the child pizza and ice cream rather than take a stand, if the child is prone to misbehave. Why is the effect more pronounced for slender kids? If a child is already overweight when the study begins, then there's not as much room to see a big change. If a child is slender and then becomes obese, the researchers will find a bigger effect among slender kids than among kids who are already overweight or obese.

Now here's a surprise. This relationship between bad behavior now and obesity later, confirmed in many studies conducted in the United States, may not hold in New Zealand. Only one prospective study on this topic has been performed in New Zealand, but in that one study, conducted in the 1990s, girls who misbehaved were somewhat *less* likely to become obese compared with better be-haved girls (boys were not studied). The researchers speculated that the badly behaved girls in New Zealand might weigh less than "good girls" because the "bad girls" were more likely to smoke cig-arettes.[38] I am not persuaded by that conjecture. Bad girls are more likely to smoke cigarettes than good girls in the United States, just as in New Zealand. I propose a different hypothesis, based on my conversations with parents and teens across New Zealand, in Auckland, Hastings, Hawkes Bay, and Christchurch. Parents there have told me that—at least in the 1990s—it would have been un-usual for a parent to allow a daughter or son to decide what's for supper. If parents in New Zealand prepared a healthy meal and happened to have a defiant and disrespectful daughter who refused to eat it, then that girl might go to bed hungry. Which, over a pe-riod of months or years, might cause her to lose some weight.

However: This New Zealand study was published in 1998, based on research done in the mid-1990s. There have been some changes in the two decades since. When I recently shared this re-search with an administrator at a school I visited in Christchurch, she said that she has observed "an increased sense of entitlement with some young people in recent years. In post-earthquake Christchurch, the level of adolescent anxiety and associated men-tal health issues may have compounded this sense of entitlement. Parents and professionals alike seem to be walking on egg shells when concerning themselves with adolescent well-being, and this fear seems to manifest itself in some overindulged teenagers, op-erating with increased levels of autonomy. Confused parents are turning more and more to schools for guidance on how to man-age disrespect and defiance in the home."[39]

So maybe we all need some help.

In Part II of the book, we will focus on concrete strategies to build your authority in the context of contemporary 21st-century culture. But those strategies will be effective only if you begin with confidence about what you are trying to teach your child. Here's what you need to teach with respect to diet and exercise:

Eat right: Broccoli and Brussels sprouts come before pizza and ice cream.

Eat less: Don't supersize. Prepare small servings and insist that kids finish everything on the plate, including vegetables, before they get second helpings.

Exercise more: Turn off the devices. Go outside. Play.

You can do this.

When parents abdicate authority and let kids decide what's for supper, one result is more kids eating pizza and French fries instead of broccoli and cauliflower. That's certainly one factor contributing to the rise in overweight and obesity among children and teens today.

It's easy to see how letting kids decide might lead to more kids who are overweight. But other important consequences are not so obvious. For example, it's not immediately obvious how the decline in parental authority might lead to more kids being diagnosed with ADHD or Oppositional-Defiant Disorder or Pediatric Bipolar Disorder, especially in the United States.

But the link is there. That's our next topic.

3

Why Are So Many Kids on Medication?

Trent is 8 years old. In my office, he is happy. He giggles when I wag my Daffy Duck puppet over my head and use my Daffy Duck voice. But his parents tell me that if Trent doesn't get his way, or if some little unexpected thing goes wrong, he erupts in a temper tantrum. "He just goes totally berserk," his mom says. "He screams. He cries. He throws things. But then 5 minutes later he's laughing again." Before I can say anything, mom continues, "I went online and researched it, and I'm thinking maybe he's bipolar. Rapid cycling."

Hmm, I nod sagely.

After a thorough evaluation, it's clear that Trent doesn't have any form of bipolar disorder, rapid cycling or otherwise. He has mood swings. He gets mad when he doesn't get his way. That's within the range of normal for an 8-year-old. But his parents seem helpless to guide his behavior or to respond appropriately to his outbursts. I begin to wonder, *How do I break the news to this mom that there is no role for medication here?* The problem lies not in Trent at all, but in his parents' failure to set and enforce consistent limits and consequences.

As I mentioned in Chapter 1, a big part of the task of enculturation is teaching Fulghum's Rules: *"Play fair. / Don't hit people. / Put things back where you found them. / Clean up your own mess. / Say you're sorry when you hurt somebody."* In the three decades between 1955 and 1985, parents could rely on the kindergarten classroom to teach these rules. In that era, even those parents who didn't work terribly hard at parenting could usually take for granted that kids knew and accepted these rules. But not anymore. In many American kindergartens today, as I said in Chapter 1, the first priority is more likely to be teaching diphthongs rather than teaching respect, courtesy, and manners.

Parents today must explicitly teach Fulghum's Rules and everything that goes with them. But many parents don't do that, for at least two reasons. First, they may not realize that they need to. Their own parents may not have preached to them on these topics 20 or 30 years ago, so why would they have to teach this stuff to their own kids? Second, parents today are less comfortable asserting authority than parents in previous generations.

I now regularly encounter parents like Trent's mom, parents who wonder whether their young child might have rapid-cycling bipolar disorder or some other neuropsychiatric explanation for bad behavior. I explain to those parents that it's normal for an 8-year-old to swing through different moods in half an hour. Sometimes in just 5 minutes. That's not rapid-cycling bipolar disorder. That's being 8 years old. I say it over and over again: *The job of the parent is to teach self-control. To explain what is and is not acceptable. To establish boundaries and enforce consequences.*

Two decades ago, that was common sense. Not anymore. At least not in the United States.

As recently as 1994, it was rare for any individual under age 20 to be diagnosed as bipolar. But by 2003, in the United States, it was becoming common. There was a fortyfold increase in the diagnosis of bipolar disorder among American children and teenagers just between 1994 and 2003. In other words, for every 1 kid diagnosed with bipolar disorder in 1994, 40 kids were diagnosed with bipolar disorder in 2003. And most of the new diagnoses were for American children under age 15.[1]

Prior to the early 1990s, pediatric bipolar disorder was rarely diagnosed in the United States or anywhere else. Before 1994, most experts agreed that bipolar disorder was characterized by episodes of depression alternating with episodes of mania. A person experiencing a manic episode is typically euphoric and energetic, often going without sleep. Episodes of mania can last for days or weeks; episodes of depression can last for weeks or months.

Beginning in the mid-1990s, a group of researchers led by Dr. Joseph Biederman at Harvard Medical School published a series of papers claiming that bipolar disorder in children is different. In children, Biederman and his colleagues argued, bipolar disorder isn't episodic at all. It is *rapid cycling*, with the phases lasting minutes instead of weeks or months. And Biederman argued further that mania in childhood doesn't look like mania in adults. Manic children are not energetic and euphoric, according to Biederman and his Harvard colleagues; instead, they are irritable.[2]

The children Biederman was describing are so different from adults with bipolar disorder that one might reasonably question whether Biederman was describing any kind of bipolar disorder at all. But Biederman insisted that this was indeed bipolar disorder and that it should be treated with the same powerful antipsychotic drugs, such as Risperdal and Seroquel, which are often used for bipolar disorder in adults.

There were, and are, skeptics. One of them, psychotherapist Dominic Riccio, believes that Biederman and colleagues are "making a diagnosis of bipolar because a child has mood switches. If a child goes from happy to sad and has impulsive outbursts, it's characterized as bipolar. But children have mood swings. To characterize this as mental illness is a serious flaw."[3] Psychiatrist Jennifer Harris was doing her fellowship in adolescent psychiatry in 2002 when Dr. Biederman was promoting the diagnosis of pediatric bipolar disorder. "We saw a huge number of kids coming in with that diagnosis," she said, but "a lot of them turned out not to have it when you did a thorough assessment." Harris concluded, "Many clinicians find it easier to tell parents that their child has a brain-based disorder than to suggest changes in their parenting."[4]

That's the situation I was in with Trent and his mom. Trent was having mood swings. When his parents didn't buy him the toy he wanted, he would scream in the toy store. But his parents had never taught him the rules of good behavior. His behavior was pretty much what you would expect of a kid who has never known consistent discipline.

Trent's mom had read a *Newsweek* cover story about pediatric bipolar disorder. The article featured Dr. Biederman and his Harvard colleagues and repeated Biederman's assertion that doctors are failing to diagnose bipolar disorder in children.[5] I could understand mom's frustration: I, Leonard Sax, am just a local family physician. Who am I to dispute *Newsweek* magazine and Dr. Biederman, the nationally renowned Harvard child psychiatrist?

Trent's mom wanted me to tell her that Trent had a chemical imbalance that could be fixed by Risperdal or Seroquel, the drugs championed by Dr. Biederman. I told mom that Trent didn't need those medications. Trent needed parents who had the confidence and authority to teach Fulghum's Rules.

Mom left the office in a huff.

Less than three weeks after that mom stormed out of my office, Dr. Biederman and his two colleagues at Harvard admitted to receiving more than $4 million from Johnson & Johnson (the manufacturer of Risperdal), AstraZeneca (the manufacturer of Seroquel), and other drug companies. The payments were discovered in the course of an investigation launched by US Senator Charles Grassley and conducted by the staff of the Senate Judiciary Committee.[6] To be clear, Biederman and his colleagues broke no law. There is no law prohibiting doctors from accepting millions of dollars from drug companies. But Dr. Biederman's action was unethical, in my judgment. I think Dr. Biederman should have told *Newsweek* and everybody else that he was, in essence, acting as a paid spokesperson for the drug companies. But he kept the money a secret, or at least it seems as though he tried to.[7]

Psychiatric social worker Elizabeth Root observes that parents are "satisfied with the quick fix" that medications offer. Parents then don't want to do the hard work of getting to the bottom of the problem.[8] Child psychiatrist Elizabeth Roberts goes even further: "Psychiatrists are now misdiagnosing and overmedicating children for ordinary defiance and misbehavior. The temper tantrums of belligerent children are increasingly being characterized as psychiatric illnesses. Using such diagnoses as bipolar disorder, attention-deficit hyperactivity disorder (ADHD) and Asperger's, doctors are justifying the sedation of difficult kids with powerful psychiatric drugs that may have serious, permanent or even lethal side effects."[9]

Kids need authority in their lives. Families need authority in order to function. But when parents abdicate their authority, a vacuum results. Nature abhors a vacuum. The doctor, armed with a prescription pad, steps in, or is sucked in. Medication fills the role of governing the child's behavior, a role that the parents ought to have filled.

For many American parents, it is now easier to administer a pill prescribed by a board-certified physician than to firmly instruct a child and impose consequences for bad behavior. That's a shame. And that, in my view, is a major factor driving the explosion in the prescribing of these medications in the United States.

This phenomenon is peculiar to North America. German researchers found that during roughly the same period in which diagnosis of bipolar disorder was exploding for children in the United States, the proportion of children diagnosed with bipolar disorder in Germany actually *decreased*.[10] In Spain, likewise, the rate of diagnosis of pediatric bipolar disorder did not change for boys, and decreased for girls, between 1990 and 2008.[11] In a study from New Zealand, the proportion of admissions for pediatric bipolar disorder decreased significantly for both girls and boys between 1998 and 2007.[12]

The Germans observed, dryly, "There is no compelling reason to presume that the frequency of bipolar disorder in children and adolescents is actually much higher in the U.S. than in Europe. Therefore, there is considerable European skepticism about the high prevalence rate of bipolar disorder in children in the U.S. The diagnosis of bipolar disorder in youngsters is fairly rare outside the United States. . . . In Germany, a diagnosis of bipolar disorder in childhood is still extremely rare."[13]

Researchers recently compared diagnoses for children in the United States and England, using comprehensive national databases for both countries. They found that—after adjusting for overall population—for every one child in England discharged with a diagnosis of bipolar disorder, 73 children in the United States were discharged with a diagnosis of bipolar disorder.[14]

I have devoted several pages to pediatric bipolar disorder because it is such a good illustration of the extent to which the United States has become an outlier among developed nations in the diagnosis of psychiatric disorders. But other psychiatric conditions are also now diagnosed in this country at rates that are many times higher than anywhere else. The most prevalent of these conditions is Attention Deficit / Hyperactivity Disorder (ADHD). Let me tell you about another patient I saw.

Dylan had been a good student throughout elementary school, with many friends. But something changed when he started middle school. He lost interest in school, in most of his friends, and in sports. His circle of friends narrowed. He now spent most of his free time with a few other boys who shared his interest in video games. He became defiant and disrespectful toward grown-ups, including his parents. He began refusing to eat supper with the family. Instead he would stay in his bedroom and play video games.

His parents made an appointment for him to see a board-certified child psychiatrist. The psychiatrist talked with Dylan and his parents and reviewed the ADHD rating scales that several teachers at the school had filled out for Dylan.

"I initially thought Dylan might be depressed, but I don't think so anymore. I now think Dylan meets criteria for two other disorders," the psychiatrist told the parents. "Oppositional-Defiant Disorder and ADHD. I think there's a good chance that you would see substantial improvement with a stimulant medication for ADHD such as Adderall, Vyvanse, or Concerta. I suggest we try one of those medications and see whether it helps."

"The medication really has helped," Dylan's mom, Sofie, told me later. "With some things. He has started paying attention in school again. He seems to listen better at home. And he's started eating supper with us again, or at least sitting with us at suppertime. He doesn't really eat much. His appetite has been terrible ever since he started taking the medication. And something else is different. There used to be a twinkle in his eye, a spark, a mischievous spark. I don't see that spark anymore."

Sofie brought Dylan to me because she was concerned about Dylan losing that spark. Talking with Sofie and Dylan, I learned that Dylan had a video-game console in his bedroom. Sofie had no idea how much time Dylan spent playing video games because his door was closed at bedtime.

After talking with Dylan, I concluded that he was sleep-deprived. He admitted that he was spending several hours late at night, almost every night, playing video games rather than sleeping. I advised no devices in the bedroom. No TV. No cell phones. No video games. He could play video games up to 40 minutes a night on school nights and 1 hour a day on other days, but the console had to be in a public space such as the living room, not in his bedroom.[15]

I also recommended that we taper and discontinue his stimulant medication. The stimulant medication "worked," I explained, because it's a powerful stimulant: it compensated for his sleep deprivation. The sleep-deprived child will have trouble paying attention, not because he has ADHD but because he is sleep-deprived. Sleep deprivation mimics ADHD almost perfectly. Medications such as Adderall and Vyvanse are amphetamines: they are "speed." The appropriate remedy for sleep deprivation, I explained to Sofie, is not prescription stimulant medication. The appropriate remedy for sleep deprivation is for the parents to turn off the video-game console and turn out the lights so that the kid can get to sleep.

One of the basic duties of a parent is to ensure that the child gets a good night's sleep rather than staying up late playing games. That's not a new idea. But 30 years ago, we didn't have Internet-enabled devices that make it easy for kids to play online with other kids at 2 a.m. Now we do. That means that parents have to be more assertive of their authority than in previous decades. But many American parents have abdicated their authority instead. The result is boys playing video games at 2 a.m. and girls staying up past midnight texting their friends on their cell phones or uploading selfies to Instagram.

Based on my experience in the office, I believe that sleep deprivation is one reason why American kids today are more likely to be diagnosed with ADHD, compared with American kids three decades ago. And the failure of parents to assert their authority is a big part of the reason why American kids are getting less sleep than they used to.

Dylan regained his spark soon after he stopped taking the medication. But other problems were not so easily solved. He had been devoting most of his social time to hanging with other gamers: kids who spend most of their free time playing video games. His parents calculated that Dylan had been spending 20 hours or more a week playing video games, an average of nearly 3 hours per day. Once his parents restricted his playing time, he pretty much stopped playing altogether. "Forty minutes a night? That's barely enough time to get online and see what's going on," he complained. "I don't see the point." He stopped hanging out with his gamer friends. But his old friends from his life before video games were not quick to take him back. They had moved on. Dylan became something of a loner, although he was a scholarly loner. His grades soared, and his relationships with his teachers improved.

I was sorry to hear that Dylan was not able to reestablish his previous friendships. Kids do need same-age friends. When I speak to parents about the importance of prioritizing family over same-age friends, some parents will respond, "But don't kids need friends their own age?" Of course they do. But here we should take a tip from the financial planners: *diversify*. If you find that all your kid's friends share one particular interest, that's not healthy. If your daughter is a soccer star and all her friends play soccer, then what will happen when she sustains a major knee injury and can't play again for 3 months, or a year, or ever? I have seen such a girl essentially abandoned by almost all of her friends. She struggled to find a new identity not bound up with the game of soccer. If her parents had encouraged her to diversify her activities, had tried to connect her with other opportunities to make friends, perhaps at the church or synagogue or mosque, perhaps at the barn (this girl used to ride horses), or even just with the girl down the street, her life would not have seemed so bleak when she couldn't play soccer anymore.

Likewise for Dylan. His parents could see what was happening. They saw how his other friendships were waning as his obsession with video games became more severe. But they felt powerless to intervene. American parents today often think they are meddling or hovering like "helicopter parents" when they try to influence their child's friendships. And I agree that it accomplishes nothing to say, *"Jacob is such a nice boy. Why don't you invite him over?"* But I think it would have been perfectly reasonable for Dylan's parents to restrict his video-game playing much earlier, before his other friendships had withered away. Such a restriction would have helped Dylan to choose for himself which friendships—that didn't involve gaming—were worth nurturing and hanging on to.

In 2013, the Centers for Disease Control and Prevention (CDC) released their figures on the proportion of American children who have been diagnosed with ADHD. Across the entire United States, nearly 20 percent of American boys and 10 percent of American girls age 14 to 17 have been diagnosed with ADHD. That means that among high school kids in the United States, 15 percent have now been diagnosed with ADHD.[16] The CDC estimates that 69 percent of American kids who are *diagnosed* with ADHD are also on *medication* for ADHD.[17] If we multiply 15 percent by 69 percent we get 10.3 percent. That means that about 103 out of every 1,000 American teenagers are now taking, or have taken, medications for ADHD.

A group of British researchers recently released comparable data from a national survey of 3,529,615 individuals across the United Kingdom. They found that among teenagers in the United Kingdom, 7.4 in 1,000 are now taking, or have taken, medications for ADHD.[18]

Let's compare. In the United States, about 103 teenagers out of every 1,000 are now taking, or have taken, medication for ADHD.

In the United Kingdom, the figure is 7.4 teenagers out of every 1,000. Comparing the United States with the United Kingdom, the odds ratio is

$$103 / 7.4 = 13.9$$

In other words, the likelihood of being treated with medication for ADHD is nearly 14 times higher for teenagers in the United States compared with teens in the United Kingdom.

For younger children, the odds ratio is less dramatic. In the United States, among children age 4 to 13, about 69 kids out of every 1,000 now take medication for ADHD.[19] In the United Kingdom, among children 6 to 12 years of age, the figure is 9.2 kids out of every 1,000. So the odds ratio, comparing the United States with the United Kingdom, is

$$69 / 9.2 = 7.5$$

The likelihood of being treated with medication for ADHD is about 7.5 times higher for elementary and middle-school children in the United States compared with elementary and middle-school children in the United Kingdom.[20]

Bottom line: On this parameter, if you're a kid, living in the United States is a major risk factor for being put on medication. And the risk increases as you move from childhood into adolescence. You'd be at much lower risk if you moved to England, although rates of diagnosis of ADHD are on the rise in England as well.[21]

I know an American family that spent several years living in England. They had one son, who was an average student: not great, but not terrible. When the family returned home to the United States, the parents enrolled him in the local public school.

Mom was startled by the continual drumbeat from teachers and other parents: *"Maybe your son has ADHD. Have you considered trying a medication?"* She told me, "It was weird, like everybody was in on this conspiracy to medicate my son. In England, none of the kids is on medication. Or if they are, it's a secret. But I really don't think many are. Here it seems like almost *all* the kids are on medication. Especially the boys."

What did the United States look like on this parameter 30 or 40 years ago? As recently as 1979, the best estimate was that only about 1.2 percent of American kids—12 out of 1,000—had the condition we now call ADHD (then known as "hyperkinetic reaction of childhood").[22] But according to the CDC data from 2013, collapsing across all age groups from 4 to 17 years of age, 110 kids out of every 1,000 have been diagnosed with ADHD. That's an increase of nearly a factor of 10, from 12 per 1,000 in 1979 to 110 per 1,000 in 2013.

Why such an increase? Why is ADHD so much more common in the United States today than it was 30 or 40 years ago? And why is it so much more common today in the United States than elsewhere?

My answer is "the medicalization of misbehavior."[23] Instead of correcting our kids' misbehavior, we American parents today are more likely to medicate our kids in hopes of fixing the behavior problem with a pill.

We parents in the United States are not doing our job of enculturation, as I explained that job in Chapter 1. Neither we the parents, nor the schools, nor the TV shows, nor the Internet are adequately teaching Fulghum's Rules, such as *"Play fair. / Don't hit people. / Put things back where you found them."* As a result: kids born and raised in the United States are now many times more likely to be diagnosed with a psychiatric disorder, and to be treated with powerful medications, compared to kids living elsewhere. In most European countries, the proportion of individuals 18 and under who are on any kind of psychotropic medication is typically 2 percent or lower, and most of those individuals are 16-, 17-, and 18-year-olds taking medications for depression or anxiety.[24] In the United States, the proportion of children and adolescents on psychotropic medications is now above 10 percent, with some surveys reporting rates above 20 percent. Many of those are children age 12 and under, taking either prescription stimulants like Adderall, Vyvanse, and Concerta, "mood stabilizers" such as Lamictal or Intuniv, or antipsychotic medications such as Dr. Biederman's favorites, Risperdal and Seroquel.[25] Between 1993 and 2009, the prescribing of antipsychotic medications such as Risperdal and Seroquel for American children 12 and under increased more than 700 percent.[26]

Today, American parents are hungry for brain-based explanations. Instead of removing the cell phone and the laptop from their kids' bedroom so their kids can get a good night's sleep, many American parents are medicating their kids with powerful stimulants such as Adderall or Concerta or Vyvanse or Metadate to compensate for their sleep deprivation, usually without any awareness that sleep deprivation, not ADHD, is the underlying problem responsible for their kids' failure to pay attention. Likewise, instead of acknowledging that their kid misbehaves and/or is disrespectful, many American parents would prefer that a doctor diagnose an imbalance in brain chemistry and prescribe Risperdal, Seroquel, Adderall, or Concerta.

Recall Dylan, the boy I described a few pages back. A board-certified child psychiatrist concluded that Dylan had both

ADHD and Oppositional-Defiant Disorder. But the psychiatrist was mistaken. Dylan had neither ADHD nor Oppositional-Defiant Disorder. The proximate cause of Dylan's lack of attention was not ADHD, but sleep deprivation. And Dylan was sleep deprived because his parents were not aware of the time he was wasting playing video games in his bedroom. When that problem was fixed, Dylan's situation improved without medication. Dylan's case illustrates how the abdication of parental authority led to a psychiatrist prescribing medication. I see that sort of thing almost every day I'm in the office.

In Australia, New Zealand, and the United Kingdom, I have seen kids who won't sit still and be quiet, just as in the United States. In the United States today, the teacher is likely to write a note to the parents or make a phone call, saying something like, *"I'm concerned about Justin. He has great difficulty sitting still and being quiet. I think you should have him evaluated."* The parents dutifully take their son to the doctor, who says, *"Let's try Adderall and see if it helps."* Sure enough, the medication "helps": once he is medicated, Justin sits still and is quiet. Everybody's happy.

In the previous chapter, when we considered the growing proportion of kids who are overweight, I mentioned that the problem of heavy-set kids and declining physical fitness now seems to be pervasive across all developed countries. But in this chapter we're talking about mental health, the diagnosis of psychiatric disorder, and the prescribing of powerful psychiatric medications. The sequence of events just described—*let's try Adderall* [or Vyvanse or Risperdal or Seroquel] *and see if it helps*—simply does not happen outside North America. I'm not saying that kids are always better behaved elsewhere. I have seen plenty of kids in Australia and

New Zealand and the United Kingdom bouncing and making buzzing noises when they are supposed to be sitting still. But the teacher does not refer the child for psychiatric evaluation. Instead the teacher—who is typically far more confident of her authority than an American teacher would be—tells the child in a firm voice that she has had quite enough of that silliness, thank you, and it is high time for it to stop.

Imagine an 8- or 10-year-old boy who misbehaves. He talks back to teachers. He is deliberately spiteful and vindictive. He doesn't listen. He seems to have little or no self-control. Thirty years ago, perhaps even 20 years ago, the school counselor or principal might have said to the parent, *"Your son is disrespectful. He is rude. He exhibits no self-control. You need to teach him some basic rules about civilized behavior if he is going to stay at this school."* Today it is much less common for an American school counselor or administrator to speak so bluntly to a parent. Instead, the counselor or administrator will suggest a consultation with a physician or a psychologist. And the physician or psychologist will look at the reports from the school and talk about Oppositional-Defiant Disorder or Attention Deficit / Hyperactivity Disorder or Pediatric Bipolar Disorder.

What's the difference between saying, *"Your son is disrespectful,"* and saying, *"Your son may meet criteria for a psychiatric disorder"*? There's a big difference. When I say, *"Your son is disrespectful,"* the burden of responsibility is on you the parent and your child. With that responsibility comes the authority to do something about the problem. But when I say, *"Your son may meet criteria for a psychiatric disorder,"* then the burden of responsibility shifts away from the parent and the child to the prescribing physician and, indeed, to the whole burgeoning medical/

psychiatric/counseling complex. And the reasonable next question from the parents is not *"What should we do to change his behavior?"* but rather, *"Should he begin taking a medication?"*

The medications work. They do change the child's behavior. That's what I find so scary. These medications are being used as a means of behavior modification to an extent almost unimaginable outside North America.

These are powerful medications. The most popular medications for ADHD are prescription stimulants such as Adderall, Ritalin, Concerta, Metadate, Focalin, Daytrana, and Vyvanse. All these medications work in the same way: they increase the action of dopamine at synapses in the brain.[27] Dopamine is a key neurotransmitter in the nucleus accumbens, the brain's motivational center. When researchers administer these medications to laboratory animals, they find that these medications damage the nucleus accumbens; similar findings have recently been reported in humans.[28] The result of long-term use of medications such as Adderall, Ritalin, Concerta, Metadate, Focalin, Daytrana, and Vyvanse may be a girl or boy who is more likely to be disengaged, and less motivated to achieve in the real world.[29]

We don't know for sure. Not yet. As I just noted, most though not all of the relevant research has been conducted in laboratory animals rather than humans. It takes a long time to achieve conclusive proof in medicine. As a parent, you have to make a decision in the face of uncertainty. In the face of that uncertainty, if you must use a medication, I recommend avoiding these potentially dangerous stimulants and instead using safer nonstimulant medications for ADHD such as Strattera, Intuniv, or Wellbutrin. (I have no affiliation with and I accept no payments from the drug companies that manufacture these or any other medications.)

The most popular medications now used to control temper tantrums and other acting-out misbehaviors in American kids are the atypical antipsychotics, especially Risperdal, Seroquel, and Zyprexa. These are the same medications that psychiatrists use to treat schizophrenia. (They are called "atypical" antipsychotics to distinguish them from the older, "typical" antipsychotics such as Thorazine and Mellaril.) The United States is an outlier among developed countries in the use of antipsychotics for children: American kids are about 8.7 times more likely to be on these medications compared with kids in Germany, 56 times more likely compared with kids in Norway, and about 93 times more likely compared with kids in Italy.[30]

The most dramatic and obvious side effects of the atypical antipsychotic medications are metabolic: kids who take these medications are much more likely to become obese and develop diabetes.[31] This risk is greater for children than for adults, and the younger the child, the greater the risk.[32] Stopping the antipsychotic medication does not reliably reverse the metabolic consequences.[33] And yet, when I meet with parents whose kids are on these medications, I find that few have been seriously counseled regarding these risks.

Aside from the serious side effects these medications can cause, I see a deeper problem: a shift of authority and responsibility away from the parents to the prescribing physician. When the child subsequently misbehaves, many parents say, *"He can't help it; he has ADHD / bipolar disorder / Autism Spectrum"* (circle one).

I saw this firsthand at a school in St. Louis, in a second-grade classroom. A boy was defying the teacher. He was running around the room making buzzing noises while the teacher was asking all the students to sit.

"I need you to sit down and be quiet so that the other students can concentrate," she said to the buzzing boy. He ignored her. "It's really not fair to the other students for you to keep buzzing around like that. How would you feel if you were trying to concentrate, and somebody else was running around the room making buzzing noises?" Still no acknowledgment from Buzz. "I really have to ask you please to sit still and be quiet. Or else."

"Or else *what*?" Buzz said in a jeering tone, pausing for a moment.

"Or else I will *make* you sit still," she said.

Buzz started running around the room again, making buzzing noises louder than before. When the teacher tried to grab him, he bit the teacher's wrist, then ran out of the room, laughing. The bite was deep. It drew blood.

The teacher called the boy's mother. When the teacher told mom what had happened—that the boy had bit her wrist, drawing blood—the mother did not apologize. She did not even express surprise. "Well, you know that he has a psychiatric diagnosis," the mother said. "He probably needs an adjustment in his medication. You should have called the psychiatrist directly. Don't you have his number?"

Teaching self-control is one of the first tasks of the parent and the teacher. As we will see in Chapter 6, a child's self-control at age 11 or 14 is a good predictor of the child's health and happiness 20 years later, when the child is in his or her 30s. But if that child has been diagnosed with a psychiatric disorder and is put on powerful medication to control behavior, then the child's self-control may be undermined. As one kid told me, "I can't help it, I have Asperger's." In fact, a psychiatric diagnosis should be a reason for parents to become more involved, more engaged, more devoted to teaching self-control and Fulghum's Rules. But I have observed firsthand how the prescribing of psychiatric medication often shifts responsibility away from the child and the family to the prescribing physician.

When the teacher and the parents are confident of their authority, then bad behavior—whether in the form of throwing a temper tantrum, or making buzzing noises, or ignoring the teacher—can be recognized as what it is: namely, *bad behavior*, which signifies a loss of self-control on the part of the student. The teacher and parents can insist that the student show better self-control. When the teacher and parents exercise their authority, most students will develop better habits and show greater self-control, because the teacher and parents require it, because they expect it, and because the student really cares what they think.

What happens when the teacher and the parents no longer have that authority? Kids misbehave in all countries. But when kids no longer respect the teacher's authority, the teacher who attempts to wield authority may encounter the same result as the teacher I observed in St. Louis. She may get bitten. So, how to maintain order in the classroom? Increasingly, the answer in the United States is to medicate the child.

Many American children and teenagers who are currently taking psychiatric medications would not be taking them if they lived in the United Kingdom or Norway or Australia. That's especially true for diagnoses such as ADHD and bipolar disorder. You and I don't want our own children to be among those taking medication if it's not absolutely necessary.

What can you do, in concrete terms, to minimize the risk that your child will be prescribed medication he or she doesn't need for a psychiatric condition he or she doesn't really have?

Recommendation #1: When appropriate, command. Don't ask. Avoid the question mark. Instead of "Do you think maybe it's time to leave the playground?" say "It's time to go home." Instead of "Won't you just *try* a bite of your peas?" say "Please eat your peas." Instead of "Don't you think pornography is demeaning to women?" say "You are not allowed to watch pornography; here's why." The question mark undermines your authority. I am amazed by the difficulty which some parents have in speaking to their children without question marks.

A mother and father brought their 6-year-old daughter to see me. The child had a fever and a sore throat. I examined the ears, which were fine. I said, "Next I'm going to take a look at your throat." But before I could look at the throat, mom asked, "Do you mind if the doctor looks in your throat for just a second, honey? Afterward we can go and get some ice cream."

The child paused, then burst into tears and said, "I don't want to! I don't want to!" What should have been a simple 2-second exam became a major ordeal lasting several minutes. In more than two decades of practice, I have learned that the key to effective examination of a sick child is simply to *do the exam.* Don't negotiate with a 6-year-old. In two sentences, the mother (1) changed my statement into a negotiable request, and (2) turned the negotiation into a bribe. The authority of the grown-ups was undermined. When you ask a 6-year-old, "Do you mind if the doctor looks in your throat?" the child hears a legitimate question, and the answer may be "I **DO** MIND" and "I WON'T LET HIM."

As your child gets older, explanation becomes more appropriate. When your 6-year-old is at the doctor's office, *command* her to comply with the doctor's requests. "Because I'm your mother, that's why." But when your child is 15 years old, then it's more reasonable to offer an explanation of your decision-making process. When you tell your 15-year-old that the family is going on a ski vacation next week, and the 15-year-old says that she would rather spend the weekend with a friend, explain that family activities are a higher priority than activities with her same-age peers. You may not persuade her, but that's not the objective. You are explaining, not negotiating. The objective is to help your child formulate her disagreement and express her position without losing her cool. And the only way for her to do that is to practice. It's reasonable to offer an explanation to a teenager. Just don't let your explanation slide into negotiation.

The general rule for authoritative, "Just Right" parents should be, Don't ask. Command. Some American parents blanch with horror when I tell them to "command" their child. I have found that the parents most horrified by that suggestion are also more likely to be medicating their kids with Adderall or Concerta or Vyvanse or Seroquel or Risperdal.

Kids need parental authority in their world. Homes without strong parental authority are more likely to be homes in which powerful medications are used to suppress unwanted behaviors.

Recommendation #2: Eat dinner with your kids. And no cell phones allowed, no TV in the background during dinner.

Every meal counts. In a recent survey of 26,078 Canadian adolescents from a wide range of backgrounds—urban and rural, affluent and low income—researchers asked each kid, "In the last seven days, how many days have you had a meal with a parent?" Kids who had more meals with parents were less likely to have "internalizing problems" such as feeling sad, anxious, or lonely. They were less likely to have "externalizing problems" such as fighting, skipping school, stealing, etc. They were more likely to help others and to report feeling satisfied with their own lives.

The difference wasn't just between kids who had 7 evening meals a week with a parent compared with kids who had none. At almost every step from zero up to 7 evening meals a week, each extra dinner a child had with a parent decreased the risk of both internalizing problems and externalizing problems and increased both prosocial behavior and the child's general satisfaction with life.[34] The change was statistically significant at almost every step. For example, when you compare kids who have 6 dinners per week with a parent to kids who have 5 dinners per week with a parent, you find that kids who have 6 dinners a week enjoy significantly better well-being, demonstrate significantly more prosocial behavior, and have significantly fewer internalizing problems (anxiety, depression) and significantly fewer externalizing problems (acting out, fighting) compared with kids who have 5 dinners a week with a parent. That 1 extra meal with a parent, the difference between 5 evening meals a week together and 6 evening meals a week together—makes a difference. (Incidentally, in a separate study, researchers found that kids who regularly eat meals with their parents are at lower risk for becoming obese years down the road.[35])

American families today are significantly less likely than families in most other developed countries to eat meals together.[36] And suppertime in the United States is different from suppertime in other developed countries. In the United States, it's common for a TV or radio, sometimes both, to be left on during a meal. In the USA, it's also common for family members to look at their cell phones at the table. I have found that to be much less common in Scotland, Switzerland, and New Zealand.

Not everybody is convinced of the benefits of family meals. Researchers at Boston University controlled for other variables, such as parents' involvement with their kids, the amount of time kids spent watching television, the parents' level of education, and so forth. When they factored in all those other variables, they found that family meals no longer predicted outcomes in their sample. "We found little evidence for beneficial effects of frequent family meals," these researchers concluded.[37] But I think that's a little hasty. I think the Boston University research suggests that parents who eat meals with their kids are more likely to be involved with their kids, less likely to allow their kids to spend 30 hours a week watching TV, and so on. In other words, the family meal may be a *marker* for a constellation of behaviors that collectively predict good outcomes: behaviors such as limiting the amount of time watching TV or on the Internet, etc.

The bottom line on family meals:

- A family in which kids often have meals with parents is likely to be a family in which parents still have authority; a family in which parents and family interaction still *matter*.
- But just insisting that everybody eat together, while the TV is blaring and the kids are texting at the dinner table, probably won't accomplish much by itself.[38]

Across North America today, both in the United States and in Canada, I find many parents who believe that their kids' participation in sports, or dance, or some other extracurricular activity is more important than time spent with the family, sitting around the dinner table. I think those parents are mistaken. The family should be a higher priority.

When family time is a top priority, parents are likely to have a better sense of what's going on in their children's lives. If you get a report from school that your son has misbehaved or your daughter has been a bully, don't rush to the child psychiatrist. Ask your child what happened. Talk with the teachers and the school administrators. Do everything you can to teach the rules of good behavior to your children. And enforce those rules. Remember that you—not the teacher, not the coach—must be the primary authority responsible for instilling in your child the rules of good behavior.

Try to adopt the European mind-set with regard to medication for kids. That means viewing medication as an absolute *last* resort after every other possible intervention has been tried. In the United States, medication has become the first resort: *"Let's try it and see if it helps."* The result of the American mind-set is a generation of kids on powerful psychiatric medications, medications whose long-term consequences are unknown.

American kids are now substantially more likely than kids in other countries to be on medication. Often that medication is prescribed in hopes of boosting academic achievement. But over the same two decades in which the prescribing of medication for children and teens soared in the United States, the academic achievement of American kids dropped dramatically, relative to kids in other countries. That's our next topic.

4

Why Are American Students Falling Behind?

American kids used to be among the world's best students. Now they trail kids in Poland, Portugal, Spain, and many other countries. How come?

It was a big disappointment for me when I discovered the truth: Australia isn't that different from the United States.

Like many Americans, my notions of Australia prior to my first visit were a confused mix of kangaroos, koala bears, and half-remembered scenes from *Crocodile Dundee*. I have now visited more than 40 schools across Australia on 6 different tours, in all 6 states as well as in the capital city, Canberra. I remember arriving in Melbourne for my first visit in 2006 and feeling disappointed when I looked through the airport bookstore and saw magazine covers featuring Brad Pitt, Angelina Jolie, and Jennifer Aniston. No different from the airports back home in the United States. I'm not sure what I expected to find: maybe magazines for hunters tracking crocodiles in the outback? But the magazine racks in Melbourne (and Sydney and Perth and Hobart and Brisbane and Adelaide and Canberra) look pretty much the same as what you would find in an American city, except that the Australian bookstores do tend to have a few more magazines devoted to the British royals.

I have met with students in Australia on many occasions. I often ask them to name their favorite TV shows. Typically they list the same shows that American students name: *The Big Bang Theory*, *Grey's Anatomy*, *Two and a Half Men*. Rarely does any program produced in Australia crack the top 5.

Mainstream Australian culture is not that different from mainstream American culture. That's one reason I felt comfortable accepting invitations to lead workshops for teachers in Australia. Because the cultures are so similar, I assumed that the issues that mattered to American teachers would be similar to the issues that mattered to Australian teachers.

That was a big mistake.

In May 2012, I led a workshop for teachers at Shore, a private school in a suburb of Sydney. From the school library, which is magnificent, there's a stunning view of the harbor and the Sydney Harbour Bridge.

I began the workshop by promising the teachers that I would share what I have learned from my visits to hundreds of schools—mostly in the United States and Canada—about how to create a culture of respect in the classroom. "Even if the majority of your kids are respectful," I said, "there are always some who will try to undermine your authority and bring you down. That's true even at the most elite schools serving the most affluent neighborhoods."

After a few minutes of this, one of the teachers, Cameron Paterson, could take it no longer. He raised his hand. I called on him. "I'm sorry Dr. Sax," he said. "But I have no idea what you are talking about. And I don't think what you are saying makes any sense to my colleagues, either. We don't have students who are trying to undermine our authority and 'bring us down.' We simply do not have this problem."

I asked for a quick poll of the other teachers who were present. Did they agree? Or did they often find themselves struggling with disrespectful students?

All the teachers agreed with Mr. Paterson. A culture of respect prevails at this school. For example, students at Shore routinely thank their teachers at the conclusion of every class. One by one, as students walk out of the class, each student says, "Thank you, sir," or "Thank you, ma'am," as the case may be. Often a student will say, "Great lesson, sir!" That would be unusual today even at the most elite schools in the United States.[1] If an American student today were to compliment a teacher at the conclusion of a lesson, other students might make fun or they might suspect that student of apple polishing. Not in Australia.

I felt silly. But I also learned something. *Don't assume that what's true in the United States is true in Australia or Scotland or the Netherlands.*

The popular culture as reflected in the magazine racks may not differ dramatically between the United States and Australia. But the culture of disrespect which is pervasive among children and teenagers throughout the United States is less prevalent in Australia. In the United States, you will find kids in almost every classroom who disrespect the teacher or who are actively trying to undermine the teacher's authority. That's true, as I told the teachers in the workshop, even at the most elite schools serving the most affluent neighborhoods. Girls text during class. Boys make belching noises.

You will find this behavior outside North America most often in schools serving low-income neighborhoods. That was the situation in our country as well, 40 or 50 years ago. American public schools serving low-income neighborhoods have often had to contend with a culture of disrespect, at least since the end of World War II. Movies such as *The Blackboard Jungle* (1955) and *To Sir with Love* (1967) depict the culture of disrespect in schools serving low-income neighborhoods in the United States and in England. These movies may have been popular in part because the disrespectful culture they depicted seemed so foreign to middle-class moviegoers.

Today, movies such as *To Sir with Love* seem quaint. The pranks those students played on Sydney Poitier's character seem playful in comparison with the mayhem that American students now commonly inflict on their teachers.

When I mentioned this recently to an American friend who has lived in England as well as in the United States, she replied that yes, perhaps American kids are less well behaved and more disrespectful compared with kids in England or Australia. But she argued that the bad behavior of American kids is the price we pay for the greater creativity of young Americans.

She's assuming that young Americans are more creative than young people in other countries. But is that assumption correct? Are young Americans, in fact, more creative than young people in other countries?

Let's consider this notion of American creativity. Irish author Eamonn Fingleton observes that American global supremacy in creativity and innovation is a relatively recent phenomenon. Ralph Gomory, former head of research at IBM, told Fingleton that up until the 1930s, the United States was regarded as an adapter of other nations' technologies.[2] In other words, prior to World War II, the United States played the role which has been played in more recent decades by East Asian countries.

The half century between 1945 and 1995 was the great era of American creativity and innovation. In the first half of that period, from 1945 through roughly 1970, Americans truly did lead the world in transportation, manufacturing, agricultural sciences and food production, and communications. In the second half of that period, from 1970 through the mid-1990s, researchers at American universities and in private corporate research and development (R&D) departments continued to lead the world in each of these fields, as well as in the newer fields of biotechnology, computing, and information technology.

But the world has changed since 1995. Silicon Valley venture capitalist Peter Thiel told Fingleton that American innovation in the past two decades has been remarkably narrow, "confined largely to information technology and financial services." For innovation in transportation, manufacturing, and even biotechnology, the leaders are now in Western Europe and Asia. Fingleton reports that "the evidence of international patent filings is looking increasingly ominous" for the United States. According to data compiled by the World Intellectual Property Organization, only 4 American companies currently rank in the Top 20 among companies filing international patents, based on the number of patents filed.[3]

Even research by American companies is increasingly conducted outside the United States. Fingleton has found that American corporations are moving their R&D operations abroad. Fully 27 percent of all employees in US multinational corporations' research departments were based abroad as of 2009, up from 16 percent in 2004. Fingleton interviewed Paul Michel, a former federal appellate judge who is an authority on patent law. Intel is launching a huge new R&D operation in China, larger than anything that the company now has in the United States. The patents developed in the new facility will be registered in the name of Intel, which is an American company. But, Michel observed, "most of the staff in these labs will be Chinese, and undoubtedly many of the resulting manufacturing jobs will be located in China."[4] The United States now ranks #11 in the world in the filing of international patents *per capita*, behind Denmark, Finland, Germany, Israel, Japan, Luxembourg, the Netherlands, South Korea, Sweden, and Switzerland.[5]

My American acquaintance defended the insubordination of American students as a supposed prerequisite for creativity. I dispute that assumption. The golden era of creativity for young Americans was 1945 through 1970, when US students were much more likely to be respectful and deferential to teachers. (The college campus sit-ins and demonstrations of the 1960s were for the most part politically motivated, often organized around opposition to the Vietnam War. And even the largest demonstrations engaged only a small fraction of the population. The silent majority[6] of Americans during the 1960s stayed home, watching *The Andy Griffith Show* or *Gidget*.) The silver era of creativity spanned 1970 through 1995, when the attitude of American students toward teachers was still much more respectful than it is today. The marked rise of the culture of disrespect over the past two decades has actually been associated with a decline in American creativity.

Kyung-Hee Kim is an educational psychologist at the College of William and Mary who has analyzed results from the Torrance Tests of Creative Thinking.[7] Kim finds that the creativity scores of American children have diminished steadily over the past two decades. According to Dr. Kim, that means that American kids have become "less emotionally expressive, less energetic, less talkative and verbally expressive, less humorous, less imaginative, less unconventional, less lively and passionate, less perceptive, less apt to connect seemingly irrelevant things, less synthesizing, and less likely to see things from a different angle."[8]

The culture of disrespect is not essential to creativity. The evidence suggests that the culture of disrespect actually undermines true creativity while strengthening same-age peer conformism.

I recently visited an American school serving an affluent neighborhood. The teacher was trying to create a more courteous and orderly atmosphere in the classroom. She explained that she would no longer tolerate students interrupting one another or interrupting her (the teacher). As she was talking, one of the boys in the back of the class belched loudly and then said, "Oh just SHUT UP."

"You see, that's exactly what I'm talking about," the teacher responded. "That was an uncalled-for interruption. That is rude."

"Oh, I'm sorry," the boy said. "*Please* shut up." Other students, both girls and boys, giggled.

Do not confuse insubordination with originality. There is nothing original or creative about an American child or teenager saying "shut up" to an adult. On the contrary, such behavior today merely signifies conformity to the prevailing American culture of disrespect.

In defense of my American acquaintance who praised the insubordination of American students as a supposed prerequisite for creativity: she grew up in the era between 1970 and 1995, when American students actually did lead the world in many measures of academic achievement. That era is gone. *Recently* gone.

The most widely accepted measure for comparing students' achievement in different countries around the world is the Program for International Student Assessment (PISA). First administered worldwide in 2000, the PISA test is offered every three years. Students take the PISA at 15 years of age.[9] Within each participating country, schools are randomly chosen. The program has received wide praise for its thoroughness and its ability to test real understanding and creativity, not just rote mastery of facts. The PISA also has maintained a constancy of methods since its first administration in 2000, so it provides a consistent yardstick over time.

As recently as 2000, when the PISA was first administered, the United States still maintained a respectable mid-rank position in the world list. Here's where we stood on the math test in 2000 (the actual PISA raw score on the math scale is shown as well):[10]

Rankings in 2000

1. New Zealand	537	
2. Finland	536	
3. Australia	533	
4. Canada	533	

5. Switzerland   529
6. United Kingdom   529
7. France   517
8. Austria   515
9. Denmark   514
10. Sweden   510
11. Norway   499
12. **United States**   493
13. Germany   490
14. Hungary   488
15. Spain   476
16. Poland   470
17. Italy   457
18. Portugal   454
19. Greece   447
20. Luxembourg   446

By 2012, we had dropped significantly among the same group of nations listed above, falling from #12 to #17:[11]

1. Switzerland   531
2. Finland   519
3. Canada   518
4. Poland   518
5. Germany   514
6. Austria   506
7. Australia   505
8. Denmark   500
9. New Zealand   500
10. France   495

11. United Kingdom   494
12. Luxembourg   490
13. Norway   489
14. Portugal   487
15. Italy   485
16. Spain   484
17. **United States** 481
18. Sweden   478
19. Hungary   477
20. Greece   453

You can't invoke the economy to explain these results. Between 2000 and 2012, Spain experienced a major economic meltdown worse than that in the United States. Yet, during that period, the United States sank below Spain in achievement on this parameter. Poland, which trailed far behind the United States in 2000, had soared far above us by 2012. Despite the fact that our per capita spending on education is more than twice what it is in Poland.[12]

Many theories have been advanced to explain the recent drop in academic achievement of American students relative to students elsewhere. In her book *The Smartest Kids in the World: And How They Got That Way*, journalist Amanda Ripley made a careful comparison of the United States with countries that outperform the United States on the PISA exam by wide margins. Ripley identifies three domains where she thinks the United States has gone wrong:

- **Overinvestment in technology:** Ripley notes that American schools, especially schools serving affluent neighborhoods, nowadays are awash in tablet computers, high-tech smartboards, and other wireless gadgets.

Teachers in these high-end schools now routinely pass out wireless clickers to students for instant polling. In the most successful countries, the classrooms are typically "utilitarian and spare" with no digital gadgets.[13] Ripley notes that in countries which outperform the United States, the board at the front of the classroom is "not connected to anything but the wall. . . . Conversely, giving kids expensive, individual wireless clickers so that they can vote in class would be unthinkable in most countries worldwide. In most of the world, kids just raise their hands and that works out fine." She concludes, "Americans waste an extraordinary amount of tax money on high-tech toys for teachers and students, most of which have no proven learning value whatsoever." In most of the countries that score ahead of us on the PISA, "technology is remarkably absent from the classrooms."[14]

- **Overemphasis on sports:** Ripley describes American schools with multiple playing fields, lots of resources for sports, and an Athlete's Hall of Fame, but less emphasis on academics. In most of the rest of the world, the first mission of the school is academics. In the United States, at many high schools, sports routinely preempt academics. Even at leading US high schools, varsity athletes are often excused from class to participate in games. That rarely happens outside the United States. "Sports are embedded in American schools in a way they are not almost anywhere else," Ripley observes. "Yet this difference hardly ever comes up in domestic debates about America's international mediocrity in education."[15]

- **Low selectivity in teacher training:** In Finland, the teacher-training colleges are highly selective. Being admitted to a teacher-training program in Finland is as prestigious as getting into medical school in the United States.[16] In the United States, almost any high school graduate can qualify to become a teacher. Ripley writes, "Incredibly, at some U.S. colleges, students [have] to meet higher academic standards to play football than to become teachers."[17]

Each of these factors is important. I would like to add one more: the culture of disrespect. In the highest-performing countries, the average student is more likely to value what his or her parents value, compared with the average American student. Ripley followed an American high school exchange student, Kim, who spent a year in Finland. At one point, Kim asked the Finnish students a question that had been on her mind: "Why do you guys care so much [about your education]?" The students in Finland were baffled by the question, "as if Kim had just asked them why they insisted on breathing so much. . . . Maybe the real mystery was not why Finnish kids cared so much, but why so many of her [American] classmates did not."[18]

I think that's right. I think the key to understanding the decline in American academic outcomes relative to those of other nations has at least as much to do with how the United States has changed as with how other nations have changed. American teachers and administrators often devote much effort to making education cool and fun in the eyes of the students. Hence all the screens, all the gadgets. *If kids don't regard education as cool and fun, then they will not be motivated to learn.* I've heard comments of this variety from many school administrators in the United States. And if students are not motivated to learn, then classroom management—getting kids to behave—consumes a disproportionate share of the teacher's time and energy.

The solution is not to purchase more and more electronic gizmos and screens so that school comes to resemble a video-game arcade. The solution is to change and reorient the culture so that students are more concerned with pleasing the grown-ups than with looking cool in the eyes of their peers.

E ven if we fixed each of the three factors highlighted by Ripley, we would still have a long way to go. Once upon a time, young Americans led the world in college graduation rates. Even today, among adults age 55 to 64, Americans still lead the world in the proportion who have earned college degrees. But today, among adults 25 to 34 years of age, Americans have dropped to 15th place internationally in the proportion of young people who have earned college degrees. On that parameter—the proportion of 25- to 34-year-olds who have earned a 4-year degree—the United States now lags behind Australia, Belgium, Canada, Denmark, France, Ireland, Israel, Japan, Luxembourg, New Zealand, Norway, South Korea, Sweden, and the United Kingdom. In other words, we dropped from #1 to #15 in just 30 years.[19] American students who *enroll* in college are now less likely than the average student in other developed countries to *graduate* from college.[20]

As a result: Even in the unlikely event that we managed to fix all the problems in K–12 education highlighted by Ripley, I am not persuaded that such a fix would translate into a substantially improved college graduation rate. The relatively high college dropout rate now seen among American young people reflects something more fundamental than just a cultural obsession with, say, technological gadgets. We could, if we chose, eliminate all the iPads and high-tech smartboards from schools tomorrow. But I'm not convinced that such a change would, by itself, markedly improve college graduation rates.

And there is new evidence that young Americans are studying less at college, and learning less at college, than they did a generation ago. Researchers Richard Arum and Josipa Roksa studied a wide range of students who were tested during their first year at college and in their final year at college. They found that the typical American college student gains very little in terms of critical thinking ability between the beginning of the freshman year and the end of the senior year. Approximately one-third of students do not improve more than 1 point on a 100-point scale.[21]

The students themselves are vaguely aware of this, but most are not especially concerned. Many told the researchers some variation of "It's not what you know, it's who you know." Quite a few of the students interviewed by Arum and Roksa concluded that the main point of college is not academic learning at all but making the right social connections.[22] Small wonder then that so many show little gains on measures of cognitive skill and reasoning.

Combining data from multiple sources, economists Philip Babcock and Mindy Marks found that American college students in the 1960s devoted an average of 25 hours per week to studying. By the early 2000s, the amount of time per week American college students spent studying had decreased to about 12 hours, roughly half the figure from the 1960s.[23] American college students now spend less time studying than students in any European country with the sole exception of Slovakia.[24]

I have already mentioned the PISA, which assesses academic achievement among 15-year-olds. There is now a comparable test for adults, the Program for the International Assessment of Adult Competencies (PIAAC, pronounced "pee-ack"). The PIAAC has been administered only once, between 2011 and 2012, so we can't directly calculate trends in PIAAC performance over time. But Kevin Carey, director of the education policy program at the New America Foundation, compared the performance of American 15-year-olds on the PISA in 2000 with that of American 27-year-olds on the PIAAC in 2012. In 2000, as I mentioned above, American 15-year-olds did respectably well on the PISA. But 12 years later, American 27-year-olds scored well below the international average. American college graduates now "look mediocre or worse compared to their college-educated peers in other nations," Carey concludes.[25]

There are at least two possible explanations for the decline in relative achievement between 2000 and 2012 among the same cohort of Americans, born around 1985. One explanation is that American colleges are now below average, compared with colleges in other nations, in their core mission of educating undergraduates. Carey observes that the vaunted reputations of America's leading universities stem largely from the accomplishments of their leading researchers, not their success in teaching introductory courses. "A university could stop enrolling undergraduates with no effect on its score" on most international rankings, because those rankings rest on metrics such as the number of Nobel Prize winners, with no input from any measure of undergraduate education. Carey asserts that the decline in scores between American 15-year-olds in 2000 and

college-educated American 27-year-olds in 2012 reflects the mediocre quality of most American higher education.[26]

That explanation is plausible. But there is another explanation:
namely, that simply being exposed to American culture in the interval between 2000 and 2012—the era of Lady Gaga, Akon, Emi-
nem, Justin Bieber, and Miley Cyrus—might have a corrosive
effect on rational thinking. It might be the case that contemporary
American culture undermines scholarship, perhaps especially for
Americans born and raised in American culture than for foreign
students who come here to study. One reader of Carey's article
who has worked outside the United States made a similar point. If
you compare American college graduates with those outside the
United States, "You may be shocked, as I am, at how good they
[the foreign graduates] are in their chosen field, and how literate
and cultured a tech worker can be. The Brits write technical design docs like they were English Lit majors at university. The average European software engineer has command of several spoken
and written languages, and approaches software engineering as
what it is, Computer Science. Not slinging code. Something you
no longer see in US graduates unless they have a masters or PhD.
You can see why this is [so] when you spend time with their families. Getting an education is a more serious enterprise than it is in
the US. Their kids spend . . . more time doing homework, and less
time complaining about what a drag school is, than American
students."[27]

These two explanations are not mutually exclusive. It might be
the case that the average American college education is now infe-
rior to the average university education overseas, and it might also
be the case that exposure to contemporary American culture undermines both cognitive achievement and conscientiousness.

Young Americans today are more likely to drop out of college compared with their parents.[28] Relative to university-educated young people elsewhere, they now seem to be losing ground academically between 15 and 27 years of age. American parents used to be able to assume that their kids were getting a good education if the family lived in a good neighborhood with good schools and the child went on to attend a selective university. That assumption is no longer valid. As a result, you need to be more involved in your child's education to ensure that your child gets an education that measures up, not to American norms, which are now mediocre among developed nations, but to international norms. In kindergarten, in high school, and beyond.

5

Why Are So Many Kids So Fragile?

Many college faculty and staff report a noticeable fragility among today's students. Some describe them as "teacups"— beautiful, but liable to break with the slightest drop.

—Jean Twenge, San Diego State University[1]

"So what led you to suggest that Aaron should try playing football?" I asked Aaron's father, Steve.

"Actually it was the nurse practitioner at the pediatrician's office who first brought it up. She showed us how his weight percentile was climbing but his height percentile wasn't changing. I remember I asked her, 'What are you trying to tell us?' And she said, 'Aaron is getting overweight.' She didn't mention football per se. She just said that Aaron needed to be more active, and she suggested after-school sports. Football was my idea. I played football all through middle school and high school, and it helped me get into shape. It helped me to get strong. So that's where I was coming from."

"You mentioned that Aaron has always had a talent for video games. How old was Aaron when you first realized that?" I asked.

"Pretty young," Steve said. "I remember. Aaron was 6 years old. We were playing Madden NFL Football. You know that game?" I nodded. "Aaron beat me. By some crazy score. I think the final score was 62 to 7."

"He had 62 points, you had 7?" I asked.

"Yep. I was pathetic. I didn't play video games much with him after that," Steve said. "I just wasn't in his league. Plus I never really saw the point. I'd rather go outside and throw a football around. An actual football."

"So what happened last fall?" I asked.

"I had been nagging Aaron for years about playing football, but he always just ignored me. Then some of his friends, guys he played video games with, announced that they were going to try out for the JV team at school. That's the first time that Aaron showed any interest in playing the game. So he and I went to the park, and we threw the ball around, did some blocking. I told him that he had potential. I wasn't lying. He's got a few extra pounds on board, but that's not a bad thing if you're playing the line. I told him how the left tackle position is one of the highest-paid positions in the NFL. He thought that was pretty interesting."

"What happened last fall?" I repeated.

"Aaron was pretty cocky when he went to the tryouts. He thought that being master of Madden NFL Football would give him an advantage. But the coach said he wanted to get a sense of who was in shape and who wasn't. So he had them do some sprints. Then he made everyone run a mile, and every boy was timed. Aaron's times in the sprints were terrible, and he took nearly 12 minutes to run a mile. One mile. The coach said, 'Son, I have no idea whether you're going to be able to play this game or not. You're out of shape. I expect to see you back here tomorrow morning at 7 a.m. with the other kids who are out of shape. You'll run another mile around the track, then we'll go to the weight room.'"

"What happened? Did Aaron go back the next morning?" I asked.

"Nope. He never went back. That was his first and last foray into any kind of after-school sport. He said, 'I'm not a jock, I'll never be a jock, I don't *want* to be a jock. I'm a gamer.' I told him that you can be *both* an athlete *and* a gamer. I mentioned that lots of the men who play in the NFL are serious gamers as well. But he wasn't interested. He just retreated into his bedroom, closed the door, and kept on playing the games."

"So what's going on now?" I asked.

"He's just playing more and more. When I ask him what he wants to do with his life, he says he wants to be a professional gamer. He shows me articles online about these guys who are earning $100,000 a year or more playing video games."

"And you say?"

"What can I say?" Steve said. "Maybe that's his passion. That's what he says he really wants. Who am I to tell him that he shouldn't go after his dream? I just want him to be happy."

Julia always had a competitive streak. She always wanted to be #1 in her class. She may have inherited some of that drive from her parents: her mother is an investment banker, and her father is a surgeon. In any case, her parents were proud of the academic honors she earned beginning in elementary school. She was attending the top independent school in the city, a school which routinely sends graduates to the most selective colleges. And she was #1 in her class, on track to be valedictorian.

She was already taking Advanced Placement (AP) courses in 9th grade and she earned an A in every one. When she started 11th grade, she decided to sign up for AP Physics, a course usually taken in 12th grade. But Julia was already thinking of an independent study program for 12th grade, to do an engineering project at the university. She had decided, on her own, that taking AP Physics in 11th grade would be just the thing to impress the various people who would have to approve her program. To take the course as a junior, she needed special permission, which she obtained.

"She has always been at the top, or very near the top, academically," Julia's mom, Jennifer, told me. "But that was just *marginal* superiority. She was earning a 99 when the other kids were earning a 98 or a 97. She wanted to do something that would catapult her into another league altogether. She wanted something that would set her apart from the rest, not only in the eyes of college admission officers but in her own eyes. So that's where this was coming from."

"What happened?"

"Physics was way harder than she expected it to be. She had never really had any serious difficulty in school before. Everything always came easily to her. Physics was the first subject where she just didn't understand the concepts the first time around."

"When did she realize there might be a problem?" I asked.

"The first quiz," Jennifer answered. "Prior to that, I think Julia had some notion that maybe everything would be OK, she would be top of the class like always. She was studying really hard. The first quiz destroyed that notion. She got one of the lowest scores in the class, a 74. The teacher met with her afterwards and told her it wasn't too late to drop the class."

"What happened?" I asked.

"It was the first week of October. I came home from work. She was in the bedroom with her door closed, which is unusual. Usually she leaves her door open. I went to the bedroom door, and I was about to knock when I heard something I had never heard before. Sobbing. I had not heard her cry like that since she was a toddler. Convulsive, gasping sobs."

"What did you do?"

"I rushed into the room without knocking. She was on the bed, face down, crying into her pillow. Can you imagine what went through my mind? I didn't know anything about the physics exam. My first thought, to be honest, was that she had been sexually assaulted, that someone had victimized her. Because I thought, what else could cause her to be so incredibly upset? So I asked her, 'Are you OK? What happened?'"

"What did she tell you?"

"It wasn't easy for her to get the words out, but she managed to explain that she had gotten a low score on the quiz. To be honest, I had to put my hand over my mouth to keep from laughing. I was so relieved. Here I thought she had been the victim of some awful crime, and it was just a low mark on a quiz. But finally I said, 'Oh honey, that's terrible. You must feel so bad. I understand.'"

"What happened next?"

"I tried to reassure her. I said that we could hire a tutor to help her. She said she didn't want a tutor. It took me a few days to realize why this was such a big deal. If she couldn't ace physics, on her own, then she wasn't the great genius prodigy she had imagined herself to be. So it was pretty wrenching for her."

"When did she start taking medication?"

"Things just snowballed. I thought that she would come to her senses and put things in perspective. We did get a tutor for her, and I think the tutor was helpful. Her score on the next quiz was a 79. Still not great, but better. She could still pass the course. 'But I'll get a C!' she wailed. 'There are worse things in life than getting a C in physics,' I said. 'You just don't understand,' she said. And the crying spells continued, except now she told me to get out of her bedroom. She didn't want me to try to comfort her. That's when I took her to see the pediatrician. He prescribed Lexapro, 10 milligrams. He said we should try it; maybe it would help."

"Did it help?"

"A little. Eventually she was able to talk about how she was feeling without bursting into tears. She was able to explain how humiliating it was for her to be near the bottom of the class. But by Thanksgiving she seemed to be slipping back, more withdrawn, moody all the time. So we decided to take her to the psychiatrist. Actually the pediatrician suggested it."

"What did the psychiatrist say?"

"The psychiatrist spent only a few minutes with us. I was hoping for a more thorough evaluation, but he didn't seem to think it was necessary. He recommended adding Risperdal. He said that when an SSRI like Lexapro doesn't work, he likes to add Risperdal on top of the Lexapro. I looked it up online, and I just freaked out when I read the side effects of Risperdal. Weight gain. Diabetes. That's why I decided to come see you, for a second opinion. I read that essay you wrote for the *New York Times* about being skeptical about medications."

I can tell you many stories which are similar to Aaron's story and Julia's story, stories which have been related to me by parents or that I have observed firsthand in my role as a physician. The common thread connecting Aaron the out-of-shape gamer to Julia the would-be engineer is *fragility*. When Aaron came home from the tryout, why didn't he take up the coach's challenge to return, to try harder? When Julia discovered that she wasn't as smart as she thought, why did she collapse? The answer in both cases is that these kids are *fragile*. It doesn't take much for them to give up and retreat, as Aaron did, or to fall apart, as Julia did.

Fragility has become a characteristic of American children and teenagers to an extent unknown 25 years ago. That's what I'm seeing in the office today—and what I did not see in the office years ago. But besides my observations and experience as a physician over the past quarter century, several lines of evidence support my claim that young Americans are more fragile in comparison with young Americans from two or three decades ago. The first and most obvious evidence is the extraordinary rise in the proportion of young Americans diagnosed and treated today for anxiety and depression.[2] In Chapter 3, we saw that young people in this country are now much more likely to be diagnosed with a psychiatric disorder, compared to young people in other countries today and compared to young people in *this* country 30 years ago.

That line of evidence is relevant in Julia's case, since two board-certified physicians—a pediatrician and a psychiatrist—treated her with medication for depression. But that line of evidence doesn't pertain in Aaron's case. Nobody has diagnosed Aaron with anything. In fact Aaron is a pretty happy guy, as long as you don't interrupt him while he's playing his video game.

But Aaron and Julia do share something in common. In each case, something inside seems to be missing: some inner strength that we took for granted in young people a few decades back but that just didn't develop in these two. How can we quantify that? Can it be measured in statistics?

Maybe it can. In Aaron's story, the end result is a young man who has retreated from the real world into his bedroom in order to play video games. I have seen the same process in young adults—more often young men than young women—who come home from college, or drop out of college, to retreat into the bedroom with a computer screen or a video game. That's often the final common pathway which I have observed in twenty-somethings: young people whose dreams don't come true, who then give up, retreat, and return home to live with their parents or (if their parents have the means) live separately from their parents but remain supported by their parents.[3]

The phenomenon of young, able-bodied adults not working and not looking for work is becoming much more common in the United States. As recently as 2000, it was rare in this country compared to other countries. In 2000, young Americans led the world in the proportion of young people who were creating new businesses and who were either working or looking for work, ahead of countries such as Sweden, Canada, the United Kingdom, Germany, France, Australia, and Poland. But just 11 years later, in 2011, the United States had dropped from first to last among the countries just mentioned, while those countries' rank order relative to one another in most cases barely budged.

Here's the listing from 2000, with each nation rank-ordered according to the proportion of young people who were either gainfully employed or actively looking for work, from highest to lowest:

1. **United States**
2. Sweden
3. Canada
4. United Kingdom
5. Germany
6. France
7. Australia
8. Poland

And here is the listing for 2011, with the rank order from 2000 shown in parentheses:[4]

1. Sweden (was #2 in 2000)
2. Canada (#3)
3. Australia (#7)
4. United Kingdom (remained #4)
5. Germany (remained #5)
6. France (remained #6)
7. Poland (#8)
8. **United States** (#1)

You can't blame this drop on the economy. Poland and France struggled during the Great Recession of 2008–2009, but those countries retained their place in the rank order, while the United States dropped from first to last. A professor of economics at Harvard called this drop "a very big puzzle."[5]

In a healthy culture, young adults drive much of the growth in the economy. They start new businesses. They are the most likely to become entrepreneurs. But contrary to a common impression, the United States has become substantially *less* entrepreneurial over the past 30 years. The US Census Bureau keeps careful track of the number of businesses launched each year. In 2014, scholars analyzed these data and determined that "the rate of new business formation in the United States has been cut in half over the past 35 years."[6] The decline is pervasive—it is seen in all 50 states and all sectors of the economy— and has become more homogeneous across the United States over time. Every region in the United States is affected. The researchers acknowledged that "the reasons explaining this decline are still unknown." As a remedy, they suggest "liberalized entry of high-skilled immigrants."[7] Here's one of the graphs from their report ("firm entry" means creation of new businesses; "firm exit" means companies going out of business):

The US economy has become less entrepreneurial: Firm entry and exit rates in the United States, 1978–2011.

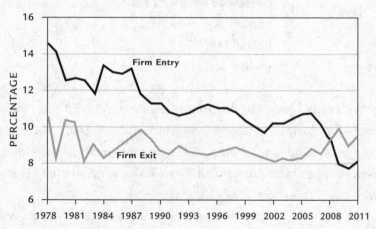

Source: Hathaway and Litan 2014.

It's easy to understand why the economists are baffled. They are looking for an answer to the riddle within the realm of economics, and they aren't finding any answers there. This phenomenon—young Americans who are fragile, who give up easily, who no longer have the drive to start new businesses—may have huge economic consequences, but the causes do not lie in economics. The causes lie in American parenting, which now creates fragile kids.

How?

Part of the answer lies in the young person's frame of reference and specifically in the shift from an adult's frame of reference to same-age peers' frame of reference. Often that young adult who is living at home, dependent on his parents, is nevertheless not too concerned with what his parents think of him. He's more interested in what his friends think. And the odds are good that many of them are living in their parents' homes as well, spending time on social media or making videos about themselves to upload to YouTube.

You can see the same dynamic in Aaron the would-be football player, the boy whose story opened this chapter. Aaron cares what his friends think. He wants to look cool in their eyes. When he's playing video games, he's top dog. His friends are impressed by his prowess. If he returned to the football field, he would be at the bottom of a different totem pole, with the athlete at the top and chubby Aaron huffing and puffing far below.

Julia is concerned about her friends' opinions, but she is mortified by her own self-assessment. She has constructed a self-concept that is all about being #1, being amazing. Her struggles in physics have popped that bubble, leading to an existential crisis. *If I am not the amazing student I thought I was, then who am I?* she asks herself. She has no answer.

In my assessment, one cause of the fragility in both Aaron's case as well as Julia's case is a weak parent-child relationship. Aaron and Julia would be the first to tell you that they love their parents. But they are not seriously concerned with what their parents think. Or more precisely, Aaron is more concerned about what his peers think than what his parents think. Julia is more concerned about her inflated self-concept than about what her parents think. *Kids need to value their parents' opinion as their first scale of value*, at least throughout childhood and adolescence. (Of course this rule cannot apply if the parents are incompetent or pathological or absent altogether. My assumption in this book is that you are a caring and concerned parent. If that assumption isn't valid, then this book is not for you.)

If parents don't come first, then kids become fragile. Here's why. A good parent-child relationship is robust and unconditional. My daughter might shout at me, "I hate you!" But she would know that her outburst is not going to change our relationship. My wife and I might choose to suspend some of her privileges for a week if she were to have such an outburst, but she would know that we both still love her. That won't change, and she knows it.

Peer relations, by contrast, are fragile by nature. Emily and Melissa may be best friends, but both of them know that one wrong word might fracture the relationship beyond repair. That's one reason why Emily is so frantic about checking her text messages every 5 minutes. If Melissa sends a text, and Emily does not promptly respond, Emily is afraid that Melissa may misinterpret her silence as indicating a lack of enthusiasm. **In peer relations, everything is conditional and contingent.**

Aaron doesn't want to look incompetent in the eyes of his peers, not for a week, not even for a single day. So he will not risk the humbling experience of being the least-fit player. Julia can't bear the thought of being anything other than a top student. So she cannot, will not, risk the humbling experience of being below-class-average in physics. Her self-concept is *conditional* on being #1. When she is no longer #1, or close to #1, her self-concept crumbles. I agree with the two other physicians who evaluated her that she meets formal criteria for the diagnosis of depression. But those other doctors failed to ask *why* she is depressed. The answer is that reality has popped the bubble of her self-concept. And the appropriate remedy for Julia, I believe, is not Risperdal, but rather the construction of a different self-concept—one rooted not in extraordinary academic achievement but in the *unconditional* love and acceptance that her parents are ready to offer her.

Children and teenagers need *unconditional* love and acceptance today no less than they did 30 or 50 years ago. But they cannot get *unconditional* love and acceptance from their peers or from a report card. That's one reason why there has been an explosion in the prevalence of anxiety and depression among American teenagers, as they frantically try to secure their attachment to other teens, as they try to gain unconditional love and acceptance from sources that are unable to provide it.[8]

Many American parents accept this situation as an inevitable consequence of 21st-century life. But they are mistaken. This phenomenon—of kids valuing their relationships with same-age peers, or their sports, or their academics, or their after-school activities, above their relationships with parents—is far more prevalent in North America than elsewhere. Most kids in Ecuador, Argentina, and Scotland still look forward to spending free time with parents, grandparents, aunts, and uncles, just as American kids might have two generations ago. As one Scotsman told me, "We don't even think much about 'generations.' We just all enjoy doing things together."

American novelist Reif Larsen recently moved with his family to Scotland. In contemporary Scottish society, Larsen observes, "family always comes first." By comparison, he is struck by the failure of contemporary American culture "to acknowledge that children actually exist." This difference is manifest not only in how kids and adults spend their free time, but also in

> an infrastructural commitment to children in public places. At the Edinburgh airport, you can find three large soft-play areas in the terminals, ample highchairs and dedicated lines for families. You can preorder baby milk, which will be delivered to you at your departure gate. There's even an entire cushy room devoted solely to nursing mothers. . . . Compare this with our experience in the United States. In the Newark airport, there is no such room. After much searching, we discovered there was approximately one highchair for all of Terminal C. We had to drag it across the airport like a family of transient Bedouins.[9]

All of us, as parents, need to establish the primacy of the parent-child relationship over peer-to-peer relationships, over academics, and over other activities. How to accomplish that?

One simple strategy is to schedule vacations just for the family. When your daughter asks whether she can bring her best friend along, the answer must be NO. If the best friend comes along, then a significant portion of time on the vacation will go to your daughter bonding with her best friend. The main purpose of the family vacation should be to strengthen the bonds between parent and child, not to give the kids an expensive playdate. Even simpler is to create rituals, such as a weekly parent-child visit to a local coffee shop. Taking a walk together to the coffee shop, if it is within walking distance, provides a good opportunity to talk and listen to whatever your daughter or son might have to say. The family supper, the family trip to the movies, and even a ride in the car all provide opportunities to strengthen these bonds.

In all your arrangements for your child, try to make connecting with adults a higher priority than connecting with your child's same-age peers or academics or after-school activities. Prioritize your extended family and your close adult friends in the life of your child. If you have the opportunity to move closer to your child's aunts, uncles, and grandparents, do it. (We did.) When you are planning a vacation, look for opportunities for your child to connect with her aunts, uncles, and grandparents. You want to give your child a different perspective. You want to connect her to your culture. That task is arguably more difficult today than at any other time in American history. Today, the default for most American kids is a primary attachment to same-age peers.

There is another important element in Aaron's story, and that is his involvement in social media, linked to online video games. I can recall boys who were in situations similar to Aaron's as recently as 15 or 20 years ago. They failed to make the team, so they worked harder, got in shape, went back the next week or the next season, and then made the team. Those stories were common 20 years ago. They are rare today. How come?

I think the online world is part of the answer. Twenty years ago, the Internet was a slow, clunky novelty. There was no such thing as an *online* video game: it took forever just to download a single photo. Playing a fast-moving game against an online opponent in real time wasn't possible on a 14K dial-up connection. But today's online world provides Aaron with an alternative culture created mostly by other young people. His parents regard Aaron's immersion in the world of video games as unusual. They wonder why Aaron is not more concerned about being out of shape physically. But Aaron's reference point is not the real world of his parents, but the online world of his video games and the associated social media sites. He is in touch with literally hundreds of other people who are roughly his own age and whose priorities are similar to his. Video games come first. In his online world, his unconcerned, laid-back style is the norm, not the exception. If he were to express an earnest desire to get in shape so that he could play sports rather than spend his time with a game controller and a video screen, he would likely get a derisive response from his online peers. Or they might think he was joking.

Aaron's father isn't sure what to do. He said to me, "Who am I to tell him that he shouldn't go after his dream? I just want him to be happy." That's a common response. The kids themselves often say something along the same lines. Another young person in a similar situation said to me, "I'm just trying to do my own thing. Whatever floats your boat, you know?" That notion—*whatever floats your boat; if it feels good, do it*—reflects a particularly American perspective. That lack of concern is one factor contributing to the rapid rise in the proportion of young Americans who are not working and not looking for work. And that rapid rise, as we have seen, is uniquely American: it has not occurred in Sweden, Canada, the United Kingdom, Germany, France, Australia, Poland, and so forth.[10]

Part of your job as a parent is to *educate desire*. To teach your child to go beyond "whatever floats your boat." To enjoy, and to want to enjoy, pleasures higher and deeper than video games and social media can provide. Those pleasures may be found perhaps in conversation with wise adults; or in meditation, prayer, or reflection; or in music, dance, or the arts.

The parent-child attachment has to be the first priority. The irony here is that the majority of middle-income and affluent American parents already know about attachment. Some of them have even read books about "attachment parenting." They know all about offering their newborn baby unconditional love and acceptance. By 6 months of age, a baby born to middle-income or affluent American parents is likely to be surrounded with nurturing and love. At 1 year, American toddlers are just as competent as toddlers in the Netherlands or in New Zealand. But after their child's second birthday, American parents begin to go astray.

Your parenting style has to change as your child grows up. Think of a high school cheerleader. Now think of Jürgen Klinsmann, coach of the American men's national soccer team, which advanced to the round of 16 in the 2014 Men's World Cup; or Jill Ellis, coach of the American women's soccer team, champions of the 2015 Women's World Cup. When your child is an infant or toddler, you play the role of the cheerleader. When your toddler stumbles and falls, then clambers back up again, you say, "Good job! Way to go!" But as your child gets older, your role must shift. Less cheerleader, more Jürgen Klinsmann and Jill Ellis.[11] You have to correct. To redirect. To point out shortcomings. If your teenage son can't think of anything to do for fun other than playing video games, then you need to turn off the devices and get him into the real world. You need to educate his desire. You have to teach your child your values rather than allowing him or her to adopt by default the values promoted by contemporary American culture.

The main mechanisms by which contemporary American culture today asserts its primacy in the hearts of American kids are the Internet and the mobile phone. Neither of these existed in the lives of American kids 25 years ago. But today, it's common to see an American 4-year-old playing with an iPad, complete with Internet access. That's particularly true in affluent communities. And it's becoming common to see an American 9-year-old with her own cell phone—again, especially in affluent communities.

Now you start to see the real harm of the 9-year-old with a mobile phone, talking to her friends or texting them. The more time she spends connecting with her friends, the more likely she is to look to them for guidance about what matters and what doesn't.

The technology and the devices further divide the generations and undermine parental authority. Kids are more likely to understand the technology than adults are. The 9-year-old easily conquers the vagaries of Instagram and Snapchat. Her forty-something parents may not even know what Snapchat is. Even if they do, they may not see the point. Your daughter and her friends are more likely than you are to know how to upload a photo from a cell phone to an Instagram page, complete with digital special effects. That's one reason why your daughter may come to value her friends' opinions over yours. Her friends seem to know more about important things than you do. And the more time she spends on Instagram, the more likely she is to think that knowing about Instagram is important.

Some countries have traditions that help to maintain parent-child bonds. In Holland, schools close at noon every Wednesday so that kids can enjoy some quality midweek time with their parents. Most Dutch employers give their employees Wednesday afternoon or even the whole day off. French kids in elementary school traditionally have Wednesdays off as well, although the government is rethinking that position.[12] In Geneva, Switzerland, the public elementary schools close for two hours at lunch, every day, so that kids can go home and eat lunch with a parent. Many Swiss employers accommodate that tradition by giving their employees 2½ hours off for lunch, so that a parent can be at home with the child for that meal.[13]

We used to do something similar in this country. Growing up outside Cleveland, Ohio, in the 1960s and 1970s, I walked home for lunch every day.[14] For me, it seemed pointless, because my mom had to work, and I was walking to an empty home. (My parents were divorced; my father lived in Los Angeles.) My mother's employer didn't give her a 2-hour lunch break so that she could be at home with her kids.

So what are we supposed to do? American employers aren't going to give us, the employees, 2 hours off for lunch. They're not going to give us every Wednesday afternoon off. So we have to fight for supper with our families. Fight for time with your child. Cancel or forego after-school activities, if need be, in order to have more evening meals together. Your kids can't attach to you if they hardly ever see you. And turn the devices off.

In Chapter 1, we considered Dr. Gordon Neufeld's observations on the disintegration of the parent-child bond over the past 20 years. His main idea is that many of the problems we see with North American kids today—the defiance, the disrespect, the disconnection from the real world—can be traced to the lack of a strong attachment between parents and their kids. Or more precisely, to the fact that kids now form their primary attachment with same-age peers rather than with parents. As Neufeld writes, "the waning of adult authority is directly related to the weakening of attachments with adults and their displacement by peer attachments."[15]

Consider an acorn. Its strong shell prevents it from growing until the time is right. If you break open the shell too early, you don't stimulate the growth of a new tree. You just have a dead acorn. As with the acorn, the key to healthy child development is to do the right thing *at the right time*. Neufeld makes a strong case that the wrong attachment style in childhood and adolescence results in the wrong attachment style in early adulthood. Throughout childhood and adolescence, the primary attachment of a child should be to the parent. If a child has a strong primary attachment to a parent from infancy through adolescence, then when the child becomes an adult, that bond will break naturally, as an acorn breaks open naturally at the right time so that a new tree can grow. Such a child, once she becomes an adult, is ready to head out confidently into the world as an independent young adult. But increasingly, Neufeld and others have found, young people across North America just are not ready to step into the adult world. The same girl who refused to talk with her mom at 13 years of age is now texting her mom 5 times a day at age 22, asking for basic guidance about adolescent concerns. The acorn, having broken open too early, does not have the strength to become a tree.

Parents have to regain the central place in the lives of their children, displacing same-age peers. Same-age friends are great for your child. But your child's first allegiance must be to you, not to her best friend. The contemporary culture of texting, Instagram, Snapchat, YouTube, Twitter, Facebook, and online video games has concealed this fundamental reality, promoting and accelerating the premature transfer of allegiance to same-age peers.

Why are American kids today so fragile? The fundamental reason is the breaking of the bonds across generations, so that kids now value the opinions of same-age peers or their own self-constructed self-concept more than they care about the good regard of their parents and other adults. The result is a cult of success, because success is the easiest way to impress your peers and yourself. But the cult of success just sets the kid up for catastrophe when failure arrives, as we saw in Julia's case. And failure will come, sooner or later.

Failure comes to us all. The *willingness to fail*, and then to move on with no loss of enthusiasm, is a mark of character.[16] The opposite of fragility, as we have discussed fragility in this chapter, is the willingness to fail. When kids are secure in the unconditional acceptance of their parents, they can find the courage to venture and to fail. When kids value the good regard of their peers or their own self-concept above the good regard of their parents, they lose the willingness to fail. They become fragile.

PART TWO

Solutions

6

What Matters?

Which of the following, measured when a child is 11 years of age, is the best predictor of happiness and overall life satisfaction roughly 20 years later, when that child has become a 31- or 32-year-old adult?

A. IQ
B. Grade point average
C. Self-control
D. Openness to new ideas
E. Friendliness

The correct answer is C, self-control.

Until recently, the answer to this question would have been a matter of opinion or guesswork. The scientific study of long-term outcomes was mired in confusion for most of the 20th century. One reason for the confusion is the sheer number of human personality traits. People can be cheerful or gloomy, generous or stingy, prudent or reckless, truthful or dishonest, rude or polite, curious or incurious, intensely driven or relaxed, sensible or silly. It took psychologists most of the 20th century to figure out that human personality can be mapped onto a five-dimensional graph. Those five dimensions are separate from intelligence, which is best understood as a factor that influences personality but is not in itself intrinsic to personality.[1] To put it another way, psychologists now tell us that your personality is separate from how smart you are, just as it's separate from how tall you are or how physically strong you are.

The five dimensions of personality are Conscientiousness, Openness, Extraversion, Agreeableness, and Emotional Stability.[2] Each of these dimensions has multiple subordinate traits. For example, some of the traits associated with Conscientiousness include self-control, honesty, and perseverance. The association is not 100 percent. You can find people who exhibit self-control and honesty but fail to persevere, to give an example. Nevertheless, this five-factor model of human personality has opened up a new era in quantitative psychological research. It is now fairly easy for a modern researcher to look for correlations between personality traits and outcomes and to separate these outcomes from other factors such as IQ, household income, race, and ethnicity.

When these correlations are studied longitudinally, over years and decades—when we consider how a trait possessed by a child at age 10 in 1980 predicts that individual's health and wealth at age 38 in 2008—then we can begin to move from statistical correlation to causal inference. We can start to say, with some confidence, *what matters*. We can begin to answer the question: What should we be doing as parents to improve the likelihood of good outcomes for our children?

In one study, researchers looked at Americans nationwide from a wide range of backgrounds: affluent and low income, urban and rural, White and Black and Asian and Hispanic. They recorded how much money each person had earned in the past year, how happy they were, how much wealth they possessed overall, and how satisfied they were with their lives. The researchers correlated those outcomes with the Big Five factors listed above and separately with intelligence. Not surprisingly, they found that intelligence predicts both income and wealth: people who are more intelligent earn more money and have a higher net worth, on average, compared with people of below-average intelligence. But intelligence does not predict happiness or unhappiness. Smart people are not happier or unhappier, on average, compared with less intelligent people. Nor does intelligence predict life satisfaction. Smarter people might have more money compared with less-smart people, on average, but they are not any more satisfied with their lives overall.

You might reasonably wonder whether *any* of the Big Five traits could predict happiness *and* wealth *and* life satisfaction. Only one does: Conscientiousness. Individuals who are more Conscientious earn and save more money, even after researchers adjust for intelligence, race, ethnicity, and education. Individuals who are more Conscientious are also significantly happier than individuals who are less Conscientious, and they are substantially more satisfied with their lives.[3] Other studies have shown that Conscientiousness predicts better health and longer life.[4] People who are more Conscientious are less likely to become obese.[5] They are less likely to develop Alzheimer's disease.[6] They are more likely to live longer and happier lives[7] and, as noted above, more likely to be satisfied with their lives.[8]

Teenagers who are more Conscientious are less likely subsequently to use drugs or alcohol or to engage in risky sexual behaviors.[9] Although it's true that more Conscientious individuals enjoy higher socioeconomic status on average compared with less Conscientious individuals, the benefit of Conscientiousness with regard to health can't be attributed to socioeconomic status for two reasons: first, the researchers in all these studies controlled for socioeconomic status; second, the magnitude of the health benefit of Conscientiousness is more than three times the benefit associated with socioeconomic status.[10] No other human trait can pull off this hat trick. No other human trait predicts significantly greater wealth *and* health *and* happiness among those who possess it compared with those who do not.

In some ways, this is not a new insight. Nearly 300 years ago, in 1735, Benjamin Franklin wrote, "Early to bed, early to rise, makes a man healthy, wealthy, and wise." Going to bed early, deliberately abstaining from the temptations of the night, and getting up early, resisting the temptation to sleep in late, are good measures of *self-control*, and self-control is the characteristic most emblematic of Conscientiousness. We can update Franklin's maxim in 21st-century English as follows: "Exercising self-control in terms of when you go to sleep and when you wake up is associated with improved health, greater wealth, and greater academic achievement." And that's a true statement, though I concede that Franklin's version sounds better.

When I ask parents whether their kids are on the right road, many respond by mentioning something about grades and/or test scores. Parents often assume that if their kid is above average as measured by these markers, then their kid has an above-average chance of achieving happiness and success. Conversely, if their kid ranks below the 50th percentile in academic achievement, many parents are frantically searching for an explanation and a remedy, perhaps medication for Attention Deficit / Hyperactivity Disorder, or some other fix.

In short, many parents have come to assume that good grades and test scores are the best measures of achievement and the most reliable key to future happiness. But they are mistaken. If you want your child to be healthy *and* wealthy *and* wise, then your first priority should not be measures of cognitive achievement, such as high grades or test scores, but measures of Conscientiousness, such as honesty, integrity, and self-control.

Let's take a closer look at the data, because these findings are so striking and so important. Let's start with drugs and alcohol. Addiction to drugs and alcohol in adulthood can be measured. If Ted has been in rehab three times, and Ted tells you that he is still struggling with addiction, and Ted's friends agree that he is struggling, then it's a good bet that Ted has a problem.

Grades and test scores at age 11 don't accurately predict whether an individual will grow up to be an alcoholic or a drug addict. The best predictor of whether your 11-year-old will grow up to have a problem with drugs or alcohol is Conscientiousness, and the best single measure of Conscientiousness is *self-control*. Researchers found that children who scored high on measures of self-control at 11 years of age were much less likely to report problems with substance abuse at 32 years of age—and their friends gave reports that confirmed the same findings. But kids who scored low on measures of self-control at 11 years of age were much more likely to have problems with substance abuse two decades later, at age 32.[11]

Again, some parents push back when I share this research. If a child is an outstanding student or artist, a real prodigy, those parents often assume that their child's gifts will protect him or her from drug addiction. That's when I find that specific stories of real people are helpful. I sometimes mention Jim Morrison, lead singer for The Doors. Morrison was an outstanding student whose high-school teachers were awed by the depth and breadth of his scholarship. And Morrison's artistic gifts as a composer and musician are beyond dispute. Morrison died in 1971, addicted to heroin, at 27 years of age.[12]

The same relationship holds for overall physical health. Kids who scored lowest on self-control at 11 years of age were most likely to be in poor physical health at 32 years of age. Likewise, kids who scored highest in self-control at 11 years of age were least likely to be in poor physical health at age 32.[13]

Let's talk about money. What factors at 11 years of age predict who's going to be earning the most money at age 32? Who's going to be in financial distress? (Incidentally, those are two separate questions. How much money you earn is not a reliable predictor of whether you will be in financial distress. People earning $300,000 a year are somewhat less likely to be in financial distress compared with people earning $50,000 a year, but only somewhat. Regardless of income, it's often a struggle for people to live within their means.) Once again, the trait of self-control as measured in childhood predicts adult wealth with uncanny accuracy. Likewise, the lack of self-control in childhood predicts a higher likelihood of financial distress when that child grows up to be an adult.

The data are clear. Kids who had the most self-control at age 11 had the highest incomes and the best credit scores at age 32 and were least likely to be struggling financially. Conversely, kids with

Self-control in childhood predicts adult wealth and credit rating.

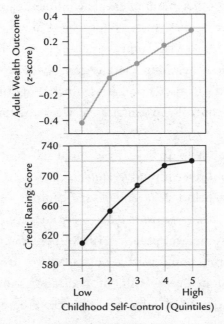

Source: Moffitt and colleagues 2013.

the least self-control at age 11 were, at age 32, the most likely to be struggling financially and the least likely to have a high income.[14] These researchers concluded, "Childhood self-control strongly predicts adult success, in people of high or low intelligence, in rich or poor, and does so throughout the entire population, with a step change in health, wealth, and social success at every level of self-control."[15]

This information is tremendously important, because you can help your child to become more Conscientious: to be more honest, to be more trustworthy, to develop better self-control.

There are many things you can't change. You can't change the color of your child's eyes. You can't change how tall he or she will be. Many other parameters that influence long-term outcomes in these studies, such as household income, also are not easily changed. Likewise, some aspects of personality are harder to change than others. But there is good evidence that you can boost your kid's Conscientiousness—including his or her honesty and self-control—in a matter of weeks, without spending any money.[16]

How do you help an 8-year-old build self-control? You say, *"No dessert until you eat your vegetables."*

How do you help a teenager build self-control? You say, *"No TV or Internet or video games until after you've done your homework."*

In my own medical practice, I have personally witnessed a child change from impulsive and out-of-control to self-controlled within a matter of weeks—without medication. All it takes is for the parents seriously to implement a simple program that builds self-control. You already know how to do this. *"Put your toys away after you play with them. No use of the cell phone until you do your household chores."*

Let me give you a tip. If you want to become a more authoritative parent, if you are going to insist on your child being honest and self-controlled, then sit down with your child and say so. Every household has rules, most of which are implicit and unspoken. Matters of habit. If you are going to change the rules, tell your child what you are doing and why. Parents who explicitly announce, "Things Are Changing As Of Today," then enforce the new rules and are not cowed when their child yells, *"You are totally ruining my life—I hate you!"* are surprised by how dramatic the change is. Not in one day. Not in one week. But after six weeks of consistent enforcement of the rules, your child will be more pleasant, and more respectful of you and of other adults. And both of you will be enjoying life more.

Your child's Conscientiousness is not hardwired. It is not determined at birth. It is something you can influence. It is something you can change.

What is true of self-control is true of the other major aspects of Conscientiousness, such as honesty, responsibility, and industriousness. There is one inescapable truth: *you must teach by example.* You can't expect your child to exercise self-control if you stay up past midnight watching TV or surfing the Web. You can't expect your child to be responsible if you don't keep your word. And you can't expect your child to be industrious if you yourself are often looking for the easy way out.

To become a better parent, you must become a better person.

Let's look at another study that followed kids from birth through adulthood. Researchers enrolled every child born at local city hospitals in April 1970, more than 17,000 babies in all. Then they followed those 17,000+ babies at regular intervals, right up through 2008, when they had reached 38 years of age.[17] Dr. James Heckman, a Nobel Laureate in economics at the University of Chicago, has analyzed the data on that large cohort of babies born in April 1970. He writes, "Numerous instances can be cited of high-IQ people who failed to achieve success in life because they lacked self-discipline, and low-IQ people who succeeded by virtue of persistence, reliability, and self-discipline."[18] Dr. Heckman's analysis of the cohort data has led him to conclude that grades and test scores "are poor predictors of success in life because they measure only one skill—cognitive achievement. . . . Far too much credit is given to cognitive skills. . . . Character skills play pivotal roles."[19]

So. One of your most essential duties as a parent is to teach Conscientiousness to your child. Let's look more closely at how to do that. I encounter some parents who act as though their job is simply to teach their child to parrot the usual clichés: *If at first you don't succeed, try again. If you try hard enough, your dream will come true.* By the age of 6, most American kids know these slogans and can produce the right answers when requested. So the parent thinks the job is done.

The job isn't even started.

Teaching Conscientiousness requires a different approach than teaching kids to be smart. Let's start with smart. What's the secret to raising smart kids? Stanford professor Carol Dweck thinks she knows. Her secret in one sentence: never tell your child that he or she is smart (identity); instead, praise him or her for working hard (behavior).[20] Many parents who have never heard of Carol Dweck have nevertheless heard of her famous experiment in which she randomly assigned young children to two groups. Each group took the same math quiz, which was easy. Most students earned a perfect score. In the first group, children were told, "You had a perfect score! You are so smart!" (identity). In the second group, students were told, "You earned a perfect score! You must have *tried really hard!*" (behavior). Then children in both groups took a more difficult math quiz. The students in the first group, who had been praised as smart, did badly on the harder quiz: they gave up too easily. But the students in the second group, who had been praised for trying hard, did better: they kept working on the harder problems until they succeeded in solving them.

Professor Dweck believes that if you praise children for being smart, they develop a "mind-set" that they have a certain amount of intelligence and that their IQ is fixed. If they then encounter a problem they can't solve, they may think, *I'm not smart enough to do this*, and give up. Professor Dweck recommends that you instead praise children for trying hard. Teach them that intelligence is not a fixed quantity but instead depends on their mind-set. If you try harder, you can become smarter.

In other words, Professor Dweck says that you should praise kids based not on their identity (smart / not smart) but on their behavior (trying hard / not trying hard). In the realm of promoting cognitive achievement—motivating kids to learn stuff in school—there is good evidence to support her belief.[21]

But teaching the virtues of Conscientiousness may be different. The students at my daughter's school were asked to bring a dollar with them one day to buy a special pencil. My daughter's friend forgot to bring her dollar. So my daughter gave her the dollar that she had brought to school to buy the same pencil, which meant that my daughter came home without the coveted pencil. Should I say to my daughter, *"That was a very kind thing you did"* or should I say *"You are a very kind person"*? Does it make any difference? If Professor Dweck's rule applies in the realm of virtue, then praising the behavior (*that was a very kind thing you did*) would be a better strategy than making a statement about identity (*you are a very kind person*). But there is now good evidence that when it comes to teaching virtue, Professor Dweck's approach is precisely the wrong way to go.

When it comes to teaching virtue, identity seems to work better than behavior. *You are a very kind person* works better than *That was a very kind thing you did*. In one study, students were less likely to cheat when they were told that the researchers were studying the prevalence of *cheaters*. The proportion of students who cheated more than doubled when researchers instead said that they were studying the prevalence of *cheating*.[22] Words make a difference. Saying, "Don't be a cheater" (identity), is a more effective instruction than saying, "Don't cheat" (behavior).[23] Apparently kids are more comfortable cheating if they don't see themselves as cheaters. Likewise, researchers have recently found that young children are more likely to help with a project if they are encouraged to "be a helper" rather than merely asked "to help."[24]

In a recent study of American high school students, more than 60 percent admitted to cheating on homework or tests in the past year. In the same study, more than 80 percent of those students said that their own personal ethics were "above average."[25] In the minds of many American students, ethical behavior no longer requires "not cheating on tests." They do not see themselves as "cheaters" even though they did, in fact, cheat. They see themselves as nice kids who occasionally cheat. But they aren't cheaters.

In reality, behavior influences identity and eventually becomes identity. If you cheat, over and over, you are—or will soon become—a cheater. Your actions will, over time, change your character. Parents used to teach these moral fundamentals, but many no longer do.

Cheating isn't new. But before roughly 1990, the kids most likely to cheat on tests or homework were not the academic high achievers. Today that's no longer the case. Today, the cream of the academic crop is just as likely, and possibly *more* likely, to engage in cheating compared with students lower down the academic totem pole.[26] According to Howard Gardner, a Harvard professor who has been studying academic integrity since the early 1990s, over the past two decades "the ethical muscles have atrophied." The attitude he now finds at the most selective universities—which he did not find there 20 years ago—is *We want to be famous and successful, we think our colleagues are cutting corners, we'll be damned if we'll lose out to them.*[27]

In defense of today's American teens: they are immersed in a popular culture that preaches that self-control is the one remaining sin in a world which has otherwise been washed free of guilt and responsibility. "Just Do It" and "Go For It" define 21st-century American popular culture. Exercising self-restraint in today's teen culture is downright un-American.

Pepsi recently launched a new marketing campaign, "Live for Now." I took photos of huge Pepsi billboards in various American cities with enormous images of Beyoncé promoting the slogan "Live for Now." I sometimes share those photos when I speak with parents about contemporary American culture. I think Pepsi accurately captured the sense of what children and teenagers in the United States today perceive as cool.

I'm not blaming Pepsi. I don't see the Pepsi marketing campaign as a *cause* of this disintegration but as a *symptom* of the disintegration. The *cause* is the collapse of American parenting. And I don't blame Pepsi for that.

Earlier I introduced you to Bill Phillips, father of four sons (remember the Breathalyzer?). Andrew is the oldest of the four. Andrew is also one of the most talented athletes I have ever met in more than two decades of medical practice. He is muscular, but also fast and agile. Early in the summer after 10th grade, he attended a weeklong football camp at the University of Maryland. At the end of the camp, the head coach of the Maryland football team called attention to Andrew as the most outstanding player at the camp. Coach Ralph Friedgen publicly announced that he would offer Andrew a full scholarship to play football at Maryland at the earliest allowable moment under NCAA rules. "I want you to come play with us. I want you to be a Terrapin," the coach said to Andrew.

Andrew told me that he was flying high at that moment. It's pretty special for the head coach of an NCAA Division I football team to call attention to how great you are when you still have two years of high school left to go.

When Bill Phillips arrived to pick up his son and heard about Andrew's new celebrity status, he made an unexpected announcement. "I don't think I mentioned this to you, but you'll be heading up to Maine next week. Your job for the rest of the summer is going to be on a fishing boat." Bill didn't ask his son, "What would you think of working on a fishing boat this summer?" He just told Andrew that's what he would be doing.

Sure enough, one week later, Andrew was in Portland, Maine, cleaning fish guts from the deck of a rusting fishing boat. (Andrew's father owned a fishing business.) Andrew's coworker was a convicted felon who had just been released from prison after serving a 15-year sentence for selling drugs. "And he was Mexican, and he had become a born-again Christian while he was in the penitentiary," Andrew told me. "So there I was on the deck of this dilapidated boat, listening to this Mexican ex-convict telling me about selling hard drugs, and getting busted, and coming to Jesus. Definitely not the kind of guy I would meet at my high school." Andrew attended an elite private high school in Maryland.

Bill Phillips didn't preach to his son about Conscientiousness and the virtues of hard work. He didn't say anything. He just signed his son up for a tough summer job. Andrew learned the lesson well. At the time, though, Andrew wasn't happy. "I did feel a little resentful. Other guys were having all kinds of fun adventures or camping trips, and there I was on this dumb boat cleaning fish guts off the deck. But now I understand why my dad made me do it. To give me a taste of the real world. To show me something about how other people live."

That's how you teach the virtue of hard work. That's also how you teach empathy: not by asking, "How would you feel if you were in that situation?" but rather by insisting that the adolescent spend a summer alongside someone from a different background, to learn the stories firsthand.

You don't teach virtue by preaching virtue. You teach virtue by requiring virtuous behavior, so that virtuous behavior becomes a habit.

There is a notion prevalent among American parents that kids need to be convinced or persuaded that an action is right before being asked to perform it. If you want kids to act virtuously, according to this assumption, you must first persuade your child of the importance of virtuous behavior. That sounds logical. It might even make sense, in some circumstances, if we were talking about grown-ups.

But even for grown-ups, there is strong evidence that the arrow of causality points in the other direction. Behaving virtuously leads people to become more virtuous, as a rule. Again, this insight is not new. More than a century ago, American psychologist William James observed, "Common sense says we lose our fortune, are sorry and weep; we meet a bear, are frightened and run; we are insulted by a rival, are angry and strike. . . . [But] this order of sequence is incorrect. . . . [T]he more rational statement is that we feel sorry because we cry, angry because we strike, afraid because we tremble, and not that we cry, strike, or tremble, because we are sorry, angry, or fearful, as the case may be."[28] There is a 2,000-year tradition along the same lines with regard to virtue. If you *compel* children to *act* more virtuously, they actually *become* more virtuous. In the biblical book of Proverbs, which scholars tell us was written more than 2,500 years ago, we read, "Train up a child in the way he should go, and when he is old he will not depart from it."[29] In other words, if you compel a child to behave virtuously, then when he is an adult he will continue to behave virtuously.

What does the published research have to say about this approach?

I think a fair summary of the empirical research would be that the book of Proverbs is too optimistic. A more accurate conclusion would be *Train up children in the way they should go, and when they grow up and move away from home, you will have **improved the odds**.* There are no guarantees. But the research strongly suggests that if you instill habits of good behavior and self-control in your son or daughter throughout childhood and adolescence, then you have improved the odds that your child will continue to do the right thing after leaving home.[30] Conversely, if you subscribe to the 21st-century-American notion that parents should leave kids free to do pretty much whatever they want, and your son is spending hours a night masturbating over pornography (which has become very common for American boys[31]), and your daughter is spending hours a night Photoshopping her selfies for Instagram and/or texting—then the odds are not good that when they arrive at college they will say, "Behold, my peers are spending much time on social media sites and playing video games, but I will nevertheless turn over a new leaf and become a more virtuous person." That's not very likely.

The Western tradition in parenting is to inculcate virtuous habits into children. Again, this goes way back. In the *Nicomachean Ethics*, Aristotle wrote that a person becomes virtuous by doing virtuous acts. Behavior becomes identity. The historian Will Durant, commenting on Aristotle, observed, "We are what we repeatedly do. Excellence, then, is not an act but a habit."[32]

The Western tradition begins not only with the Greeks and the Romans but also with Judaism. For that reason I will ask your permission to quote one more time from the Hebrew Bible, this time from the book of Deuteronomy. God has just given the commandments at Mount Sinai, and the text reads *V'shinantam l'vanecha*: וְשִׁנַּנְתָּם לְבָנֶיךָ. Those two Hebrew words are usually translated into English as "Teach them diligently to your children," or something along those lines. But that's not what the Hebrew says. The Hebrew says, "*Inscribe* them on your children."

The verb *shanan*, which I am translating as "inscribe," could also be translated as "incise"—it literally means to cut with a knife.[33] "Teach them diligently" is watered down.

I am not preaching or proselytizing here. I am not a missionary. I am a family doctor trying to understand what I am seeing in the office and across this country and why I didn't see it 25 years ago when I started my practice.

You teach virtue by requiring children to behave virtuously. In other words, you ask them to pretend that they are virtuous before they really are. As psychologist Adam Grant observes, "People often believe that character causes action, but when it comes to producing moral children, we need to remember that action also shapes character."[34]

As I have already emphasized, this is not a new idea. Aristotle wrote about it more than 2,000 years ago. In the mid-20th century, the British writer C. S. Lewis put the same idea this way: "The pretence leads up to the real thing. When you are not feeling particularly friendly but know you ought to be, the best thing you can do, very often, is put on a friendly manner and behave as if you were a nicer person than you actually are. And in a few minutes, as we have all noticed, you will be really feeling friendlier than you were. Very often the only way to get a quality in reality is to start behaving as if you had it already."[35]

Very often the only way to get a quality in reality is to start behaving as if you had it already. Lewis wrote those words more than a half century ago. They express wisdom that was common knowledge then, but no longer.

How you act influences the kind of person you are and the kind of person you are becoming. If we act virtuously, consistently, for long enough, we become more virtuous. But this process works the other way as well. William Deresiewicz interviewed graduates of elite American universities who had little sense of what they wanted to do with their lives. Some of them decided to get a job working for a Wall Street investment bank or management consultancy. If you don't know what your passion is or what you really want to do, they said, then "you might as well go to Wall Street and make a lot of money if you can't think of anything better to do."[36] And I have heard similar comments from young graduates of selective colleges and universities. Nobody has ever taught them that *what you do influences the kind of person you will become*. After a year or two in the Wall Street culture, working hard for companies that are all about making money, many of these kids will absorb that culture, which, after all, is well aligned with American popular culture: *Get what you can while the getting is good*. These attitudes, once formed, are hard to change and will likely influence a young person's choices long after she has left Wall Street.

Back in Chapter 2, when we were discussing the school lunch program, I mentioned that it is unrealistic to expect that simply *offering* kids healthier choices will consistently and reliably lead to kids *making* healthier choices. Now you can see that point in a larger context. The 21st-century assumption—implicit in many aspects of our society, such as the National School Lunch Program—is that if you give kids a choice between right and wrong and show them why they should make the right choice, then that is the choice they will make. This assumption is not based in evidence. It's based on a 21st-century guess about human nature.

The evidence suggests that such an approach is unlikely to work consistently. A more reliable and effective approach might be to *require* kids to eat the healthier food, for years, to inculcate healthy habits—and at the same time to educate them in the virtues of healthy eating. But merely hoping that kids will eat foods that are not their first choice is not likely to be effective in a culture where kids believe that their own desires should be paramount.

A regular contributor to the *New York Times*, Jennifer Finney Boylan, recently published a column in which she asked the question: What is school for? What does "getting an education" actually mean? What should it mean? Boylan offers two contrasting ideals, one old and one new. The old ideal, as she describes it, is about "handing down shared values of the community to the next generation." This ideal she disparages. In its place, she promotes a new ideal, which she describes as: "enlightening our children's minds with the uncensored scientific and artistic truth of the world. If that means making our own sons and daughters strangers to us, then so be it."[37]

That may sound brave and noble to some. It is certainly vintage 21st-century American. But the moment you begin to unpack it, questions arise. What precisely is the "artistic truth of the world"? Is the music of Mozart and Beethoven and Brahms and Stravinsky and Copland closer to the "artistic truth of the world" than the music of Katy Perry and Nicki Minaj and Lil Wayne and Justin Bieber and Miley Cyrus? Are the ethics of Lehman Brothers circa 2007 better or worse than the ethics of Mother Teresa circa 1977? Who gets to decide? If one simply sets kids loose in the chaos of 21st-century culture in the hopes that they will discover the "artistic truth of the world," what those kids will discover is most likely the popular culture of the Internet, social media, online video games, and pornography. They will have no standard by which to judge Miley Cyrus or Nicki Minaj in comparison with Stravinsky or Copland, no standard by which to compare the accounting gimmicks at Lehman Brothers with the altruism of Mother Teresa, because no authoritative teacher will have instructed them in a scale of value. Self-control is not innate. Honesty is not innate. These virtues have to be taught. If you don't teach them, who will? You can't rely on schools to do this job. Not in the United States. Not in this era.

In fact, the abdication of authority that Boylan and others put forward as enlightened wisdom is not wisdom at all. It is a dereliction of duty. It is a retreat from adult responsibility. As social critic Roger Scruton recently observed, the end result is that an American education, conceived in this way, is nothing more than "a rite of passage into cultural nothingness," with no clear guidance about what is worthwhile and what is not.[38]

I am not singling out Boylan personally. On the contrary, I have heard the sentiments she expresses presented at leading universities across the United States, during school board meetings in the United States, and from the heads of leading public and private schools across the United States.

Across the United States, but not elsewhere. This peculiar notion—that the best schools are those that most completely sever the bonds between parent and child, that most completely undermine parents' values and traditions—is uniquely American.

Reject the notion of virtue promoted by Boylan & Co. Think carefully about the virtues you want your children to possess, and teach them diligently. Inscribe them on your children. That means, among other things, that you yourself must demonstrate the virtues you want your child to develop. Teach your child self-control and restraint, which is no easy task in a culture where billboards scream "Live for Now." The stakes are the highest imaginable: the health and happiness of your child. This matters.

7

Misconceptions

When I meet with parents, some questions come up again and again. Parents want to do the right thing, but they are sometimes reluctant to try because certain misconceptions get in the way. We now have the foundation in place to address each of these misconceptions.

Here's the first:

I'm worried about a rebound effect. If I try to be the kind of parent you describe, and I force my child to behave "virtuously"—whatever that means—then when she goes away to college and she's on her own, I'm worried she will do all kinds of crazy things that she wouldn't have done otherwise, because I have prevented her from doing stuff she wants to do. She won't have learned how to make good choices on her own.

Longitudinal studies, such as those we considered in the previous chapter, are helpful in addressing this misconception. Those studies show that, in general, well-behaved kids are more likely to grow up to be well-behaved adults. Kids raised by more permissive parents are more likely to get into trouble as adults: trouble with alcohol, trouble with drug abuse, trouble with anxiety and depression.

In the early 1990s, researchers in the United States launched an ambitious study of more than 20,000 American kids drawn from every part of the United States: urban and rural, Asian, Black, Latino, and White, affluent and low income, East Coast and West Coast and Midwestern and Southern, and so forth. They gathered data on the teenagers in 1994, when most of these kids were 12 to 14 years old, and then periodically through 2008.[1] Researchers who have analyzed these data have found that the children of authoritative parents do better in school, are less likely to get drunk, and are less likely to engage in unsafe sexual practices—not only in their early teenage years but also in their 20s, compared to the children of parents who are less authoritative.[2] They go on to have healthier, happier romantic relationships in young adulthood.[3] As adults they have healthier babies, even after adjusting for demographic variables such as race, ethnicity, and household income.[4]

Diana Baumrind and her colleagues and students have published studies over the past 40 years addressing some of the same issues. Baumrind and her colleagues assessed how parents interacted with their kids when the children were young, then studied the outcomes many years down the road. Baumrind divided parenting styles into three categories, which we can refer to as "Too Hard," "Too Soft," and "Just Right."[5]

"Too Hard" parents rarely show any kindness or love to their child. They often make unrealistic demands. The children of these harsh parents are more likely than others to become abusive parents themselves 20 years down the road. The children of "Too Hard" parents are also more likely, as adults, to have difficulty sustaining romantic relationships.

"Too Soft" parents are usually good at expressing love and affection for their child, but not so good at enforcing rules.[6] The children of "Too Soft" parents are more likely, as adults, to have problems with drug and alcohol abuse; to struggle financially, regardless of their actual income, because they find it difficult to live within their means; and more likely to be convicted of a felony.

"Just Right" parents communicate their love for their child, but they also enforce rules fairly and consistently. The rules may bend on occasion, when necessary, but they don't break. Over more than four decades of research, Baumrind accumulated overwhelming evidence that the healthiest parenting style is the "Just Right" style. The children of "Just Right" parents are the most likely to have good outcomes, no matter which outcome you look at. "Just Right" parents are strict, within reasonable bounds, and also loving.[7]

When I present these three categories, almost all parents say that they want to be "Just Right." But what they consider "Just Right" is different from what their parents would have considered "Just Right." Over the past 30 years, the American notion of "Just Right" has shifted steadily away from authoritative to permissive. Baumrind herself recently noted that there has been "a definitional drift" in the way scholars use her categories. She cites one group of scholars who included "easy-going" as one of the characteristics of "authoritative" parenting; the same scholars neglected to include any parameter related to strictness, which Baumrind considers essential to authoritative parenting.[8]

Many parents today perceive a tension between "strict" and "loving." They think you can be *either* strict *or* loving but not both. Baumrind's research proves that notion to be wrong. The parents whom she found to be "Just Right" were *both* strict *and* loving.[9] If you are not enforcing the rules—if your kids regard you as loving but not strict—then you are "Too Soft." As I said, there has been a shift in American parenting from "Just Right" to "Too Soft" as measured by the standards of 1985. This shift helps to explain the misconception of the parent who is concerned that her daughter's behavior will "rebound" if the parent enforces a virtuous code of behavior while the daughter is in middle school and high school. Many parents today seem to believe that stricter parenting now will result in a "rebound" into degenerate behavior when their kids go away to college. Sometimes this belief is an after-the-fact rationalization for less authoritative parenting. In other words: it's a way of justifying what the parent is going to do anyhow. When I ask parents *why* they believe that stricter parenting now will result in more reckless behavior by their child a few years down the road, they often respond by citing a movie about a teenager who had puritanical parents or by mentioning something they saw years ago on *Oprah*.

I answer these parents by pointing out that the research provides no support for this notion. Indeed, the research flatly contradicts it. But rather than harp on the scholarly studies, I ask the parents to consider whether this same notion would make sense in any other context.

Suppose you are hiring a new employee, and you have to choose between Sonya and Vanessa. Sonya's previous employers tell you that she always shows up for work on time, never cheats or steals, never uses company time for personal chores. Vanessa's previous employers tell you that Vanessa often shows up an hour or two late for work, she has stolen office property and then lied about it, and she often visits Instagram on a company computer when she is supposed to be working. Would you say, *"I'm sure Vanessa has gotten rid of all her bad impulses, so now is the time to hire her"*? Would you say, *"I won't hire Sonya because she is so repressed, odds are good that she is going to 'rebound' sometime soon"*? No you wouldn't.

In this example, the prospective employer is following a rule which used to be well known to American parents: **virtue begets virtue, and vice begets vice.** The employee who has a record of honesty and virtue in the past is more likely to be honest and virtuous in the future. In the workplace, most Americans understand this.

But at home, they forget. This notion of "rebound" is based not in evidence but in the popular culture of the early 21st century: not a reliable source of information. And this notion is propagated, I believe, in part by the desire of at least some parents to justify to themselves their own less authoritative parenting style.

Don't accept this notion of "rebound." Don't believe it. As I said in the previous chapter: if you train your son or daughter in the way they should go, then when they grow up and leave home, you have significantly improved the odds that they will behave wisely. Virtue begets virtue. Vice begets vice.

Next misconception:

I'm worried that if I follow your advice, my child will be an outcast. He will be the only one who isn't allowed to play Halo *or* Grand Theft Auto. *I'm worried that he will be unpopular, and he will blame me for that. And he will be right. I'm trying to find the right balance here.*

I recently was a guest on the *TODAY* Show alongside Dr. Meg Meeker, author of *Strong Fathers, Strong Daughters* and *Strong Mothers, Strong Sons*. Dr. Meeker is also an experienced pediatrician who happens to have four kids of her own, three daughters and one son, Walter. She always told Walter, "No video games. No video-game devices. You're not wasting your time on that." (Her daughters didn't have much interest in video games to begin with.)

Walter complained. "All the other boys are playing *Call of Duty*. I'm the only one who isn't allowed to."

Mom said, "Too bad."

When Walter turned 18, he said, "I'm an adult now. I have money that I have earned from my job. I'm going to go and buy a PS3 and some video games like *Call of Duty*."

Mom said, "Fine."

One year later, near the end of his freshman year at the University of Dayton, Walter called his mom. "I just made $400!" he told his mom. "Guess how I did it?"

Mom said, "No idea."

"I sold my PS3 and all my video games. They were just gathering dust anyhow," Walter said. He explained that he saw so many other guys at college who had started playing these games many hours a week at 10 or 12 or 14 years of age. These boys defined themselves as gamers. Their sense of self was tied up with their proficiency at playing video games. They expected Walter to be impressed by their video-game skills.

But Walter was not impressed. He had a different perspective. During those crucial adolescent years when he was *not* allowed to play video games, he had developed a wide array of hobbies and interests, as well as people skills, which the gamers were less likely to have. He observed that the gamers were often clumsy in real-life social situations.

Age matters. If a boy starts playing video games when he is 9 or 12 or 14 years old, those games may "imprint" on his brain in a way that they won't if he starts playing at 18. Before puberty is complete, the brain is enormously plastic, as discussed in Chapter 1. That's both good and bad. The plasticity of the brain before and during puberty allows it to change in fundamental ways as circumstances require. But the areas of the brain responsible for judgment and perspective aren't mature. Once the process of puberty is fully complete—once the boy becomes a man or the girl becomes a woman—the areas of the brain responsible for anticipating consequences and thinking ahead are stronger.[10]

Now let's return to the question at hand: Do the benefits of restricting what video games your son plays outweigh the (assumed) costs of his being less popular as a result?

I gave a presentation to parents in which I shared recent research on video games. I focused on longitudinal research in which investigators followed a large cohort of kids over several years to see, after adjusting and controlling for all other variables, how and whether the kids changed as a result of the kinds of video games they played.[11] This research strongly suggests that kids who spend many hours a week playing violent video games such as *Grand Theft Auto* and *Call of Duty* become more hostile, less honest, and less kind. Not right away, not after a week or a month, but after years of playing those violent games.

After reviewing multiple studies on the long-term outcomes of playing first-person-shooter video games such as *Grand Theft*

Auto, I recommended banning those games from the household. If your son wants to shoot things, have him join a local skeet club instead. And if your child is going over to a friend's house, call the parents ahead of time and ask whether the kids will be permitted to play violent video games there. If the other parents allow those games to be played, then you should not allow your child to go to that friend's house. That child can be invited to your house instead, where you are in charge.

This recommendation struck one parent as harsh. She said that my recommendation was "totally unrealistic. There is no way I can police what my son is going to do at someone else's house." In addition, she worried that if she even tried to enforce a ban on violent first-person-shooter games such as *Call of Duty* and *Grand Theft Auto*, then her son would be less popular because he would be the only boy who wasn't allowed to play those games. She said, "I'm trying to find the right balance here."

Let's unpack the multiple assumptions driving this parent's concerns:

- **Assumption #1:** *It's important for my child to be popular.* False. Being popular in the United States in the 21st century often entails unhealthy behavior and attitudes, beginning with a disregard for parental authority. Recent evidence suggests that being popular in the United States at age 13 today may actually be a major risk factor for bad outcomes in early adulthood.[12] You need to be clear in your own mind about what's important. Helping your child to become kind, well behaved, and self-controlled is important. Your child being popular with lots of same-age peers is not.

- **Assumption #2:** *It's unrealistic for me to hold my child responsible for behavior outside my home.* Also false. I have observed many "Just Right" parents closely and at firsthand over the past 20 years in my medical practice, first in Maryland and more recently in Pennsylvania. All of the "Just Right" parents I have known expect their child to behave outside the home as he or she does when at home. There is a word for that consistency of behavior: the word is "Integrity." Integrity is one of the traits linked to Conscientiousness. "Just Right" parents do not hesitate to call or even occasionally to drop in without warning at their kids' friends' homes to check on what their kids are doing. That's one way to teach Integrity.

- **Assumption #3:** *Parents should find a balance between "Too Hard" and "Too Soft."* True, but misunderstood. The parent who asked this question had accepted the contemporary American notion that parents have to choose between being strict *or* loving. As a result, she thinks it's unrealistic to try to be strict *and* loving. She is mistaken.

This particular parent was talking about video games. But the same analysis applies across different domains. If your daughter spends too much of her free time Photoshopping her selfies for Instagram, or if your son spends all of his time surfing the Internet, it's your job to unplug the device and get your child or teen reconnected to the world of real experience—whether that experience is talking with another human being face-to-face, playing field hockey, or splashing in a pond to chase tadpoles.

A parent in Sandy, Utah (near Salt Lake City), told me that she didn't allow any of her children to have cell phones, period, right through high school. "I just never saw the need for it," this mom told me. And the other kids didn't have a problem with it. No big deal. But the other *parents* gave this mom a hard time. "Why are you making her the odd girl out?" they would ask her.

Whether you live in Utah or California or Florida or New York: Do what's best for your child. Don't be too concerned about what other kids or other parents might say.

Next misconception:

I want my child to be independent. So when she talks back to me or is disrespectful, I try to see that in a positive light, as a sign that she is becoming more independent. And I support that.

It is never acceptable for your child to be disrespectful to you. That doesn't mean she has to agree with you. It's fine for her to say, "I don't agree. I think you are making a mistake." But it is never acceptable for her to say, "Shut up. You don't know what the f*** you're talking about." Yet that sort of language has become commonplace in the United States, in affluent communities as well as in low-income communities. Disrespectful language has also become common on the most popular American television programs. Don't allow such language in your house.

But true independence of thought is useful. How to cultivate that independence without encouraging disrespect? Most of the "Just Right" parents I have known are able to accomplish this feat. One strategy revolves around suppertime conversation. Long rides in the car also provide a good opportunity. For younger kids, it could be talking about a favorite food or about movies. Ask your kids to name their favorite movie among those they have seen recently and to explain why it's their favorite. Describe how and why your opinion differs. Show them that two people can disagree about preferences for one movie over another or about their taste in food without disrespecting or disliking one another.

For teens, you might choose a controversial topic from the news. Ask your teen to express an opinion about nuclear power versus conventional power versus solar or wind power. Or ask your teen a question about the Palestinian-Israeli conflict. Listen carefully and respectfully to your child's position. Then state how your opinion differs and why you don't agree with your child's position. For purposes of this exercise, stay away from personal topics such as whether your child should be allowed to stay up late playing video games or surfing the Internet. The point of the exercise is to develop the skill of disagreeing respectfully—of building independence without hostility. Once that skill is honed, you and your child or teen should be able to navigate more personal disagreements with less likelihood of the discussion degenerating into an argument.

Next misconception:

I just want my son to be happy. What makes him happy is different from what makes me happy. I'm thinking I may just have to accept that.

This mom has a teenage son who spends at least 20 hours a week playing video games. For months she tried to restrict his playing time to refocus his attention on academics. He's doing OK in school but not as well as he could be. She kept saying things like, "If you want to get into a top college, you need to do better in school. I know you can do better but you're wasting too much time on video games. You should spend more time on schoolwork and less time playing video games."

Finally one day he exploded. "I DON'T GIVE A S**T whether I get into a top college!" he yelled. "I don't want to GO to college. Look, you don't know anything about *World of Warcraft*, but I am a celebrity because of this game. I'm level 85. I am Guild Master. You don't even know what that means. It means that there are people in Singapore and Johannesburg and Tokyo who basically worship me. That's worth something. I can monetize that. I don't care about trigonometry or Spanish or American History or any of the rest of that crap they teach at school. I. DON'T. F***ING. **CARE**. So just leave me alone, will you?"

Mom was stunned into silence. Her son was right about one thing: she had no idea what it meant to be Guild Master in the online video game *World of Warcraft* (*WOW*). She went online and learned how huge *WOW* is. She discovered that some young men actually earn real money playing *WOW* full-time. It had never previously occurred to her that some boys and young men might value achievement in virtual online worlds such as *World of Warcraft* more than they value achievement in the real world of school and face-to-face friendships.

In the weeks between her son's outburst and her conversation with me, she had come to question her own position. The contemporary world is different from the world of 20 years ago, she reflected. Twenty years ago, *WOW* did not exist. Twenty years ago you couldn't earn money creating and selling accessories for combat in imaginary online worlds. But today you can. So maybe she should stop worrying about her son's suboptimal academic achievement and instead support him in whatever he wants to do. "I just want him to be happy," she said to me more than once.

I told mom that she was confusing *happiness* with *pleasure*.[13] That's common today. A trip to the video arcade may be a source of pleasure, but it will not give lasting and enduring happiness. This mother's son derives pleasure from playing video games, but playing video games in an online world is unlikely to be a source of real fulfillment. The pleasure derived from a video game may last for weeks or even months. But it will not last many years, in my firsthand observation of many young men over the past two decades. The boy either moves on to something else, or the happiness undergoes a silent and malignant transformation into addiction. The hallmark of addiction is decreasing pleasure over time. Tolerance develops. Playing the game becomes compulsive, almost involuntary. It no longer gives the thrill and pleasure it once did. But the addict can no longer find pleasure in anything else.

Pleasure is not the same thing as happiness. The gratification of desire yields pleasure, not lasting happiness. Happiness comes from *fulfillment*, from living up to your potential, which means more than playing online video games.

This mom should trust her instincts. Her son, playing *World of Warcraft* 20 hours a week, is not fulfilling his potential. He is indulging a desire, an uneducated desire. Mom needs to disconnect the video game and redirect her son.

Such redirection is not fun. It is not easy. Your son will not thank you for it now, or next week, or next month. Maybe he will in 5 years. Maybe. But you aren't doing this job in order to win your son's approval. You are doing this job because *it is your job*, as a parent, to help your child to find and to fulfill his or her potential. That is never simple because neither you nor your child can know in advance precisely where your child's potential lies. But it surely doesn't consist in spending 20 hours a week playing online video games.

Turn off the device.

Again, this recommendation doesn't apply just to video games. The same considerations hold if your child or teen says that he or she is happiest when uploading photos to Instagram or surfing the Web or sending and receiving text messages. Part of the task of the parent is, and always has been, *educating desire*: teaching your child to desire and enjoy things that are higher and better than cotton candy. Video games, Instagram, and text messages are the cotton candy of American popular culture today.

In the United States our popular culture today puts a premium on the satisfaction of personal desire. "Live for Now." "Whatever floats your boat." You are trying to teach Conscientiousness: honesty, self-control, and integrity. You are battling the culture.

It's a challenge to raise a child in opposition to the culture in which you live. As David Brooks recently observed, "We all live within distinct moral ecologies. The overall environment influences what we think of as normal behavior without [our] being much aware of it."[14] Today the assumption which pervades American culture is the belief that your child's personal fulfillment is roughly equivalent to the fulfillment of your child's desires. A child presumably knows her own desires better than her parents possibly can. If the key to human fulfillment is the satisfaction of immediate and uneducated desire, then the authority of the parent becomes subordinate to the whim of the child.

As I have said, one assumption that now drives American culture, as experienced by kids born and raised in this country, is *If it feels good, do it. Inhibitions just hold you back. Whatever floats your boat, go for it.* Arthur C. Brooks, president of the American Enterprise Institute, recently commented on the American slogan "If it feels good, do it." He observed that this slogan equates the existential goals of a human being with those of protozoa.[15]

We are human beings, not protozoa. Being a human being means more, and *should* mean more, than mere gratification of desire. Service to others. Mastery of the arts. Faith in something greater than oneself. Discipline in pursuit of a higher goal. All these and more have traditionally been recognized as the proper aims of human life. Gratification of uneducated desire—*if it feels good, do it*—has historically been seen as a distraction, a temptation to stray from the goal of true fulfillment, not the goal itself. The result of the cultural acceptance of this notion—"Live for Now"—is the infantilizing of American culture, compounding the cult of youth that is already one of our greatest weaknesses.

The solution is mindfully to create an alternative culture. To build a subversive household in which the dinner table conversation is actually conversation, with the screens switched off. To value family time together above time that kids spend with same-age peers. To create a space for silence, for meditation, for reflection, so that your child can discover a true inner self that is more than the mere gratification of impulse.

It's not easy to battle the weight of the culture. But it can be done.

Next misconception:

If I love my child, then that means I also trust my child, right? If she says she didn't cheat on the test, and if I love her, then I have to trust her, right? You can't have love without trust.

Again, this misconception is easier to understand if you know the context. This girl was taking a test at school. The teacher caught the girl looking at her cell phone during the test and copying answers from it. The teacher confiscated the cell phone and sent the girl to the principal's office. The girl insisted that the teacher had made a mistake. The phone just happened to be in her lap, but she wasn't looking at it. So she said. The principal supported the teacher's decision to mark the test a zero.

The parents went ballistic. They swooped in like prosecuting attorneys. "It's just the teacher's word against the word of our daughter," the father said. "Our daughter said she didn't do it. And our daughter would never lie to us."

Mom took a more reflective, less adversarial tone than her husband. That's when she said, "If I love my child, then that means I also trust my child, right? If she says she didn't cheat on the test, and if I love her, then I have to trust her, right? You can't have love without trust."

Short answer to mom's question: **the rules of love between parent and child are different from the rules between adults.** Maybe it's true that love between adults requires blind trust. It's certainly not true of a parent's love for a child. The father in this case said, "Our daughter would never lie to us." I don't know that family, but I know that father is wrong. Any parent who says such a thing is wrong. *Your daughter (or son) is more likely to lie to you than to anyone else,* because she doesn't want to disappoint you. She doesn't want to let you down. And she hopes that you will think well of her, even if she does value her peers' opinions more highly than yours.

Which brings us back to cheating. In the previous chapter we discussed the rise of cheating among American kids, including "good" kids who work hard and get good grades. American kids today usually consider cheating to be no big deal. Almost every-body's doing it or they know someone who is. But many kids also have an uneasy feeling—which happens to be correct—that their parents were raised in a different era, an era in which good kids did not cheat. So the temptation to lie to parents about cheating is very strong.

A generation ago, there was an alliance between parents and the school. If a teacher, or the principal, notified the parents that their child had been caught cheating, the parents would likely im-pose penalties at home to reinforce the school's discipline. In the United States, that alliance is broken. Today, when a student is caught cheating and the school seeks to impose some semblance of discipline, the parents often act as adversaries, challenging the school's authority.

I spoke on this topic at a middle school in Menlo Park, Califor-nia, an affluent community in Silicon Valley. I was speaking to an audience of about 300 parents. A woman in the front row raised her hand. I called on her. She said,

> Dr. Sax, I would like to share a story with everyone here. Last year I caught a girl cheating on a test, very similar to the situation you just described. I reprimanded her for cheating, in front of the class, and I marked her test a zero. But it turns out that her parents are venture capitalists who have millions of dollars. They have friends on the school board. They donate to the school district. After I reprimanded their daughter, they made some phone calls. About two weeks later, I was called into the principal's office. I was told that as a condition of my continued employment, I would have to apologize to this girl, in class, in front of all the other students. So that's what I did. I wasn't ready to quit.

So do you want to know what I did this fall, when the new school year began? I told all my students, "Go ahead and cheat if you want to. I'm not even going to try to enforce the rules, because I have learned that the district doesn't want me to. I hope you won't cheat, but if you do, I won't say a word about it."

Many times in recent years, I have heard stories like this one. But usually they are whispered to me. Once a teacher actually pulled me into the janitor's closet and closed the door to tell me her story. What was unusual about the story the teacher shared in Menlo Park is that she had the courage to tell it out loud, to an audience of about 300 of her neighbors.[16]

Don't say, "My daughter would never lie to me." In more than 20 years of clinical practice, I have found that whenever a parent says, "My child would never lie to me," you can be fairly sure that child is doing just that: lying to the parent.

One final misconception:

I'm worried that if I follow your advice, my child won't love me anymore.

Read your job description. Your job as a parent is to raise your child to be the best person she or he can be. Your reward comes from knowing that you have done your job well. As wonderful as it is to receive a loving hug or a spontaneous and unasked-for "I *love* being with you" from your child, such shows of affection can't be your main objective.

Many parents are in marriages or long-term relationships that have frayed. Other parents are single, without a loving partner.

The parent without a partner or whose partner is unloving may look to the parent-child relationship for warmth and affection. I understand that. My own mom was a single mom who spent the last half of her life looking for the right partner. She never found him. In my adult patients, I see the loneliness of the single parent or of parents who are stuck with partners whom they no longer love or who no longer love them.

But trying to get your child to give you more affection, in order to fill the void that an adult partner should fill, greatly undermines your authority as a parent. In a relationship with an adult partner, everything is negotiable. You are equals. You can't give each other orders. Your relationship with your child is different. You have to set the rules and enforce them, even if your child doesn't agree that vegetables should come before dessert. It's confusing to everybody involved if one moment you are trying to be the affectionate "cool" parent and the next moment you are trying to be the "Just Right" parent. The most common result is that parents slip from being "Just Right" into being "Too Soft," because they don't want to jeopardize the affection they hope to gain from their child.

Abigail, a mom living near Tampa, Florida, shared with me a story that I think illustrates the right priorities. Her 14-year-old daughter Kasey wanted to go to Cancun for spring break with her friends. But parents were not invited. Her mother pointed out that Cancun has become a popular spring break destination for American college students. And although Kasey was 14, she could easily pass for 18—the process of sexual maturation was complete. "How is a young man supposed to know that you are underage?" mom asked.

"Mom, stop being so paranoid," Kasey said. "We will be totally fine. We will stay together. We'll have our cell phones."

"I don't think it's safe," mom said.

"It's totally safe," Kasey said.

"You're not going," Abigail said.

"Mom! You are going to like totally *ruin* my whole *life*! All my friends are going! Everybody is going!"

"You're not going," Abigail repeated.

"I hate you!" Kasey screamed. "I hate you! I never want to talk to you again as long as I live!"

"Well," Abigail answered, "to be honest, sometimes I'm not so fond of you either. But I'm your mother. That means my #1 job is keeping you safe. And I know more than you do about the behavior of drunk college boys. You're not going."

And Kasey didn't go.

Over more than two decades as a family physician, I have been involved professionally in a handful of cases of sexual assault, each with a girl as victim. In one case, my only involvement was to sit with mom after the fact. "I knew I shouldn't have let her go," this mom said to me. "She's just 15 years old. It was a party for college kids. I knew I shouldn't have let her go."

One part of me wanted to shake the mom and yell, "**THEN WHY DID YOU LET HER GO??**" But of course I didn't do that. Because I already knew the answer. This mom wanted her daughter to like her. She didn't want her daughter to be upset with her.

If you are doing your job as a parent, then sometimes you will have to do things that will upset your child. If you are concerned that your child won't love you anymore, that concern may keep you from doing your job.

Do your job.

8

The First Thing: *Teach Humility*

When I meet with parents, I sometimes ask, in regard to their children: "What is most important to you? What are you trying to help your children to become?" Parents often answer, "I want my kids to be happy, to be fulfilled, to be kind."

"That's great," I say. But when I ask, "How are you going to help your child get from here to there? What will it take for your child to reach that goal—to grow up to be a kind person, an honest person?" many parents aren't sure how to respond. Particularly in the United States, parents are likely to confuse fulfillment with success. The assumption seems to be that if the child goes to a good college and gets a good job, then personal fulfillment is assured. When I point to the evidence that professional achievement is no guarantee of personal fulfillment or life satisfaction, many parents don't know what to say.

What do you need to teach your child? My answer: the first job of the American parent has to be to teach humility.

Why humility? **Because humility has become the most un-American of virtues.** And partly for that reason, humility today is the most essential virtue for any kid growing up in the United States. **Because so many American parents have confused virtue with success.** The only real sin, for many middle-income and affluent parents today, is failure. Teaching humility, and trying to practice what you preach, is the most useful corrective. Most American parents are fine with the idea of teaching openness, agreeableness, and so forth. But humility? They don't know where to start, or how, or why. Some parents no longer even understand what the word "humility" means. Those parents think that humility means trying to convince yourself that you're stupid when you know that you are smart. That's not humility. That's psychosis: a detachment from reality. The fact that the psychosis might be pursued with good intentions does not make it any less psychotic.

No. Humility simply means being as interested in other people as you are in yourself. It means that when you meet new people, you try to learn something about *them* before going off on a spiel about how incredible your current project is. Humility means really listening when someone else is talking, instead of just preparing your own speechlet in your head before you've really heard what the other person is saying. Humility means making a sustained effort to get other people to share their views before trying to inundate them with yours.

The opposite of humility is inflated self-esteem. I recently visited an elementary school where the third-grade students were required to write five words to describe how amazing they were. Each student then attached the words to a big cut-out of his or her own name. Everything was taped up on the wall for all to see. I took a photograph of one boy's poster. He chose these words to describe himself:

- Marvelous
- Awesome
- talented
- exellent [*sic*]
- a Geenius [*sic*]

I don't mean to pick on this boy. After all, he was just doing the assignment the teacher had given him. I share this story to illustrate how little awareness there is in some schools of the way in which a puffed-up ego at age 8 or 14 can lead to resentment at age 20 or 25.

I recently took another photo at an American public school of a flowery poster with the words "Dream until your dreams come true." That's bad advice. That advice cultivates a self-righteous sense of entitlement. Better advice might be, **Work** *until your dreams come true.* That might not sound as good, but it would be one notch closer to reality. A truer statement, possibly suitable for framing, would be, *Work in pursuit of your dreams, but realize that life is what happens while you are making other plans. Tomorrow may never come or may be unrecognizably different.*[1]

I debated this point recently with Charlene, an American high school student. Charlene hopes and expects to be a famous novelist someday. She's a teenager who has experienced the usual slings and arrows of adolescence and has used those experiences as grist for her fiction. Her teachers have praised her writing. She has sent manuscripts to agents but has received only rejection notices.

Charlene has very high self-esteem. I don't think that's such a good thing. Her high self-esteem at age 15 is setting her up for disappointment and resentment at age 25. I have witnessed this trajectory many times. Soaring self-esteem in childhood and adolescence, carefully nurtured by parents and teachers, predictably leads to a crash after college, typically about 3 to 5 years after graduation, when it slowly dawns on the young adult—the same adult who had been so talented as an adolescent—that she's actually not as talented as she thought. She discovers that just because she was repeatedly told that she is amazing does not mean that she is, in reality, amazing.[2]

Put bluntly, **the culture of self-esteem leads to a culture of resentment**. If I am so wonderful, but my talents are not recognized and I'm still nobody at age 25, working in a cubicle—or not working at all—then I may feel envious and resentful of those who are more successful than me. *How come that other young writer got her novel published, and she was on the* TODAY *Show and I can't even get an agent?*

One parent recently said to me, "Kids need self-esteem. I want my daughter to have the courage to apply for that big job, her dream job. And that requires self-esteem."

Not quite, I answered. Taking appropriate risks requires *courage*, first and foremost. Again, many parents confuse self-esteem with courage, just as some parents tend to confuse humility with timidity and cowardice. To be courageous means that you recognize the risks and your own limitations, but you find the resolve to move forward anyhow. The young person with bloated self-esteem, unaware of her own deficiencies, is unlikely to do well in the job interview. But the young person who is genuinely interested in what the recruiter has to say is more likely to get the job.

The right kind of humility helps you to recognize your own shortcomings. To be better prepared. To understand the risks. And to take those risks courageously, when necessary.

The antidote to the culture of bloated self-esteem is the culture of humility. If I am in the culture of humility, then I rejoice at the success of others, and I am happy with my portion. **The culture of humility leads to gratitude, appreciation, and contentment.** The key to lasting happiness is contentment.

This conclusion is now grounded in some compelling research. Investigators have recently found that if an individual has a grateful attitude toward life, that individual is more likely to be satisfied with life, more contented, and happier.[3]

Again, this is not exactly a new insight. Traditionally, American parents taught this truth to their children with sayings such as "Count your blessings" and "Be grateful for what you have." It's less common to hear American parents say such things today, except as consolation after their child isn't picked to star in the school play or when their teen gets the thin envelope from Stanford.

The sequence of events matters here. Many of us regard gratitude as a *result*. Santa Claus brings the child an unexpected wonderful present, and the child is grateful to Santa Claus. But researchers are discovering that a grateful attitude is a *cause* of happiness, psychological well-being, and a sense of personal mastery.[4]

Gratitude and humility. These are key virtues that American kids today are unlikely to possess after years of indoctrination in their own awesomeness. These are the virtues you want to teach your child or teen *before* disappointment comes.

I understand that this may rub some of you the wrong way. I went through an Ayn Rand phase myself as a teenager. (Ayn Rand won fame for her novels *The Fountainhead* and *Atlas Shrugged*, which feature strong, unabashedly selfish protagonists who pursue their own self-interest relentlessly and without apology. When I looked at those novels again as an adult, I noticed that none of the major protagonists is a parent. Rand herself never raised a child.) Such a phase can be a normal part of adolescence, part and parcel of the relentless egocentrism of the young. But as you mature into adulthood—and certainly when you become a parent—you realize that the world is, and should be, bigger than you. It's not about you. And once you realize and accept that, gratefully, you can breathe a sigh of relief.

Think back to Aaron and Julia, the two kids whose stories I shared in Chapter 5. Aaron was the gamer who gave up on football after one day of tryouts. Julia was the star student whose self-concept crumbled when she found that she had to struggle to pass AP Physics. Think how different their experiences might have been if their parents had taught them something about humility beforehand. Aaron might have learned to persevere, might have gotten in shape, might have made the team—which in turn might have grounded his self-concept in something more real than the world of video games. Julia might have crafted a self-concept that was more mature, less about her personal awesomeness. She might also have gotten closer to figuring out whether she was taking AP Physics as a junior because of a genuine interest in physics or because she wanted to impress people by taking AP Physics as a junior.

In every era and in every culture, warnings abound regarding the errors to which that culture is least prone. In puritanical eras, pastors preach about the dangers of indulging the flesh. In indulgent eras, TV talk show hosts warn about the dangers of puritanism. In an era of "walk tall" and "stand proud," it takes courage to teach humility. And it won't earn you many friends.

How do you do it? How do you teach your kid to walk *humbly* in an era when every other parent you know is trying to boost their kids' self-esteem?

My first answer is: chores. Require your kids to make their beds. Wash the dishes. Mow the lawn. Feed the pets. Set the table. Do the vacuuming.

I have previously mentioned the late Bill Phillips, his wife, Janet, and their four sons. Bill Phillips was a successful businessman and, separately and simultaneously, a successful Washington lawyer and lobbyist. His family enjoyed an affluent lifestyle. But he and his wife insisted that their four sons devote several hours every week, most often on Sunday, to household maintenance.

His oldest son, Andrew, explained it to me this way. Their usual Sunday morning routine was to go to church as a family. After church they had brunch. After brunch, they changed into work clothes, and everyone went outside to do chores. The family's large estate near Potomac, Maryland, required lots of maintenance.

"It literally required an army to keep that place running," Andrew wrote in an e-mail to me.

Typically there would be one major task for the day. I remember doing things like moving piles of brush, felling trees, removing bushes, rebuilding fences, cleaning and maintaining the pool, mulching, power washing, planting flowers, weeding, painting, cleaning vehicles, moving debris, weed whacking, replacing bricks from our walkway, etc. My dad had a hard line policy of *"if you're here on a Sunday, you're working."* I remember several occasions where friends of ours would have spent the night, but they didn't because they didn't want to have to do the chores the next day. My dad made it clear that having a friend over was not an excuse for missing work Sunday. Frankly it made for some awkward interactions with friends who were clearly less than excited at the prospect of spending two hours mulching before their parents picked them up. In fact very few things would get you excused from Sunday chores. I have distinct memories of us all trying really hard to get out of stuff with, "But I have SO much homework!" and similar excuses.

Janet and Bill could have afforded a landscaping service. Most of the families living on large estates around Potomac employ professional landscapers. Why didn't Janet and Bill just hire a landscaping crew? I posed that question to Janet. Here is her answer:

It would have been easier, for sure. Writing a check and leaving all that work to professionals would have been easier than leading the boys to do it. But I thought understanding the value of labor should be a major part of their upbringing, as it was for me. I grew up working every Sunday on a family "project."

Remember, I grew up in a small town in southwestern Minnesota. My dad was the local town lawyer. Every Sunday after church our entire family would go into town. We lived on a small farm on the edge of town, and we'd pile into the family station wagon and head into dad's small office. As a family we cleaned his office. It never struck me as odd. I thought that's what all practical families did. But I hated it! "Time to go to town" would interrupt our usually great game of kick-the-can on our front field. I so hated this family ritual that once I hid in our chicken coop hoping that mom and dad would think I was kidnapped and head into town with the rest of the crew and forget about me. No such luck. I learned that if you resisted, you got assigned the worst job— mopping the tile floor, which during mud season was torture. I was embarrassed that my friends would see us. I was worried that if dad's clients saw us cleaning, and not employing "professionals," they'd think he wasn't a good lawyer.

Eventually my dad became a local judge and I remember being so relieved we didn't have to clean the municipal building after he was elected.

As I grew up I realized what I learned from those Sunday afternoons together. First of all, I learned how to clean. That left me with a life-long appreciation for clean spaces and those who keep them so. I also remember thinking that our family could always survive if the world got turned upside down because we knew how to do things. My parents taught me not to rely on others, unless it involved an electrical current. Our family Sundays were also the source of many, many of our favorite family stories because we were all together.

I wanted my boys to know the same strength. Life is not so scary if you know how to do things, even simple things.

Some parents, especially affluent parents, have told me that they are happy to hire a housekeeper or a landscaping service, or both. They would rather have their child devote their time to schoolwork or extracurricular activities rather than household chores. I think those parents are making a mistake. You can hire a landscape service, I suppose, if you must and if you can afford it, but you must still require your child to do some household chores. By exempting your child from all chores, as many affluent American families now do, you are sending the message, "Your time is too valuable to be spent on menial tasks," which easily morphs into the unintended message "*You* are too important to do menial tasks." And that unintended message puffs up the bloated self-esteem that now characterizes many American kids. I see it often.

I have known Beth Fayard, her husband, Jeff Jones, and their children for more than 20 years. Beth and her husband are "Just Right" parents, in my judgment—a judgment which is based on many years of observation in my role as both their family physician and their neighbor. Beth and Jeff are both strict *and* loving. And they are keen observers with real insight into what has happened in American culture, at least in suburban Maryland just outside Washington, DC, where I practiced for more than 18 years.

I met with Beth and her oldest daughter, Grace (who was born in 1989), to ask their thoughts about some of the issues I raise in this book. Grace told me, "My parents taught me early on that I wasn't going to be the cool kid. And I didn't mind that much, because what really mattered to me most was not what other kids thought about me. What mattered to me most was what my parents thought about me."

Beth chimed in, "For an American girl to be 'cool' nowadays means dressing in a provocative and inappropriate way, disrespecting your parents, and staying out late at night. None of which my girls were allowed to do."

I asked Beth what her policy was about her kids doing chores. She explained that her kids starting helping around the house at age 4 or even younger. "Even as toddlers, they helped us. Dusting for example. I would say, 'Watch what I do. This will be your job.' So that by the age of 4, they really can help with the dusting. There's no great mystery to this."

"What do other parents in the neighborhood think of your approach?" I asked.

"Most of them don't approve," she said bluntly. "Here's something that just happened recently. After my son's game, the other parents wanted all the kids to go out for pizza together. I said, 'No, we can't go out for pizza because we have to go home and clean house. Clean the chicken coop.'" The Fayard-Jones family has been raising chickens for many years, mostly for the eggs, which they eat. They currently have 12 chickens. "The other parents said, 'Oh come on Beth, are you going to keep him from his friends? Don't you think you're being a little extreme?' But these chores have to be done. The game was his leisure time."

Different parents will differ on best practice here. Even some "Just Right" parents might think that Beth is being too strict in this situation. But I think Beth is teaching her kids an important lesson. *The world doesn't revolve around you. You are a member of this family with obligations to this family, and those obligations are paramount.*

The actor Denzel Washington tells a story that illustrates this point. "I remember coming home one time and feeling full of myself and talking, 'Did you imagine all this? I mean, I'm a STAR,'" he said. "[My mom] said, 'First of all, you don't know how many people been praying for you and for how long.' . . . So then she told me to get the bucket and the squeegee and clean the windows."[5]

Teach humility. In addition to having your kids do chores, I also recommend limiting kids' use of social media: Instagram, Facebook, ask.fm, Twitter, and so on. Many other authors have made a similar recommendation, though on different grounds. Some are concerned about sleep deprivation resulting from too much screen time. Others are concerned about cyberbullying or sexting via social media. Still others are concerned about the way kids' use of social media seems to undermine social skills in the real world.[6]

These concerns are valid. But I am making a different point. I have observed that even when kids use social media appropriately—no cyberbullying, no sexting—the culture of social media is the antithesis of the culture of humility. Social media, as those media are actually used by children and teenagers, are all about self-promotion: *Here I am at the party, having a great time. Here I am getting dressed for the prom. Here I am sticking my finger up my nose.*

Here I am. Look at me. It's all about broadcasting and aggrandizing the self.

I am well aware that social media *can* be used to call attention to the plight of the poor and the homeless. But that's not the way most American kids are using these sites. I have encountered kids whose parents are trying to do everything right according to the guidelines laid out in this book, but the kids are still disrespectful, disengaged from parents, and defiant. Increasingly I am finding that the root cause in these cases is the kids' involvement with social media.

Meanwhile, the parents debate whether or not they should be their kid's Facebook friend; whether or not they should follow their kid's Instagram feed. My answer is that if your son or daughter is bound up in the American culture of disrespect, then maybe your son or daughter should not be on Facebook or Instagram at all.

Turn off the device and take your child for a walk through the woods or on a hike up a mountain. Go on a camping trip. Late at night, when it's absolutely dark, take your child's hand and ask her to look up at the stars. Talk with her about the vastness of space and the tininess of our planet in the universe. That's reality. That's perspective.

It's also a good way to begin to teach humility.

9

The Second Thing: *Enjoy*

I see it almost every day I'm in the office: parents who don't really enjoy their time with their son or their daughter. Often the parent doesn't have good insight on this point. I say to the parent, "You need to enjoy the time you spend with your child."

The parent gives me a blank look, then says, "But I *do* enjoy the time I spend with her."

"When's the last time you and your daughter did something totally fun together?" I ask. "Something both of you really enjoyed?"

Another blank look. Finally mom says, "We've just been so busy recently. She has so many afterschool activities. And then there's homework. We did go to Disney over spring break though."

Enjoy the time you spend with your child. On first blush, that advice seems so bland, so trivial, as to be almost devoid of content. But it's not. The surprising truth is that most American parents, especially mothers, do not enjoy much of the time they spend with their children.

Nobel Prize–winning economist Daniel Kahneman and his colleagues surveyed working women in the United States. Here is how those women rated their enjoyment of various activities in their lives. The most-enjoyed are at the top; the least-enjoyed are at the bottom:

1. Intimate relations
2. Socializing outside work
3. Supper
4. Lunch
5. Exercising
6. Praying
7. Socializing at work
8. Watching TV at home
9. Talking on the phone at home
10. Napping
11. Cooking
12. Shopping
13. Housework
14. Time with children
15. Working for pay

As you can see, child care was near the bottom of the list: below cooking, below housework.[1]

Kahneman and his team subsequently compared American women in Columbus, Ohio, with French women in Rennes, France. The team "expected to find substantial differences between the determinants of life satisfaction and experienced happiness in the two cities, and were instead surprised by their remarkable similarity."[2] The American women did not differ significantly from French women in how much they enjoyed active leisure, passive leisure, eating, talking, working, and commuting to work. In other words, the women were similar to one another. French culture and American culture are not as different as one might have thought.

But there was a big difference in how much the women in both countries enjoyed being with their kids. As Kahneman's team summarized their findings, "The American mothers spent more time focused on child care, but enjoyed it less." Time spent with a child was negatively associated with enjoyment for American women but positively associated with enjoyment for French women. Having a spouse mitigated the negativity somewhat for American women, but, Kahneman and colleagues concluded, "the corresponding values when children were present suggest that the presence of the spouse hardly makes American children less annoying to their mother."

"The relative unhappiness of American mothers obviously demands further study," Kahneman's team concluded drily. "Our French team member suggested that French children are simply better behaved."[3]

I suspect that the French team member was correct.

Note also that Kahneman surveyed only *women* in these studies. In her book *All Joy and No Fun: The Paradox of Modern Parenthood*, Jennifer Senior suggests that men enjoy parenting more than women do. That's partly because men are more likely to be doing the fun stuff while the women do the less fun stuff. Dad tosses the baby in the air to make the baby laugh. Mom changes the diapers. Dad takes his daughter to a father-daughter dance. Mom irons the dress for the occasion.[4]

Mothers used to spend much more time with kids than fathers do, but that gender difference is diminishing. Between 1975 and 2010, the amount of time married American fathers spent with their kids tripled, from 2.4 hours per week in 1975 to 7.2 hours per week in 2010.[5] But there's still a big gap in *how* fathers and mothers spend time with their kids. As Senior observes, fathers typically spend more time *playing* with their kids, while moms spend more time doing routine activities such as toothbrushing, bathing, and feeding. "Ask any parent which type of child care they prefer," Senior writes.[6] Most of us would rather play with our kids than help them brush their teeth. That may be part of the reason why American fathers enjoy parenting more than moms, on average: because the dads are playing, not working.

But Jennifer Senior hones in on another, more fundamental reason why American moms don't enjoy parenting. American mothers multitask. They try to be moms at the same time that they are trying to do housework or professional work. The men interviewed by Senior were less likely to attempt this multitasking. Senior notes that women with children are more than twice as likely to feel rushed "sometimes or always," compared to women without children. But American fathers are no more likely to feel rushed compared to American men without children.[7]

Senior's accounts of women who try to integrate housework or professional work with parenting strikes a chord with me, because I have heard so many similar accounts from women in my own practice and in conversations with parents across the United States. They tell me how they're trying to get something accomplished in their adult lives and at the same time to spend time with their child. They're trying to answer a text message from a friend or an e-mail from work at the same time as they're playing *Candyland* with their kid.

Don't do that. It's no fun. When you are with your child, devote yourself completely to your child. When I am on duty watching my daughter, I try to do something outdoors, partly so that I won't feel the temptation to steal a look at the computer screen for an e-mail. I once insisted that my daughter and I go play miniature golf. She had never played miniature golf before and she did not want to go. But I insisted. We drove to the miniature golf course with her protesting all the way. But once there, we had a great time. Just this morning, she and I took a walk through some nearby woods and pretended that we were marooned far from civilization.

"We don't have anything to eat. We don't have anything to drink," she said.

"Yes. We're probably going to die," I said.

We had a great time.

Sometimes it's not easy to enjoy time with your child. Sometimes your child may not even want to be with you.

Kayden was 4 years old when his parents divorced. His mother won full custody in part because Kayden's father, James, had been convicted on marijuana charges several years earlier. Four years later, when Kayden was 8, Kayden's mother was arrested and convicted of selling illegal drugs herself. The social worker called

James and told him that the court was giving full custody to him, the father.

From the first day he came to live with his father, Kayden was unhappy. He missed his mother. He resented his father. "Every day was difficult," James told me.

No matter what I did, nothing worked. If I tried to be nice, he ignored me. If I tried to be the tough guy and speak firmly, he would start screaming so loudly that I was worried the neighbors would hear. And he could tell I was worried about that.

So about three weeks after he came to live with me, I said, "We're going tubing." He said, "What?" He didn't know what tubing was. When I explained that we would go down a snowy mountain in a rubber tube, he yelled that he didn't want to go. But I said, "Too bad, you're going."

It's about an hour's drive to Blue Mountain. The first 20 minutes or so he was yelling and crying about how he didn't want to go. The next 40 minutes he didn't talk at all. But when we got there, he didn't fight me getting out of the car. I think he was interested in the mountain. He'd never been any place like that before.

After I bought the lift tickets and he looked up the mountain and he saw the kids coming down the hill, his face lit up. He still didn't say anything, but I could see he was excited. When we got in the tube, he didn't even pretend to be upset anymore. He was absolutely thrilled. When we got to the bottom he said, "Let's do it again!"

We spent the whole day on the mountain. And it changed everything. He saw me in a totally new light after that. He discovered that we could have fun together. So when we got home, we started doing rough-and-tumble play, throwing the ball around outside, wrestling inside, everything. We're good now. And it all started with that day on the mountain.

Spending fun time together with your child is not an optional elective to be squeezed in after the day's required work is done. It's essential. You have to plan for it. You have to insist on it. You must make time for it.

Kayden was 8 years old when his father was able to change his attitude with one day on the mountain. If Kayden had been 15, it might not have been so easy or happened so quickly. The younger the child, the easier it is to change the child's attitude about fun and about you. Teenagers are often more of a challenge. But not always.

Bronson Bruneau* is an all-American teenage success story. As captain of his high school basketball team, he led the team to the Minnesota state championship. He was also an All-Conference football player (he played tight end). He graduated with the #2 grade point average in his class. The girl who graduated with the #1 GPA happened to be his girlfriend. He was awarded eight different scholarships by local community groups. He earned extra cash by mowing his neighbors' lawns. Other community groups gave him their top awards for community service.[8] He is now attending Duke University, where he is playing football as a walk-on.

As befits a successful student athlete in the United States, Bronson is popular. He could have spent every night of his senior year in high school at a party or a friend's house. But when we

---

*His real name.

spoke by telephone during his senior year, he told me that his favorite free time activity was just hanging out with his parents. On more than one occasion he declined invitations to parties in order to stay home and play board games with his parents, or watch old movies with them.

Having spoken with both Bronson and his older sister, Marlow,* I'm pretty confident that their parents are "Just Right" parents, in the sense that they are both strict and loving. Marlow told me how upset she sometimes was with her parents when she was a teenager. She wasn't allowed to get her ears pierced until she turned 13. She was never allowed to see an R-rated movie until she was 17, and she had to give her parents advance notice of the movies she was going to see. She was never allowed to be home alone with friends; at least one parent always had to be present. Her father insisted on interviewing every boy before the boy was allowed to date Marlow. She was never allowed to bring a boyfriend upstairs, even though her friends were engaging in all sorts of private trysts in *their* bedrooms.

"All through high school, I told my parents, 'I'm going to be in therapy for the rest of my life because of all the terrible things you're doing to me,'" Marlow told me. "I was always the odd girl out, the girl who wasn't allowed to do stuff that everybody else was doing. Then I went to the University of Virginia, and after about two years there, seeing all the kids who were falling apart and who were doing all kinds of crazy things to wreck their own lives, I suddenly realized, *I'm NOT going to have to be in therapy now or later, because of the way my parents raised me.*"

---

*Her real name.

Despite—or perhaps because of—their parents' strictness, both Marlow and Bronson enjoy spending time with their parents. The Bruneaus (mom and dad) don't do anything extraordinary. They play board games with their kids. Monopoly. They watch old movies together. They play a family baseball game. Dad and Bronson like to shoot pool or play golf together.

Little things make the best happiness.[9]

Enjoy the time you have with your kids. That means no devices at mealtime. When you are sitting at the table together, the focus should be on interaction. Listen to your child and talk with your child.

We try to enforce this rule strictly in our home. No screens at the dinner table. No glancing at cell phones. No TV on in the next room. No iPads. Sometimes we make up silly rhymes. Last night we created a limerick. Other nights we sing Hollywood show tunes, or Leonard Cohen's "Hallelujah," or early Taylor Swift songs—and see how many words we can remember. Sometimes we just play word-association games. The oldest person at the table is 80, and the youngest is 9, so some explanation may be required. Once, when I absent-mindedly reached for my phone to ask Google for a definition, my daughter raised her eyebrows and said, "No screens at the table!"

Likewise: no headphones or ear buds allowed in the car. When my wife and I went to buy a car recently, she wanted heated rear seats. It turns out the only way to get heated rear seats is to purchase the entertainment package, which includes an entertainment system for the rear seats. I kept the promotional material from the car dealer. One photo shows a mom in the front passenger seat, looking back and beaming at her two children in the rear seats. Both children are wearing headsets and watching a video. The mom seems to be saying, "Isn't this great! We can drive for hours, and I never have to talk with my kids at all!"

Everybody's in a rush. Take advantage of every moment you can. The time in the car should be a time for kids and parents to talk. Don't permit your child to separate herself or himself from you by putting on a headset or earbuds in the car or anywhere that you are together.

Following this advice—not multitasking, devoting yourself 100 percent to your child when you are with her—requires time. A significant investment of time. Beyond time spent in the car together, how do you find the time to follow these guidelines?

It's all about balance. Balance in your life and in the life of your child. You may have to cut back on your schedule and on your *child's* schedule. I have discussed this problem with many working parents and I have become convinced that many of us are just trying to do too much and our kids are trying to do too much. One mom in our neighborhood mentioned that she is so busy every afternoon, chauffeuring her kids to their various activities, that they almost never have time for a meal at home. Instead they order sandwiches on the run and eat in the car, between ballet class and soccer practice. By the time they get home it's time for homework and then bed.

What message is being sent here? The unintended message is that relaxed time together as a family is the lowest priority of all.

Parents are overscheduled as well, trying to do too much in too little time, not getting enough sleep. But instead of cutting back on our own schedules, many of us—American parents—act as though the answer is to book up our kids' schedules so that they are as stressed and overwhelmed as we are.

This sort of behavior is more common in the United States than elsewhere. Outside North America, it's unusual to find adults who boast about how busy they are and how little sleep they get. Outside North America, it's rare to find full-time parents who spend their days chauffeuring their children from one activity to another, even over the summer holiday.[10] As essayist and cartoonist Tim Kreider observes, "If you live in America in the 21st century you've probably had to listen to a lot of people tell you how busy they are. . . . It is, pretty obviously, a boast disguised as a complaint." He describes a friend who left New York City and moved to France. She "described herself as happy and relaxed for the first time in years. She still gets her work done, but it doesn't consume her entire day and brain. . . . What she had mistakenly assumed was her personality—driven, cranky, anxious and sad—turned out to be a deformative effect of her environment. It's not as if any of us wants to live like this. . . . It's something we collectively force one another to do."[11]

I recently spoke with a woman who has a daughter, Darby. Darby works hard at school. Her mother and father both support her academic ambitions, but they are cautious about giving her too much help with her homework. They don't want to be helicopter parents. She has soccer practice every Saturday and every Tuesday afternoon, dance class on another day, and a computer coding class another day.

Darby is 8 years old.

When I asked Darby's mom why Darby is doing so much, she answered, "Because Darby really enjoys all those activities."

"That's great," I said. "But don't you think you need to teach her something about *balance*, about not being overscheduled? Something about the joy of a quiet moment, maybe just lying on your back on the grass and looking at the sky?"

Mom paused. She could see where I was going with this. "Computer coding is a really valuable skill," she said. "Especially for girls."

I didn't pursue the argument. I didn't have much hope of actually changing that mom's mind, and I don't see the point of arguing just to argue. Of course computer coding is a valuable skill. Especially for girls. But by cramming a child's life full of activities, with little time for reflection, with no quiet time for a relaxed parent-child supper, this mom is sending an unintended message: *what you **do** is more important than who you **are**.* And this parent is teaching her daughter that becoming more accomplished, honing her skills in this activity and that activity, matters more than free time, more than relaxation, more than good conversation and listening to others. More than family.

The focus on after-school activities for kids, like the culture of Instagram and Facebook, is all about boosting the ego and inflating the self. *Look at my kid: she's an accomplished dancer, a skilled soccer player, and a whiz at computer coding.*

The same is true for parents: I have found many who are stretched thin with commitments at work, volunteering, and other chores that leave too little time for a relaxed meal at home with their child. Too many parents want to say, "Look at me: I'm a successful professional, a great parent, and blah blah blah."

Like mother, like daughter. Like father, like son.

Americans have everything backwards. Forget about the accomplishments. Don't push your child to live her life as though she were continually preparing her college application. Teach her not to worry about being amazing in the eyes of other people. That means doing less and becoming more.

Making these changes may require some big adjustments both personally and professionally. You may have to move from one state to another in order to find a less demanding job or to live comfortably on a smaller income. That's OK. You have to be clear about what the priorities are.

You have to teach the meaning of life.

10

The Third Thing:
The Meaning of Life

When I visit schools, I often meet with students, in groups both large and small. When I meet with middle or high school students, I sometimes engage them in semi-Socratic back-and-forth questioning. I pose questions and call on students who raise their hands.

What's the point of school? I ask. Why bother?

To get into a good college—that's the answer I most often hear from American high school students.

So what's the purpose of college? I ask.

To get a good job, to earn a living, the students answer.

This dialogue is the basis for what I have come to call "the middle-class script." The script reads as follows:

1. *Work hard in school so you can get into a good college.*
2. *Get into a good college so you can get a good job.*
3. *Get a good job and you will make a good living and have a good life.*

187

There are several problems with this script. The first problem is that every line in it is false.

1. Working hard in school is no guarantee of admission to a top college. We all know stories of kids who worked hard, earned good grades, and didn't get into any of their top choices.

2. Getting into a good college is no guarantee of a good job. The media and the blogosphere are full of stories of young people who have earned bachelor's degrees from Princeton and Harvard and who are now waiting tables or simply unemployed.[1]

3. Getting a good job is no guarantee of having a good life.

More about #3 in a moment. But first you and I need to ask the question, more seriously: What is school for?

I find that parents in the United States, more than in any other country, have bought into the middle-class script. In Germany and Switzerland, for example, there is no shame if a 15-year-old chooses to train to become an auto mechanic rather than embarking on the university track. And that's true even if both parents are university professors. Mechanics in those countries are respected and they earn good money.

Mechanics can earn good money in the United States as well, but there is a stigma, a lack of respect, attached to "blue-collar" work in the United States today, which is utterly lacking in *Mitteleuropa*. In the United States, it is hard to imagine the child of two professors choosing to go straight into "vocational training" to be a mechanic unless that child has been diagnosed with some sort of learning disability. Most Americans today regard "vocational training" as a low-prestige option for below-average-IQ kids or for kids with learning disabilities.

At some level, sometimes subconsciously, many Americans—both parents and students—have accepted the idea that a primary purpose of K–12 schooling, maybe even *the* primary purpose, is to get accepted into a selective college and to prepare for college. That's a mistake. The primary purpose of education should be to prepare for *life*, not for more school. And many of the skills needed to succeed in life are different from the skills needed for admission to a top college.

In order to be admitted to a highly selective university, it is usually necessary to have a good grade point average as well as good test scores. The student will also need to have participated in extracurricular activities that will impress the admissions staff. So, a rational student will avoid classes that might interest her but in which she is less certain of getting an A; instead she enrolls in familiar classes that she knows she can ace. She may sign up for an after-school activity not primarily because it interests her but because she thinks it will look good on her college application. In short she is not *living* so much as she is *performing*, putting on a show to impress the college admissions office. And it breaks my heart to see so many parents aiding and abetting this puppet show in the belief that they are acting in their kids' best interest.

There are a few life trajectories—but only a few—in which this approach might make sense. If you are absolutely certain that you want to be a doctor, and you are sure that nothing else will bring you fulfillment, then the middle-class script might be a good fit for you. Work hard in school; get into a selective college. Work hard in college; get into medical school. Work hard in medical school; get into a good residency. Work hard in residency; get a job with a good practice. Simple. The medical profession is a popular choice among college students, in part because the path it offers to a good life seems clear at 18 years of age.

As a practicing physician, I can tell you that many of my colleagues never did the hard work of figuring out, in childhood or adolescence, the answers to the really important questions: *Who am I? What do I really want? What would make me happy?* Those are not trivial questions. The great American psychologist Dr. Abraham Maslow observed that many adults never answer those questions.[2] I have seen some such adults among my own physician colleagues. This man may be regarded as a successful surgeon; he may earn $600,000 a year; but he's miserable. He's unhappy because he is working 80 hours a week at a job he has come to loathe.

If you are working 80 hours a week at a job which shrivels your soul, then you are a slave. I don't care whether you are earning $600,000 a year or more. Life is precious. Each minute is a priceless gift. No amount of money can reclaim lost time. If you are wasting your time on work you detest, you may come to feel resentful about the time you are losing. If you are a physician, you may come to resent your patients. I have learned to recognize such physicians, and I try to steer my patients away from them.

According to some labor force experts, in the 21st century, most Americans will bounce from one job to another, even from one career to another, several times throughout their lives.[3] That sort of life, the bouncing-from-job-to-job life that most of our children will lead, demands a very different skill from the skill set which works well in school. Your child will have to be willing to try different things, to go in different directions, in order to find their niche, their calling, their vocation. And their niche, calling, or vocation may change over time. If you and your kid are playing by the middle-class script, then school isn't preparing your kid for real life. Instead, school is making your kid *less* prepared for real life, by pushing your kid to be unduly cautious and risk averse.

The rules for success in life are different from the rules for getting admitted to Princeton or Stanford. The *willingness to fail* is one key to success in real life. To be a top student, you need to earn top marks in all your courses, or at least most of them. The values inculcated at most schools today, both public and private, reinforce a reluctance to take risks, a reluctance to fail.

Your job as a parent is not to reinforce the middle-class script, but to undermine it. Empower your daughter or your son to take risks and congratulate them not only when they succeed but also when they *fail*, because failure builds humility. And the humility born of failure can build growth and wisdom and an openness to new things in a way that success almost never does. Steve Jobs said something similar in his 2005 commencement speech at Stanford: "I didn't see it then, but it turned out that getting fired from Apple was the best thing that could have ever happened to me. The heaviness of being successful was replaced by the lightness of being a beginner again, less sure about everything. It freed me to enter one of the most creative periods of my life."[4]

Over the past 15 years, I have visited more than 380 schools. I have been trying to understand what kids need and how schools help, or don't. I have often been disappointed. Many schools I have visited, especially in the United States, completely embrace the middle-class script. As a result, they often make kids more fragile rather than less. But some schools have slipped free of that script. One of those schools is Shore, the Australian school I mentioned earlier.

Robert Grant, sixth headmaster at Shore, was fond of making one particular remark to the parents of students newly enrolled at the school. He liked to say, "I hope your child will be *severely disappointed* during his time at this school." The parents were often confused. *Why would the headmaster wish for my child to be severely disappointed?* Grant would explain that if a student does not experience real disappointment at school, then he will be unprepared for disappointment when it comes in real life.

And disappointment will come. Dreams will be crushed. Loved ones will die. Relationships will end. The right education, alongside the right kind of upbringing, should prepare your son or daughter to handle disappointment and failure, to slip loose of a dream when the dream is over, to move to another field of endeavor with no loss of enthusiasm. A few schools teach this explicitly and well. But in the United States, there are only a very few. Some of the American schools regarded as "the best" because many of their graduates attend highly ranked colleges don't even attempt to teach these skills, the skills needed for success in *life*. Those schools are too busy preparing their students to get the best grades and the best test scores.

Flashdance was a popular motion picture when it premiered in 1983. It's about a teenage girl who dreams of auditioning for a prestigious dance company. But she lacks the training and resources of many of the other girls. She is discouraged. At one point in the movie, she is ready to give up. Then her boyfriend, Nick, tells her, "When you give up your dream, you die." So she perseveres, and her dream comes true.

Many American parents and kids today are caught in the grip of what I call the *Flashdance* illusion. Movie as metaphor. Even if they have never seen *Flashdance*, American kids have seen dozens of other movies with the same theme. *Go for your dream. If you work hard enough, it will happen. If you build it, they will come.* And the parents often are stuck in the same script.

But it's a toxic script. It leads kids to focus on one trajectory, one story line: *initial failure must be met with the resolve to try harder in the same domain, leading to ultimate success. Flashdance* might have been more interesting as a movie and more instructive for real life if, halfway through, Jennifer Beals's character had said, "You know, maybe I'm not such a great dancer after all. Maybe I'll forget about dancing and instead go to Colorado and try my luck as a ski instructor. Or maybe I'll open a bed-and-breakfast in Nova Scotia."

The *Flashdance* metaphor is toxic for reasons similar to why the culture of Instagram and Facebook is toxic. It's all about *me*. It's all about what I'm doing, my success. For many middle-income and affluent American parents, the deepest meaning of life they can offer their children is this notion of personal success. Winning the jackpot of fame and fortune has become the new American dream. Success equals fulfillment, or so many Americans now seem to believe. As *New York Times* columnist David Brooks recently observed, American culture today is based on the premise "that career and economic success can lead to fulfillment," an assumption that Brooks calls "the central illusion of our time."[5]

The flipside of the dream is what Mark Shiffman, professor of humanities at Villanova, calls "the game of fear": the concern so many young Americans now have that they will not find their place, that they will be less successful than their parents. "It has always been hard to answer life's deep and abiding questions," observes Shiffman. But he believes that contemporary American culture "makes it hard to ask them at all." He points out that young adults today have become accustomed to relying on institutionalized criteria to validate and affirm themselves. The result is a focus on what kids *do*, what they achieve, instead of on who they *are*, their character.

It's part of your job as a parent to help your child develop character, self-control, Conscientiousness. To help your child to learn what does and does not matter. Doing so, Professor Shiffman concludes, will give your child "clearer bearings amid life's uncertainties, a place to stand outside the game of fear. It also addresses what might be the deepest fear of all, which is that endless achievement might not add up to a meaningful life, that winning the races of academic and professional competition might not bring genuine happiness."[6]

The antidote to the culture of *Flashdance* and Facebook is to teach humility and gratitude. It's no longer all about *me*. It's about service to others. Integrity. Even if my service and integrity are never noticed by anybody and never result in any morsel of fame or fortune. It's finally about the person you truly are, not the person you are pretending to be.

Real life does not conform to conventions of the movies. American kids and their parents need to break free of this idea of life as some sort of movie about personal success. Let it go. Find another dream. The movie is not a good metaphor.

One of the most difficult obligations of responsible parenthood is telling your son or your daughter that their dream isn't going to come true, that they need to find another dream. Parents unsure of their own authority, whose top priority is pleasing their child, will never speak these difficult truths. But if you don't, who will?

W hich is more important, achievement or happiness? It's a flawed question.

Many parents have heard about "Tiger Moms" who are focused on their children's achievements. They know some "Irish Setter Dads" who just want kids to have fun.[7] They wonder, *Should I push my kid harder to achieve? Or should I loosen up and let them relax?*

But this question—achievement versus happiness—is based on false premises. There is no point in pushing your kid harder to achieve if he or she has no goal or sense of purpose that gives some context to that achievement. Likewise, there isn't much point in letting your kids relax and do whatever they desire if you have not first *educated* their desire.

One of your tasks as a parent is to instill a sense of meaning, a longing for something higher and deeper. Without meaning, life comes to seem pointless and futile. Without meaning, young people are more likely to become anxious and depressed.

Once children have a sense of meaning, they can pursue achievement with confidence because they know *why* that achievement is worth pursuing. Once desire has been educated, young people can enjoy free time more deeply and more fully, whether reading a book, listening to music, or taking a walk through the woods. Or, a fishing trip in Alaska.

In the previous chapter, I mentioned the importance of enjoying the time you spend with your child. Schedule a vacation with the objective of strengthening the parent-child bond. That's what Bill Phillips was doing on the morning of August 9, 2010, when he and his youngest son, Willy, climbed aboard a 12-seater amphibious floatplane in a remote corner of southwestern Alaska, on their way to some of the best salmon and trout fishing in the world, where the Nushagak River joins Lake Nerka. It would be a great adventure.

The plane—a single-engine DeHavilland DHC built in 1957—never reached its destination. The pilot, Theron "Terry" Smith, 62 years old, had survived a stroke four years earlier and was grieving the recent death of his son-in-law, who had died in a plane crash.[8] The group boarded the floatplane around 11 a.m. Staff at their lodge called the fishing camp around 5 p.m. to ask when the party would be returning for dinner.[9] That's when the staff learned that the nine people on board the plane had never arrived at the fishing camp. Both civilian and Alaska Air National Guard aircraft were quickly dispatched to search the flight path.

One of the pilots spotted the wreckage of the plane. He thought, *No one could have survived this crash.* The wreckage lay on a 40-degree slope. There was a scar on the hillside where the plane had impacted and skidded up the steep hill. The scar was about 75 yards long. The front of the aircraft had been sheared completely off.[10]

Then another pilot radioed that he had spotted a survivor. *Someone at the scene of the crash is waving for help.* That waving hand converted a recovery mission into a rescue mission. The pilots alerted the medical chain of command: *There is at least one person still alive down there.* But how to execute a rescue? There was no place for a helicopter to land. And time was short. Conditions on the hillside were cold and damp. A doctor and medical support staff were helicoptered to the closest landing spot about 1,000 feet away and forced a path to the crash site through dense brush "as fog and cold rain blanketed the area and nightfall set in," according to one news report.[11]

Willy Phillips, 13 years old, had survived. His father, Bill Phillips, was dead. Willy had broken his foot and had other injuries as well. In the confusion and horror immediately following the impact—which the four survivors agreed occurred with no warning—Willy realized, first, that his father was dead; second, that he himself was injured; third, that the plane was a tangle of debris. (Later rescuers had to cut open the steel fuselage to extract the other three survivors.) But Willy managed to crawl out of the jumble of the broken aircraft, slippery with oil and fuel and cold rain, and jump down to the ground to wave at the first search aircraft flying low overhead, even though that jump further compounded his own injuries.

It's hard to imagine a stress much worse than witnessing the death of a beloved father and at the same time being in agonizing pain from broken bones. No one could have faulted Willy if he just crumpled into a ball next to his father's corpse. But instead Willy heroically sought to summon help.

Most American parents do not prepare their child in any serious way for disappointment, for failure, for heartbreak. Bill and Janet did prepare their four sons, I believe. And that made all the difference.

I have mentioned my visit to Shore, a private school in Sydney, Australia. During my visit, I had a conversation with the current headmaster, Dr. Timothy Wright. I asked him the question that I often ask students: *What's the purpose of school?*

He immediately answered, "Preparation for life." That's not a trivial answer. Dr. Wright constantly reminds his teachers, his students, and their parents that the main purpose of school is not to get into a top university but to prepare for life. The skills needed to get into a top university are not the same as those needed for success in life, as we discussed a moment ago.

I said, "OK, preparation for life. So what's the purpose of life?" Dr. Wright responded without hesitation:

1. Meaningful work
2. A person to love
3. A cause to embrace

I paused. "That's persuasive," I said at last.

I'm not saying that Dr. Wright is a guru. I'm not suggesting that his formula is the answer we all must accept. But it is an answer. And I believe that *you must have an answer* when your child asks you, "Why should I work hard at school?" You must have some answer that's bigger than "getting admitted to Stanford" or "making a good living." You must offer a bigger picture. Some concept of what it's all about. Some understanding that experiences with people matter more than the acquisition of things.[12] And you must have the authority to communicate that big picture to your child. In order to do that, you have to matter more in the life of your child than his or her peers.

The most serious consequence of the shift from a parent-oriented culture to a peer-oriented culture is that *parents no longer are able to provide that big picture to their children.* By age 10, an American child is more likely to look to peers than to parents for guidance about what really matters in life. But children are not competent to guide other children. That's what grown-ups are for. The shift from a parent-oriented society to a peer-oriented society has turned K–12 education into a "race to nowhere," to borrow the title of a recent documentary. Children and teenagers from middle-income and affluent homes feel that they are in a rat race trying to get good grades, to get into a good college, but they have no idea *why*, beyond the vague promise of a comfortable job at the end of the rainbow and the lack of any coherent alternative.

Without strong guidance from parents, children and teenagers turn to the marketplace for guidance about what counts. And today, the American marketplace—the mainstream culture in which most American children and teenagers take part—is focused narrowly and relentlessly on fame and wealth. In the culture of Justin Bieber and Miley Cyrus and Lady Gaga and Kim Kardashian, fame and money and looking cool matter most. But the pursuit of fame and wealth and good looks for their own sake impoverishes the soul.

Being a good parent means—among other things—helping your daughter or son to find and fulfill their true potential. Dr. Wright's answer provides a road map for thinking about what that might mean, concretely. *Meaningful work. Someone to love. And a cause to embrace.* What work might your child find most meaningful? How can you prepare your child to give and receive love in a lasting relationship? How can you help your kids find a cause, something larger than themselves, that they can champion with enthusiasm?

The Conscientious child or teen is more likely to develop into a Conscientious adult: a woman or man mature enough to set meaningful goals and work toward them with integrity. To serve others. And to love, honestly and faithfully.

To find the meaning of life.

Conclusion

You and I are not the only ones trying to raise kids right in a culture that is likely to steer them wrong. I have met like-minded parents across the United States and around the world. Together, you and I and other parents like us can create a community of parents who understand the challenges, who are trying to build a culture of respect that works in the context of the 21st century.

We need to reevaluate our values.[1] Fifty years ago, our popular culture celebrated the lives of ordinary people in television shows like *I Love Lucy*, *The Dick Van Dyke Show*, and *The Andy Griffith Show*. The characters depicted in those shows were not famous or wealthy. But they were good role models for children, because they were good people. Today, popular American culture—especially the culture of children and teenagers—celebrates famous entertainers or would-be entertainers in shows like *iCarly*, *The X Factor*, *So You Think You Can Dance*, *The Voice*, and *American Idol*. As journalist Alina Tugend recently observed, we parents "end up convinced that being average will doom our children to a life that will fall far short of what we want for them." The very word "ordinary" has become a derogatory term. Brené Brown, a professor of social work, suggests that in 21st-century America, "an ordinary life has become synonymous with a meaningless life."[2]

We Americans have gone far astray in the past three decades with regard to understanding what kids need to become fulfilled and independent adults. We have undermined the authority of teachers and parents. We have allowed kids to be guided by same-age peers rather than insisting on the primacy of guidance from adults. As a result, American kids now grow up to be less imaginative, less adaptive, and less creative than they could be.

But you can change that, in your own home, starting today.

If you live in the United States and you want your child to grow up to be happy, productive, and fulfilled, then you will have to parent your child differently than many of your neighbors. Your neighbors may not understand. They may whisper to one another about how out-of-touch you are. You don't allow your 11-year-old son to play violent video games like *Grand Theft Auto* or *Call of Duty*. He must feel so Isolated! Your 12-year-old daughter is one of only three girls in her class who doesn't have her own smartphone, who doesn't have her own Instagram page. How Awful!

You will be *so* uncool.

Don't be intimidated. Lend your neighbor your copy of this book. But meanwhile, you will have to be courageous, for the sake of your child. So that he or she can grow up to be brave.

And humble.

Like you.

Throughout the world, parents in developed countries are increasingly confused about their role. Should they be their child's best friend or their child's authoritative guide? Many parents are twisting themselves in knots trying to be the cool peer one moment and the authoritative parent the next. My advice is, Don't do that. Your job is to be the authoritative parent, not the cool peer. The parent-child relationship differs from the relationship between same-age peers. Understand the differences. I have found that advice to be every bit as necessary in Edinburgh, Auckland, and Brisbane as it is in Dallas, New York, and Seattle.

But other challenges are uniquely American. In this book I have highlighted three:

1. **Culture:** The culture of disrespect is mingled with the culture of "Live for Now." When one sees the Pepsi "Live for Now" billboard in England or New Zealand, it's easy to recognize the message as an American import that anyone can freely accept or reject. But here in the United States, "Live for Now" is our native culture. It is the default culture that American kids encounter if we set them loose to navigate on their own, as some notables would have us do.[3] Without authoritative guidance, it is the culture that they will adopt as their own.

2. **Medication:** In the United States, it has become common to medicate children with powerful psychiatric drugs as a first rather than a last resort. As I explained in Chapter 3, that's a big reason why American kids are now much more likely to be on medication compared with kids outside

North America. We are experimenting on children in a way that has no precedent, with medications whose long-term risks are largely unknown.

3. **Overscheduling:** As I mentioned in Chapter 9, we Americans like to boast about how busy we are. The nonstop grind of school and activities and homework begins early in the morning and continues late into the night. That's not healthy. Find a different perspective. Boast about how you and your child spent an afternoon lying on the grass, looking up at the sky, finding shapes in the clouds.

To be a wise parent in the United States today, you must understand these challenges. Be the authoritative guide; introduce your child to a worldview more meaningful than "Live for Now." Resist the pressures to medicate your child except as a *last* resort rather than as the first intervention. Don't give in to the temptation to overschedule; teach your child that spending relaxed time with family is more important than cramming two or three more extracurricular activities into the week.

Every human relationship is characterized by responsibilities; but the responsibilities differ depending on the relationship. A physician has responsibilities to a patient: to evaluate the patient's signs and symptoms, to make a diagnosis, and to explain the treatment. A friend has responsibilities to a friend: to be kind, to be trustworthy, to be available to the best of her ability in times of need. A husband has responsibilities to his wife, and a wife to her husband. Each has made a commitment to cherish one another, forsaking all others, lifelong.

Each of these human connections—between physician and patient, between friends, and between husband and wife—is vital. But there is no greater responsibility between human beings than that of a parent to a child. It is the parent's responsibility not only to feed, clothe, and shelter the child but also to acculturate the child, to instill a sense of virtue and a longing for integrity, and to teach the meaning of life according to the parent's best understanding.

Contemporary mainstream culture has undermined the authority of parents to do their job. The result has been a collapse of parenting worldwide, perhaps more so in North America than elsewhere. The collapse of parenting has led, not surprisingly, to an explosion in anxiety and depression among children and teenagers and to an extraordinary rise in the proportion of kids who are fragile in ways unknown to previous generations.

For the sake of your child, you have to create an alternative culture in your home.

You have to assert without apology the primacy of the parent-child relationship over relationships between same-age peers.

You have to teach that family comes first, despite living in a culture where family ties are seldom respected.

You must teach your child that every choice he or she makes has immediate, far-reaching, and unforeseen consequences.[4]

You must help your child to find meaning in life that is not about their latest accomplishment, or how they look, or how many friends they have, but about who your child is, their truest self.

You must judge your success as a parent not by how many friends your child has, not by grade point average or test scores or athletic prowess, not by an acceptance letter from a famous college or university, but by whether your child is on the road to fulfillment, capable of governing his or her needs and desires instead of being governed by them.

Do not allow yourself to be paralyzed by your own inadequacies. You may not be a perfect model of honesty and integrity. Neither am I. There may be dark places in your own soul, things that you are ashamed of. I have them too. You may feel silly trying to preach to your child about virtue and character because you know how far astray you have gone in the past, including the recent past. I have often felt the same way.

But too bad. To borrow an analogy from the classroom: Raising your child to know and care about virtue and character is not a special extra credit assignment reserved for the superior parent. It is mandatory for all parents. And when you are given a mandatory assignment, you must do your best, regardless of your own shortcomings.[5] Regardless of whether your peers—other parents—are paying attention to the assignment or not.

There is no greater responsibility.

I wish you all the best—for you and for your child. And I hope we will be in touch.

Acknowledgments

My first debt is to the parents and children who have come to see me in the office, from 1989 to the present, in Maryland and in Pennsylvania. Conducting more than 90,000 office visits with children and parents from diverse backgrounds has provided me with a firsthand education that cannot be found in any book, on any website, or at any Facebook page.

My next debt is to the more than 380 schools, across the United States and worldwide, whose leaders invited me to visit between 2000 and 2015. Observing classrooms, talking with students and teachers, meeting with school administrators, and listening to parents have all been invaluable in working through the issues in this book. See my website (www.leonardsax.com) for lists of my school visits from 2006 to the present.

I am grateful to the families and individuals who have agreed to let me quote them by name in this book: to Janet Phillips and her four sons, Andrew, Colter, Paul, and Willy; to Beth Fayard, her husband, Jeff Jones, and their children, Grace, Claire, and Roland; to Dr. Meg Meeker and her son, Walter; and to Bronson Bruneau and his sister Marlow Phillips (wife of Andrew).

Throughout this book, I contrast the United States with other countries. I am most indebted to those hosts outside North America who have invited me to visit their schools or their communities and who have taught me something about the lived experiences of children and teenagers in other countries. I am especially grateful to Josep Maria Barnils of Barcelona, Spain; Jan Butler of Hobart, Tasmania, former head of the Australasian Girls' Schools Alliance; Rebecca Cody, former principal of Woodford House in New Zealand and now principal of Methodist Ladies' College near Perth, Australia; Melanie L'Eef of Christchurch, New Zealand; Anne Everest, Head of St George's School for Girls in Edinburgh, Scotland; Andrew Hunter, headmaster at Merchiston Castle School in Edinburgh, Scotland, especially for putting me up at his home on two occasions and for teaching me so much about how Scotland differs from England; Christine Jenkins, principal of Korowa Anglican Girls' School in Melbourne, Australia; Robyn Kronenberg of Hobart, Tasmania, with special thanks for a crash course in Australian football at the Melbourne Cricket Ground; Barnaby Lenon, former headmaster of Harrow School in Middlesex, England; Dr. Jane Muncke of Zurich, Switzerland; Judith Poole, headmistress of Abbotsleigh in Wahroonga, Australia, who, as an American, has a special gift for explaining Australian culture to Americans like me; Belinda Provis, former principal of Seymour College in Adelaide, Australia, and current principal of All Saints' College in Perth; Karen Spiller, principal of St Aidan's Anglican Girls School near Brisbane, Australia; Dr. Ralph Townsend, headmaster of Winchester College in Winchester, England; Dr. Timothy Wright, headmaster of Sydney Church of England Grammar School, aka "Shore," and his colleagues David Anderson and

Cameron Paterson; and Garth Wynne, headmaster of Christ Church Grammar School in Perth, Australia. Each of these individuals has taught me something about how his or her culture differs from American culture. However, my mention of these individuals here does not imply that they endorse anything I have written in the book. I just wanted to say thank you.

Dr. Gordon Neufeld is a key authority cited in this book. I am grateful that he agreed to meet with me face-to-face during the writing of the book, and I especially appreciate his insights into how Anglophone Canadian culture is growing more similar to, but is still distinct from, mainstream American culture.

Felicia Eth has been my agent for more than a decade. This is our fourth book together. I am grateful for her patience, her guidance, and her advocacy.

I thank the whole team at Basic Books, but most especially Lara Heimert, publisher, for believing in the book and my ability to write it, and for her editorial insights and suggestions, which have greatly improved it. I also thank her for bringing on Roger Labrie to undertake a careful line-by-line edit, which was immensely helpful. Any errors that remain are solely my responsibility. I also am indebted to senior project editor Sandra Beris; and I thank her colleague, Jennifer Kelland, for suggesting the title to Chapter 4.

The director of my residency program, Dr. Nikitas Zervanos, often remarked that the most important measure of any person's life is neither income, nor professional achievement, nor even happiness, but the quality of that person's closest personal relationships. He urged us to make our spouse and our children our highest priority. Family should come before work, Dr. Zerva-nos taught us.

I think he's right. And I have tried to live according to that rule. How well I have succeeded is not for me to judge; you will have to ask my wife, Katie, or my daughter, Sarah. I am indebted to Katie for any common sense that might be found in this book, and for her careful reading of many versions of the manuscript. She is my most trusted critic, my *ezer k'negedo*. I am indebted to my daughter, Sarah, for giving me a reason to research and write this book, a project I undertook in hopes of becoming a better father. I can't wait to see what she does next.

I am also thankful for my wife's parents, Bill and Joan, who live with us. My daughter is fortunate to have not one, not two, but four adults in the home who love her.

That's my family. Everything I do, I do for them.

Finally, I want to remember my late mother, Dr. Janet Sax, who, as a pediatrician, devoted her professional life to teaching parents how to guide their children. In the years before her death, she and I had countless conversations about the topics I address here. She had a vast depth and breadth of firsthand experience with children and adolescents acquired in more than 30 years of clinical practice. Throughout the book, I have often wondered, *What would Mom have said?*

Wherever you are, Mom, I hope you like the book.

Notes

Introduction: Parents Adrift

1. Lists of my events from 2006 to the present are available on my website (www.leonardsax.com).

Chapter 1: The Culture of Disrespect

1. See "How to wean kits from the doe," Florida 4-H, http://florida 4h.org/projects/rabbits/MarketRabbits/Activity8_Weaning.html.

2. See "The age of sexual maturity in rabbits," Florida 4-H, http://florida4h.org/projects/rabbits/MarketRabbits/Activity8_Maturity .html.

3. According to the website JustRabbits.com, the largest rabbits live to be about 5 years old, while the smaller breeds can live to be 10 to 12 years old.

4. On ages for horses, see "Horse breeding," Horses and Horse Information, www.horses-and-horse-information.com/articles/horse-breeding.shtml.

5. Katherine Blocksdorf, "How long do horses live?" About: Horses, http://horses.about.com/od/understandinghorses/qt/horse age.htm.

6. For purposes of our discussion here, bottle-feeding can substitute for breast-feeding. Most babies are weaned from the bottle by 12

months of age, with solid food introduced into their diet at around 6 months of age. The American Academy of Pediatrics recommends that parents discourage bottle-feeding after 12 months of age, because a child who knows that a bottle will be available may skip meals. See "Discontinuing the bottle," HealthyChildren.org, www.healthychildren.org/English/ages-stages/baby/feeding-nutrition/Pages/Discontinuing-the-Bottle.aspx.

In hunter-gatherer communities, the child may be breast-fed until age 2, 3, or even 4 years of age. See Melvin Konner, "Hunter-gatherer infancy and childhood," in *Hunter-Gatherer Childhoods: Evolutionary, Developmental, and Cultural Perspectives*, edited by Barry Hewlett and Michael Lamb (Chicago: Aldine, 2005), pp. 19–64. Those communities deploy prolonged breast-feeding in part because foods that a young child can easily eat are not readily available.

7. Susanne Cabrera and colleagues, "Age of thelarche and menarche in contemporary US females: A cross-sectional analysis," *Journal of Pediatric Endocrinology and Metabolism*, volume 27, pp. 47–51, 2014.

8. Grace Wyshak and Rose Frisch, "Evidence for a secular trend in age of menarche," *New England Journal of Medicine*, volume 306, pp. 1033–1035, 1982. In my book *Girls on the Edge*, I devote a chapter to considering how the earlier onset of both menarche and puberty has adversely affected girls. But that's not our topic here.

9. I am aware that the statistic for life expectancy at birth can be misleading when infant mortality is high. For example, in 1900 life expectancy at birth was 47 years, while in 1998 it was 75 years, an increase of 28 years. But in 1900, infant mortality—the proportion of newborns who will die in their first year of life—was roughly 150 deaths in every 1,000 live births. By 1998 that figure had dropped to just 7 deaths in 1,000 live births. As Rohin Dhar and his colleagues observe, "In 1900, life expectancy for someone who made it to her 20th birthday was about 63. In 1998, this number rose to 78. So while life expectancy from birth increased 28 years from 1900 to 1998, life expectancy from age 20 only increased 15 years." (All figures in this

paragraph are taken from "Why life expectancy is misleading," Priceonomics, December 11, 2013, http://priceonomics.com/why -life-expectancy-is-misleading.) Even when we take these factors into consideration, however, the fact remains that childhood has shortened over the past two centuries, while adulthood has lengthened.

10. For life expectancy at birth in the United States, as of 2010, please see the Centers for Disease Control and Prevention, "Table 22. Life expectancy at birth, at age 65, and at age 75, by sex, race, and Hispanic origin: United States, selected years 1900–2010," online at www.cdc.gov/nchs/data/hus/2011/022.pdf.

11. See, for example, Rhoshel Lenroot and Jay Giedd, "Sex differences in the adolescent brain," *Brain and Cognition*, volume 72, pp. 46–55, 2010. I invited Dr. Giedd, the lead investigator on this study, to speak at a conference I hosted in Lincolnshire, Illinois. At the conference, Dr. Giedd made a joke based on these findings. He said, "Hertz and Avis have the best neuroscientists." He was referring to the fact that Hertz and Avis will sometimes charge a renter a substantial additional fee if the renter is 24 years old, whereas they do not impose any surcharge on a renter who is age 64. The 24-year-old, on average, will have better hearing and better eyesight than the 59-year-old, but, Dr. Giedd explained, Hertz and Avis understand that the 24-year-old is not yet a mature adult. The risk of a motor vehicle accident is more closely tied to judgment and maturity than to better hearing and eyesight.

12. Yes, this means that I am defining a 24-year-old male as an adolescent. I devote much of my book *Boys Adrift* to explaining why this definition now makes sense (see also the previous note). But, as I say, let's not quarrel about the numbers; the exact numbers are not central to the argument here.

13. See, for example, Barry Bogin, "The evolution of human growth," in *Human Growth and Development* (New York: Academic Press, 2012), pp. 287–324. Bogin asserts that we should consider four periods in the early development of humans: infancy, childhood, juvenility,

and adolescence. He denotes the juvenile period as spanning ages 7 to 10 for girls and 7 to 12 for boys. The juvenile period ends, in Bogin's schema, with the onset of puberty. For our purposes, it's simpler to think of Bogin's "childhood" as early childhood and Bogin's "juvenile" period as later childhood.

14. For more on this point, see Melvin Konner, "Enculturation," part 4 of *The Evolution of Childhood* (Cambridge, MA: Harvard University Press, 2010), pp. 595–727.

15. For an introduction to the scholarly debate regarding whether any nonhuman species truly have "culture," see Konner, *The Evolution of Childhood*, especially the section titled "Does nonhuman culture exist?" pp. 579–592.

16. Thibaud Gruber and colleagues, "Wild chimpanzees rely on cultural knowledge to solve an experimental honey acquisition task," *Current Biology*, volume 19, pp. 1806–1810, 2009.

17. Josep Call and Claudio Tennie, reviewing the findings of Gruber and colleagues in "Wild chimpanzees rely on cultural knowledge to solve an experimental honey acquisition task," liken the differences between the two communities of wild chimpanzees to human differences in table manners. See their article "Animal culture: Chimpanzee table manners?" *Current Biology*, volume 19, pp. R981–R983, 2009.

18. See Konner, *The Evolution of Childhood*, for a lengthy defense of this statement. If you like, you can jump directly to part 4, "Enculturation," pp. 595–727.

19. When I refer to the buzz about neuroplasticity, I am thinking of articles such as Shufei Yin and colleagues, "Intervention-induced enhancement in intrinsic brain activity in healthy older adults," *Scientific Reports*, volume 4, 2014, www.nature.com/srep/2014/141204/srep07309/full/srep07309.html; Eduardo Mercado, "Neural and cognitive plasticity: From maps to minds," *Psychological Bulletin*, volume 134, pp. 109–137, 2008; and C. S. Green and D. Bavelier, "Exercising your brain: A review of human brain plasticity and

training-induced learning," *Psychology and Aging*, volume 23, pp. 692–701, 2008.

20. See, for example, Jacqueline Johnson and Elissa Newport, "Critical period effects in second language learning: The influence of maturational state on the acquisition of English as a second language," *Cognitive Psychology*, volume 21, pp. 60–99, 1989. For a recent reevaluation of the critical period hypothesis, see Jan Vanhove, "The critical period hypothesis in second language acquisition: A statistical critique and a reanalysis," *PLOS One*, July 25, 2013, http://journals.plos.org/plosone/article?id=10.1371/journal.pone.0069172#pone-0069172-g009.

21. Robert Fulghum, *All I Really Need to Know I Learned in Kindergarten: Uncommon Thoughts on Common Things* (New York: Ivy, 1988).

22. All quotations are from Yamamoto Tsunetomo, *Hagakure: The Book of the Samurai*. Because the book is nearly 300 years old, it is widely available in public-domain versions online. This particular version, translated by Lapo Mori, is online at http://judoinfo.com/pdf/hagakure.pdf. For another book which provides a similar insight into samurai culture and belief, see Thomas Cleary's book *Code of the Samurai: A Modern Translation of the Bushido Shoshinshu of Taira Shigesuke* (Tokyo: Tuttle, 1999). For a more scholarly overview of Japanese life in the era from the establishment of the Tokugawa Shogunate in 1603 to the Meiji Restoration of 1868, see Charles Dunn, *Everyday Life in Traditional Japan* (Tokyo: Tuttle, 1969).

23. The Reagan-era federal report titled *A Nation at Risk* (1983) expressed American anxiety about the perceived decline in achievement of American students versus their Japanese and German counterparts in particular. For a perceptive critique of this report and of the early-1980s anxiety about American education, see Richard Rothstein's "A Nation at Risk twenty-five years later," Cato Unbound, April 7, 2008, www.cato-unbound.org/2008/04/07/richard-rothstein/nation-risk-twenty-five-years-later.

24. For more about why American schools switched their emphasis from socialization to early literacy and numeracy, please see Chapter 2 of my book *Boys Adrift: The Five Factors Driving the Growing Epidemic of Unmotivated Boys and Underachieving Young Men* (New York: Basic Books, 2007), and Chapter 5 of my book *Girls on the Edge: The Four Factors Driving the New Crisis for Girls. Sexual Identity, The Cyberbubble, Obsessions, Environmental Toxins* (New York: Basic Books, 2010).

25. Jerry D. Weast, Superintendent of Schools for Montgomery County, Maryland, "Why we need rigorous, full-day kindergarten," from the May 2001 issue of *Principal Magazine*.

26. The literal translation would be "status insecurity" or "status uncertainty," but "role confusion" is a more idiomatic translation considering the context.

27. This paragraph summarizes the relevant aspects of Norbert Elias's essay "Changes in European standards of behaviour in the twentieth century," in *The Germans: Power Struggles and the Development of Habitus in the Nineteenth and Twentieth Centuries*, edited by Michael Schröter, translated by Eric Dunning (New York: Columbia University, 1998), pp. 23–43.

28. James S. Coleman, *The Adolescent Society: The Social Life of the Teenager and its Impact on Education* (New York: Free Press, 1961), pp. 5–6. The actual figures were: 49.2 percent said that they would "probably not join," and 12.3 percent said that they would "definitely not join" if their parents disapproved. Thus, a solid majority of 61.5 percent said that they would probably or definitely not join if their parents disapproved. These figures are provided in Edwin Artmann's doctoral dissertation, "A comparison of selected attitudes and values of the adolescent society in 1957 and 1972," North Texas State University, 1973.

29. The study entailed Ellen Galinsky's interviews with 1,000 American adolescents, which she documents in her book *Ask the Children: The Breakthrough Study That Reveals How to Succeed at Work and Parenting* (New York: HarperCollins, 2000). In *All Joy and*

No Fun: The Paradox of Modern Parenthood (New York: Ecco [HarperCollins], 2014), Jennifer Senior summarizes Galinsky's findings as follows: "During adolescence, that ingratitude is additionally seasoned with contempt" (p. 194).

30. This is a central theme of Gordon Neufeld's book, written with Gabor Maté, *Hold On to Your Kids: Why Parents Need to Matter More Than Peers*, second edition (Toronto: Vintage Canada, 2013). I explore Dr. Neufeld's perspective at greater length in Chapter 5.

31. For this purpose I used the list at www.tvguide.com/top-tv -shows.

32. This is not the whole story. I have posted other thoughts about the possible reasons behind the transfer of authority from parents to children at www.leonardsax.com/afterthoughts.htm.

33. There has been a slew of books about the lead-up to World War I as we observe the various centennials. My favorite treatment of this topic—the sunny optimism of Europeans before the actual outbreak of war in August 1914, their confidence that history is a story of smooth and continual progress—actually comes from an earlier book, Niall Ferguson, *The Pity of War: Explaining World War I* (New York: Basic Books, 2000), especially Chapter 6, "The last days of mankind: 28 June 1914–4 August 1914," pp. 143–173.

34. These quotes are from Nicolás Gómez-Dávila's *Scholia to an Implicit Text*, edited by Benjamin Villegas, translated by Roberto Pinzón (Bogotá: Villegas Editores, 2013). Gómez-Dávila, a citizen of Colombia educated in France, was careful to maintain a European mind-set in contradistinction to the *latinoamericana* culture, which he disdained. I do not share or condone his negative attitude toward *latinoamericana* culture; I include mention of his attitude only to indicate that Gómez-Dávila would not want to be referred to as a "Latin American philosopher." The passages quoted in the text come from *Scholia to an Implicit Text*, pp. 55 and 137. In the second passage I have departed from Pinzón's English translation. Here is the original Spanish: "El Progreso [capital *P* in the original, hence my use of quotation marks around 'Progress'] se reduce finalmente a

robarle al hombre lo que lo ennoblece, para poder venderle barato lo que le envilece."

35. For this analysis of Megan's behavior, I am indebted to Dr. Gordon Neufeld and his book *Hold On to Your Kids*, cited above in note 30. I explore Dr. Neufeld's perspective at greater length in Chapter 5.

36. Neufeld and Maté, *Hold On to Your Kids*, p. 7.

37. Neufeld and Maté, *Hold On to Your Kids*, pp. 15–16 (emphasis in original).

Chapter 2: Why Are So Many Kids Overweight?

1. These figures come from Cheryl Fryar and colleagues, "Prevalence of obesity among children and adolescents: United States, trends 1963–1965 through 2009–2010," Centers for Disease Control and Prevention, September 13, 2012, www.cdc.gov/nchs/data/hestat/obesity _child_09_10/obesity_child_09_10.htm. The figure titled "Prevalence of obesity among American children and teenagers" is adapted from "CDC grand rounds: Childhood obesity in the United States," Centers for Disease Control and Prevention, January 21, 2011, www.cdc.gov /mmwr/preview/mmwrhtml/mm6002a2.htm#fig1.

2. Some parents are confused about when to use the terms "obese" and "overweight." Several have chided me for using the word "obese" because they think it is derogatory. "You should say 'overweight' instead," they tell me. But the two terms have precise definitions, which differ. In the United States, the term "overweight," for children, applies to individuals with a body mass index (BMI) in the 85th to 95th percentile for the age- and sex-specific reference values established by the Centers for Disease Control and Prevention (CDC) in its growth chart published in 2000. The term "obese," for children, applies to those with a BMI above the 95th percentile on the 2000 CDC growth chart. See Cynthia Ogden and Katherine Flegal, "Changes in terminology for childhood overweight and obesity," CDC, June 25, 2010, www.cdc.gov/nchs/data/nhsr/nhsr025.pdf. You can download 2000

CDC growth charts at CDC, "2000 CDC growth charts for the United States: Methods and development," May 2002, www.cdc.gov/growth charts/2000growthchart-us.pdf. BMI calculators are widely available on the Internet—for example, at National Heart, Lung, and Blood Institute, "Calculate your body mass index," National Institutes of Health, www.nhlbi.nih.gov/guidelines/obesity/BMI/bmicalc.htm.

Some examples may help make this more concrete. A 15-year-old boy who was 5'8" would be obese if he weighed more than 180 pounds. If he weighed 155 pounds, he would be overweight but not obese. A 15-year-old girl who was 5'4" would be obese if she weighed 168 pounds or more. If she weighed 142 pounds, she would be over-weight but not obese. Remember that these rules apply to children and adolescents, not adults.

3. For example, see Sabrina Tavernise, "Obesity rate for young children plummets," *New York Times*, February 26, 2014.

4. Mark Bittman, "Some progress on eating and health," *New York Times*, March 4, 2014, www.nytimes.com/2014/03/05/opinion /bittman-some-progress-on-eating-and-health.html.

5. Jaime Gahche and colleagues, "Cardiorespiratory fitness levels among U.S. youth aged 12–15 years: United States, 1999–2004 and 2012," NCHS Data Brief 153, May 2014, www.cdc.gov/nchs/data /databriefs/db153.htm.

6. The quotes from Dr. Fulton and Dr. Blackburn are from Gretchen Reynolds, "This is our youth," *Well* (blog), *New York Times*, July 9, 2014, http://well.blogs.nytimes.com/2014/07/09/young -and-unfit.

7. I also note that this boy's public school district has cut back on PE to save money and devote more time to reading, writing, and math. When he does have "physical education" in his schedule, what passes for PE may just be a health class on puberty, the virtues of safe sex, and the like, all conducted with the children sitting in chairs. In this case, it was clear that this child was simply out of shape: his lungs were clear, and his peak flow was normal. In similar cases, I have seen children diagnosed with "exercise-induced asthma." Many

parents and even some physicians seem to believe that exercise-induced shortness of breath equals exercise-induced asthma even in the absence of true wheezing. But that's not true. Many kids who have exercise-induced shortness of breath are simply out of shape. Yet I know several physicians who seem to find it easier to say, "Your child has exercise-induced asthma," and prescribe an inhaler, than to say, "Your child is out of shape because he doesn't get enough exercise."

I am not the only physician to express concern that American kids are being diagnosed with "exercise-induced asthma" when the correct diagnosis is "exercise-induced breathlessness" due their being out of shape. See, for example, Yun Shim and colleagues, "Physical deconditioning as a cause of breathlessness among obese adolescents with a diagnosis of asthma," *PLOS One*, April 23, 2013, doi: 10.1371 /journal.pone.0061022.

8. My comments about Australia, Canada, Finland, Germany, the Netherlands, Spain, Sweden, Switzerland, and the United Kingdom are based on a seminal article describing the worldwide character of this problem: Youfa Wang and Tim Lobstein, "Worldwide trends in childhood overweight and obesity," *International Journal of Pediatric Obesity*, volume 1, pp. 11–25, 2006. The trend toward increasing overweight and obesity is clear internationally only among children age 6 and older; the trend is not clear among children age 5 and under. For more on this point, see A. Cattaneo and colleagues, "Overweight and obesity in infants and pre-school children in the European Union: A review of existing data," *Obesity Reviews*, volume 11, pp. 389–398, 2009. The Dutch studies referenced in this paragraph are A. M. Fredriks and colleagues, "Body index measurements in 1996–7 compared with 1980," *Archives of Disease in Childhood*, volume 82, pp. 107–112, 2000; R. A. Hirasing and colleagues, "Increased prevalence of overweight and obesity in Dutch children, and the detection of overweight and obesity using international criteria and new reference diagrams," *Nederlands Tijdschrift voor Geneeskunde*, volume 145, pp. 1303–1308, 2001.

Here are some recent updates on this topic, country by country:

Australia: Michelle Haby and colleagues, "Future predictions of body mass index and overweight prevalence in Australia, 2005–2025," *Health Promotion International*, volume 27, pp. 250–260, 2012.

England: E. Stamatakis and colleagues, "Childhood obesity and overweight prevalence trends in England: Evidence for growing socioeconomic disparities," *International Journal of Obesity*, volume 34, pp. 41–47, 2010.

France: S. Péneau and colleagues, "Prevalence of overweight in 6- to 15-year-old children in central/western France from 1996 to 2006: Trends toward stabilization," *International Journal of Obesity*, volume 33, pp. 401–407, 2009.

Scotland: Sarah Smith and colleagues, "Growing up before growing out: Secular trends in height, weight and obesity in 5–6-year-old children born between 1970 and 2006," *Archives of Disease in Childhood*, volume 98, pp. 269–273, 2013.

Spain: E. Miqueleiz and colleagues, "Trends in the prevalence of childhood overweight and obesity according to socioeconomic status: Spain, 1987–2007," *European Journal of Clinical Nutrition*, volume 68, pp. 209–214, 2014.

United States: Cynthia Ogden and colleagues, "Prevalence of obesity and trends in body mass index among US children and adolescents, 1999–2010," *Journal of the American Medical Association*, volume 307, pp. 483–490, 2012.

9. See, for example, D. Cohen and colleagues, "Ten-year secular changes in muscular fitness in English children," *Acta Paediatrica*, volume 100, pp. 175–177, 2011. See also Helen Peters and colleagues, "Trends in resting pulse rates in 9–11-year-old children in the UK 1980–2008," *Archives of Disease in Childhood*, volume 99, number 1, pp. 10–14, 2014; D. Moliner-Urdiales and colleagues, "Secular trends in health-related physical fitness in Spanish adolescents," *Journal of Science and Medicine in Sport*, volume 13, pp. 584–588, 2010.

10. For more evidence regarding the role of endocrine disruptors in promoting overweight—as well as suggestions for how to protect

your child from these substances in foods, beverages, creams, lotions, and shampoos—please take a look at Chapter 5 of my book *Boys Adrift* and Chapter 4 of my book *Girls on the Edge*. For an introduction to the research on the role of gut bacteria in obesity, see the review by Kristina Harris and colleagues, "Is the gut microbiota a new factor contributing to obesity and its metabolic disorders?" *Journal of Obesity*, 2012, article ID 879151, doi: 10.1155/2012/879151.

11. Richard Troiano and colleagues, "Energy and fat intake of children and adolescents in the United States," *American Journal of Clinical Nutrition*, volume 72, pp. 1343s–1353s, 2000, http://ajcn .nutrition.org/content/72/5/1343s.full. See also Joanne Guthrie and Joan Morton, "Food sources of added sweeteners in the diets of Americans," *Journal of the American Dietetic Association*, volume 100, pp. 43–51, 2000.

12. Simone French, Mary Story, and Robert Jeffery, "Environmental influences on eating and physical activity," *Annual Review of Public Health*, volume 22, pp. 309–335, 2001. The factoid about the 200 percent increase is on p. 312.

13. Kelsey Sheehy, "Junk food axed from school vending machines," *US News & World Report*, July 1, 2013, www.usnews.com /education/blogs/high-school-notes/2013/07/01/junk-food-axed -from-school-vending-machines.

14. These figures are taken from Nicholas Confessore, "How school lunch became the latest political battleground," *New York Times*, October 7, 2014, www.nytimes.com/2014/10/12/magazine/how-school -lunch-became-the-latest-political-battleground.html.

15. Pete Kasperowicz, "Michelle Obama's school lunch rules leading to healthy, hunger-free trash cans," *The Blaze*, October 14, 2014, www.theblaze.com/blog/2014/10/14/michelle-obamas-school-lunch -rules-leading-to-healthy-hunger-free-trash-cans-2.

16. National School Boards Association, "New poll validates concerns about federal school meals," press release, October 13, 2014, www.nsba.org/newsroom/press-releases/national-school-boards -association-celebrates-national-school-lunch-week-new.

17. Mrs. Obama's remarks were widely reported, for example by Annika McGinnis of Reuters in "Michelle Obama expands push to get Americans to drink more water," *Huffington Post*, July 23, 2014, www.huffingtonpost.com/2014/07/22/michelle-obama-water_n _5611501.html.

18. See Samreen Hooda, "#BrownBagginIt trending on Twitter as Pittsburgh students protest school lunches," *Huffington Post*, October 2, 2012, www.huffingtonpost.com/2012/08/31/pittsburgh -students-are-brownbagginit_n_1846682.html. See also Confessore, "How school lunch became the latest political battleground."

19. Megumi Hatori and colleagues, "Time-restricted feeding without reducing caloric intake prevents metabolic diseases in mice fed a high-fat diet," *Cell Metabolism*, volume 15, pp. 848–860, 2012. See also Amandine Chaix and colleagues, "Time-restricted feeding is a preventative and therapeutic intervention against diverse nutritional challenges," *Cell Metabolism*, volume 20, pp. 991–1005, 2014. Those studies concern mice. For evidence that the same phenomenon holds true in humans, see M. Garaulet and colleagues, "Timing of food intake predicts weight loss effectiveness," *International Journal of Obesity*, volume 37, pp. 604–611, 2013. For a useful overview of the practical implications of this research, see Gretchen Reynolds, "A 12-hour window for a healthy weight," *New York Times*, January 15, 2015, http://well.blogs.nytimes.com/2015/01/15/a-12-hour-window -for-a-healthy-weight. The quote from Dr. Panda comes from Reynolds's article.

20. John P. Robinson, "Television and leisure time: Yesterday, today, and (maybe) tomorrow," *Public Opinion Quarterly*, volume 33, pp. 210–222, 1969. This survey was conducted in 1965; the paper was published in 1969. Robinson collected data only from adults, not children. Children's viewing time was likely significantly lower than that reported for adults, because most TV programming in 1965 targeted adults, with the exception of Saturday morning cartoons. And, as noted, most households had only one TV. As a result, popular evening programs such as *Gidget* were

intended for a family viewing audience, meaning that adults and children watched together.

21. In 1965, only 19.4 percent of American households with a television had 2 or more, and 7.4 percent of American households did not have even 1 set, according to the Television Bureau of Advertising (TBA), "TV Basics: A report on the growth and scope of television," www.tvb.org/media/file/TV_Basics.pdf (accessed May 6, 2015). The figure of 19.4 percent comes from the table titled "Multi-set and VCR households," and the figure of 7.4 percent comes from the table titled "TV households," both on p. 2.

22. Kaiser Family Foundation, "Generation M2: Media in the life of 8 to 18 year olds," January 2010, http://kff.org/other/poll-finding/report-generation-m2-media-in-the-lives. In their October 2013 guidelines for use of media by children and teenagers, the American Academy of Pediatrics cited this Kaiser Family Foundation report as the most definitive recent survey of media use by American children and adolescents. See the American Academy of Pediatrics, Council on Communications and Media, "Children, Adolescents, and the Media," October 28, 2013, doi: 10.1542/peds.2013–2656; I have posted these guidelines at www.leonardsax.com/guidelines.pdf.

23. For a thoughtful review of how play has changed for American kids and why kids need more unsupervised play, see David Elkind, *The Power of Play: Learning What Comes Naturally* (Boston: Da Capo, 2007).

24. See, for example, "Dodgeball banned after bullying complaint," *Headline News*, March 28, 2013, www.hlntv.com/article/2013/03/28/school-dodgeball-ban-new-hampshire-district. For an earlier report, see Tamala Edwards, "Scourge of the playground: It's dodgeball, believe it or not. More schools are banning the childhood game, saying it's too violent," *Time*, May 21, 2001, p. 68.

25. Noreen McDonald, "Active transportation to school: Trends among US schoolchildren, 1969–2001," *American Journal of Preventive Medicine*, volume 32, pp. 509–516, 2007.

26. In a meta-analysis of studies involving 30,002 children age 2 to 18 and 604,509 adults over 18, Francesco Cappuccio and his colleagues found that decreased sleep was more strongly associated with obesity for children than for adults. Specifically, the odds ratio was 1.89 for children and 1.55 for adults. See Francesco Cappuccio and colleagues, "Meta-analysis of short sleep duration and obesity in children and adults," *Sleep*, volume 31, pp. 619–626, 2008. For an especially persuasive longitudinal study, see Julie Lumeng and colleagues, "Shorter sleep duration is associated with increased risk for being overweight at ages 9 to 12 years," *Pediatrics*, volume 120, pp. 1020–1029, 2007, http://pediatrics.aappublications.org/content/120 /5/1020.full.

27. See, for example, Shahrad Taheri and colleagues, "Short sleep duration is associated with reduced leptin, elevated ghrelin, and increased body mass index," *PLOS Medicine*, December 7, 2004, www .plosmedicine.org/article/info%3Adoi%2F10.1371%2Fjournal.pmed .0010062. See also Chantelle Hart and colleagues, "Changes in children's sleep duration on food intake, weight, and leptin," *Pediatrics*, volume 132, pp. e1473–e1480, 2013.

28. Katherine Keyes and colleagues, "The great sleep recession: Changes in sleep duration among US adolescents, 1991–2012," *Pediatrics*, February 16, 2015, doi: 10.1542/peds.2014–2707.

29. The National Institutes of Health (NIH) tries to establish a national consensus among experts on many topics. These figures are drawn from the National Heart, Lung, and Blood Institute, "How much sleep is enough?" NIH, February 22, 2012, www.nhlbi.nih.gov /health/health-topics/topics/sdd/howmuch.html.

30. These figures are taken from Figure 3 in Eve Van Cauter and Kristen Knutson, "Sleep and the epidemic of obesity in children and adults," *European Journal of Endocrinology*, volume 159, pp. S59–S66. See also the National Sleep Foundation, "Children and Sleep," March 1, 2004, www.sleepfoundation.org/sites/default/files/FINAL %20SOF%202004.pdf.

31. Lisa Matricciani and colleagues, "In search of lost sleep: Secular trends in the sleep time of school-aged children and adolescents," *Sleep Medicine Reviews*, volume 16, pp. 203–211, 2012.

32. See, for example, Jennifer Falbe and colleagues, "Sleep duration, restfulness, and screens in the sleep environment," *Pediatrics*, volume 135, pp. e367–e375, 2015.

33. I have posted the full text of the AAP guidelines at www .leonardsax.com/guidelines.pdf. The exact text of the recommendation I am citing here is "Keep the TV set and Internet-connected electronic devices out of the child's bedroom" (p. 959). I note that a mobile phone with Internet access counts as an "Internet-connected electronic device."

34. Hundreds of American media outlets picked up this Associated Press story in the last week of October 2013. See, for example, Lindsey Tanner, "Docs to parents: Limit kids' texts, tweets, online," *Huffington Post*, October 28, 2013, www.huffingtonpost.com/2013/10/28 /doctors-kids-media-use_n_4170182.html.

35. Marshall Connolly, "Futile report? Pediatricians advise limiting kids to 2 hours on Internet, TV," *Catholic Online*, October 28, 2013, www.catholic.org/health/story.php?id=52916.

36. For an overview of this topic, see Daphne Korczak and colleagues, "Are children and adolescents with psychiatric illness at risk for increased future body weight? A systematic review," *Developmental Medicine and Child Neurology*, volume 55, pp. 980–987, 2013. Some of the articles that demonstrate this phenomenon—of the defiant child being more likely to become overweight or obese— include (in alphabetical order): Sarah Anderson and colleagues, "Externalizing behavior in early childhood and body mass index from age 2 to 12 years: Longitudinal analyses of a prospective cohort study," *BMC Pediatrics*, volume 10, 2010, www.biomedcentral .com/1471–2431/10/49; Cristiane Duarte and colleagues, "Child mental health problems and obesity in early adulthood," *Journal of Pediatrics*, volume 156, pp. 93–97, 2010; Daphne Korczak and colleagues, "Child and adolescent psychopathology predicts increased

NOTES TO CHAPTER 2

adult body mass index: Results from a prospective community sample," *Journal of Developmental and Behavioral Pediatrics*, volume 35, pp. 108–117, 2014; Julie Lumeng and colleagues, "Association between clinically meaningful behavior problems and overweight in children," *Pediatrics*, volume 112, pp. 1138–1145, 2003; A. Mamun and colleagues, "Childhood behavioral problems predict young adults' BMI and obesity: Evidence from a birth cohort study," *Obesity*, volume 17, pp. 761–766, 2009; Sarah Mustillo and colleagues, "Obesity and psychiatric disorder: Developmental trajectories," *Pediatrics*, volume 111, pp. 851–859, 2003; Daniel Pine and colleagues, "Psychiatric symptoms in adolescence as predictors of obesity in early adulthood: A longitudinal study," *American Journal of Public Health*, volume 87, pp. 1303–1310, 1997, www.ncbi.nlm.nih.gov/pmc/articles/PMC1381090; B. White and colleagues, "Childhood psychological function and obesity risk across the lifecourse," *International Journal of Obesity*, volume 36, pp. 511–516, 2012.

37. The study I am citing here is Lumeng and colleagues, "Association between clinically meaningful behavior problems and overweight in children." Although these authors use the term "overweight," their definition of "overweight" is actually the 2010 definition for "obese" (see note 2 above). They found that the odds ratio for kids who misbehaved subsequently becoming obese was 2.95. An odds ratio of 3.0 would mean that the kids who misbehaved were exactly 3 times more likely to become obese. When they restricted their analysis to kids who were of normal weight at baseline, the odds ratio increased to 5.23. In other words, normal-weight kids who misbehaved were more than 5 times as likely to become obese, compared to normal-weight kids who did not misbehave.

38. Anna Bardone and colleagues, "Adult physical health outcomes of adolescent girls with conduct disorder, depression, and anxiety," *Journal of the American Academy of Child and Adolescent Psychiatry*, volume 37, pp. 594–601, 1998.

39. Melanie L'Eef, e-mail, May 2, 2015.

Chapter 3: Why Are So Many Kids on Medication?

1. See Benedict Carey, "Bipolar illness soars as a diagnosis for the young," *New York Times*, September 4, 2007, www.nytimes.com /2007/09/04/health/04psych.html. The *New York Times* article describes a study published by C. Moreno and colleagues, "National trends in the outpatient diagnosis and treatment of bipolar disorder in youth," *Archives of General Psychiatry*, volume 64, pp. 1032–1039, 2007.

2. See, for example, Joseph Biederman and colleagues, "Pediatric mania: A developmental subtype of bipolar disorder?" *Biological Psychiatry*, volume 48, pp. 458–466, 2000.

3. Dominic Riccio is quoted in Rob Waters, "Children in crisis? Concerns about the growing popularity of the bipolar diagnosis," *Psychotherapy Networker*, September 24, 2009, www.psychotherapy networker.org/component/k2/item/675-networker-news.

4. Dr. Harris is quoted in Waters, "Children in crisis?"

5. The *Newsweek* cover story, written by Mary Carmichael, is titled "Growing Up Bipolar," *Newsweek*, May 17, 2008, www.newsweek .com/growing-bipolar-maxs-world-90351.

6. See, for example, Gardiner Harris and Benedict Carey, "Researchers fail to reveal full drug pay," *New York Times*, June 8, 2008, www.nytimes.com/2008/06/08/us/08conflict.html.

7. When the news broke about the millions of dollars paid to Biederman and his two friends, the only penalty which Harvard Medical School imposed was a one-year embargo on receiving more money from drug companies. Biederman never had to pay the money back. At this writing, years after the disclosure became public, he still retains his position as chief of research in pediatric psychopharmacology at the Massachusetts General Hospital. The MGH website still prominently mentions his various honors but makes no mention of the fact that he accepted a great deal of money from the drug companies and failed to disclose that fact until Senator Grassley forced him to.

8. Elizabeth Root, *Kids Caught in the Psychiatric Maelstrom: How Pathological Labels and "Therapeutic" Drugs Hurt Children and Families* (Santa Barbara, CA: ABC-CLIO, 2009), p. 40.

9. Elizabeth Roberts, "A rush to medicate young minds," *Washington Post*, October 8, 2006, www.washingtonpost.com/wp-dyn /content/article/2006/10/06/AR2006100601391.html.

10. Martin Holtmann and colleagues, "Bipolar disorder in children and adolescents in Germany: National trends in the rates of inpatients, 2000–2007," *Bipolar Disorders*, volume 12, pp. 155–163, 2010, http://onlinelibrary.wiley.com/doi/10.1111/j.1399–5618.2010 .00794.x/full. The German researchers found a significant increase in the diagnosis of bipolar disorder for adolescents 15 to 19 years of age and a small, "nonsignificant" decline in the diagnosis for children under 15 years of age. It may have been a "nonsignificant" decline from the German perspective, but nevertheless it was a *decline*, not a huge increase as was observed in the United States. On page 159 of their paper, Holtmann and colleagues cite a rate of 204 per 100,000 adolescents in the United States discharged with a diagnosis of bipolar disorder, compared with 5.22 per 100,000 adolescents in Germany. Let's calculate the odds ratio, comparing the USA to Germany: 204 / 5.22 = 39.1. In other words, an adolescent in the United States is nearly 40 times more likely to be diagnosed with bipolar disorder than an adolescent in Germany.

11. Juan Carballo and colleagues, "Longitudinal trends in diagnosis at child and adolescent mental health centres in Madrid, Spain," *European Child & Adolescent Psychiatry*, volume 22, pp. 47–49, 2013.

12. Kirsten van Kessel and colleagues, "Trends in child and adolescent discharges at a New Zealand psychiatric inpatient unit between 1998 and 2007," *New Zealand Medical Journal*, volume 125, pp. 55–61, 2012.

13. Holtmann and colleagues, "Bipolar disorder in children and adolescents in Germany," pp. 156, 159.

14. Anthony James and colleagues, "A comparison of American and English hospital discharge rates for pediatric bipolar disorder, 2000 to 2010," *Journal of the American Academy of Child and Adolescent Psychiatry*, volume 53, pp. 614–624, 2014.

15. These guidelines are based on the research of Professors Craig Anderson and Doug Gentile. I present their research and explain the guidelines at greater length in Chapter 3 of *Boys Adrift: The Five Factors Driving the Growing Epidemic of Unmotivated Boys and Underachieving Young Men* (New York: Basic Books, 2007). Basic Books published an updated edition in June 2016.

16. Alan Schwarz and Sarah Cohen, "A.D.H.D. seen in 11% of U.S. children as diagnoses rise," *New York Times*, March 31, 2013, www.nytimes.com/2013/04/01/health/more-diagnoses-of-hyperactivity-causing-concern.html.

17. In my firsthand experience as a prescribing physician in Maryland and Pennsylvania, the proportion is higher than 69 percent. In most cases in which I have been involved, when a doctor diagnoses ADHD, the doctor also writes a prescription for a medication. But let's accept the CDC estimate of 69 percent. Here's the source for that figure: CDC, "Attention-Deficit / Hyperactivity Disorder (ADHD): Data and Statistics," November 13, 2013, www.cdc.gov/ncbddd/adhd/data.html.

18. Suzanne McCarthy and colleagues, "The epidemiology of pharmacologically treated attention deficit hyperactivity disorder (ADHD) in children, adolescents and adults in UK primary care," *BMC Pediatrics*, volume 12, 2012, www.biomedcentral.com/1471-2431/12/78.

19. According to the CDC data from March 2013, 10 percent of American children between 4 and 13 years of age—that would be 100 out of every 1,000—have now been diagnosed with ADHD. The CDC separately estimates that 69 percent of American children diagnosed with ADHD have been prescribed medication for the disorder. These statistics together indicate that 69 children out of every 1,000 have been prescribed medication for ADHD.

20. The age grouping is not precisely the same: 4 to 13 in the United States compared with 6 to 12 in the United Kingdom. But it will suffice to give us an order-of-magnitude comparison.

21. Peter Conrad and Meredith Bergey, "The impending globalization of ADHD: Notes on the expansion and growth of a medicalized disorder," *Social Science and Medicine*, volume 122, pp. 31–43, 2014.

22. Gabrielle Weiss and Lily Hechtman, "The hyperactive child syndrome," *Science*, volume 205, pp. 1348–1354, 1979.

23. I first used the phrase "the medicalization of misbehavior" in my book *Why Gender Matters* (New York: Doubleday, 2005), p. 199.

24. Here are reports from:

Denmark: H.-C. Steinhausen and C. Bisgaard, "Nationwide time trends in dispensed prescriptions of psychotropic medication for children and adolescents in Denmark," *Acta Psychiatrica Scandinavica*, volume 129, pp. 221–231, 2014.

France: Eric Acquaviva and colleagues, "Psychotropic medication in the French child and adolescent population: Prevalence estimation from health insurance data and national self-report survey data," *BMC Psychiatry*, volume 9, 2009, www.biomedcentral.com /1471–244X/9/72.

Germany: M. Koelch and colleagues, "Psychotropic medication in children and adolescents in Germany: Prevalence, indications, and psychopathological patterns," *Journal of Child and Adolescent Psychopharmacology*, volume 19, pp. 765–770, 2009.

Italy: Antonio Clavenna and colleagues, "Antidepressant and antipsychotic use in an Italian pediatric population," *BMC Pediatrics*, volume 11, number 40, 2011, www.biomedcentral.com/1471 –2431/11/40. (These authors observe that this study did not include stimulant medications such as Ritalin, Concerta, Metadate, Focalin, and the like because methylphenidate—the active ingredient in those medications—was not even licensed for sale in Italy until 2007.)

United Kingdom: Vingfen Hsia and Karyn Maclennan, "Rise in psychotropic drug prescribing in children and adolescents during

1992–2001: A population-based study in the UK," *European Journal of Epidemiology*, volume 24, pp. 211–216, 2009.

25. See, for example, Laurel Leslie and colleagues, "Rates of psychotropic medication use over time among youth in child welfare / child protective services," *Journal of Child and Adolescent Psychopharmacology*, volume 20, pp. 135–143, 2010. These researchers found that more than 22 percent of youth in child welfare had been prescribed psychotropic medication within the previous three years. One might conjecture that the use of psychotropic medication would be higher among children in child welfare; however, this conjecture was tested and proven false by Jessica Wolff, Russel Carleton, and Susan Drilea, "Are rates of psychotropic medication use really higher among children in child welfare?" (presentation at the 26th Annual Children's Mental Health Research and Policy Initiative, March 4, 2013), http://cmhconference.com/files/2013/cmh2013–16b.pdf. Nevertheless, Kathleen Merikangas and her colleagues have argued that psychotropic medications are actually underutilized in American children and adolescents; see Kathleen Merikangas and colleagues, "Medication use in US youth with mental disorders," *JAMA Pediatrics*, volume 167, pp. 141–148, 2013. In a commentary, David Rubin questioned some of the assumptions made by Merikangas and colleagues; see David Rubin, "Conflicting data on psychotropic use by children: Two pieces to the same puzzle," *JAMA Pediatrics*, volume 167, pp. 189–190, 2013.

26. Mark Olfson and colleagues, "National trends in the office-based treatment of children, adolescents, and adults with antipsychotics," *JAMA Psychiatry*, volume 69, pp. 1247–1256, 2012, http://archpsyc.jamanetwork.com/article.aspx?articleid=1263977.

27. When I rattle off the list of stimulant pharmaceutical medications—Adderall, Ritalin, Concerta, Focalin, Metadate, Daytrana, and Vyvanse—it sounds as though I am mentioning seven different medications. In fact, these seven medications are just two medications. Adderall and Vyvanse are two proprietary amphetamines. Ritalin, Concerta, Focalin, Metadate, and Daytrana are all different versions

of methylphenidate. There is consensus that methylphenidate works by increasing the action of dopamine in the synapse; see, for example, Nora Volkow and colleagues, "Imaging the effects of methylphenidate on brain dopamine: New model on its therapeutic actions for attention-deficit/hyperactivity disorder," *Biological Psychiatry*, volume 57, pp. 1410–1415, 2005. And it has long been recognized that amphetamine mimics the action of dopamine in the brain and that the dopamine system is key to ADHD; see, for example, James Swanson and colleagues, "Dopamine and glutamate in attention deficit disorder," in *Dopamine and Glutamate in Psychiatric Disorders*, edited by Werner Schmidt and Maarten Reith (New York: Humana Press, 2005), pp. 293–315.

28. For background information about Adderall, Ritalin, Concerta, Focalin, Metadate, Daytrana, and Vyvanse, please read the previous note. Many scholarly studies have now demonstrated that methylphenidate and amphetamine, the active ingredients in these medications, can cause lasting changes to those areas of the developing brain where dopamine receptors are found. The disrupting effects appear to be centered on the nucleus accumbens. This is not surprising, because the nucleus accumbens has a high density of dopamine receptors. See three papers that Harvard's William Carlezon, an early investigator in the field, coauthored on this topic: "Enduring behavioral effects of early exposure to methylphenidate in rats," *Biological Psychiatry*, volume 54, pp. 1330–1337, 2003; "Understanding the neurobiological consequences of early exposure to psychotropic drugs," *Neuropharmacology*, volume 47, Supplement 1, pp. 47–60, 2004; "Early developmental exposure to methylphenidate reduces cocaine-induced potentiation of brain stimulation reward in rats," *Biological Psychiatry*, volume 57, pp. 120–125, 2005. For more information on the central role of the nucleus accumbens in motivation, see Dr. Carlezon's "Biological substrates of reward and aversion: A nucleus accumbens activity hypothesis," *Neuropharmacology*, volume 56, Supplement 1, pp. 122–132, 2009.

Terry Robinson and Bryan Kolb at the University of Michigan were among the first to demonstrate that low-dose amphetamine leads to damage to dendrites in the nucleus accumbens. They first documented this finding in "Persistent structural modifications in nucleus accumbens and prefrontal cortex neurons produced by previous experiences with amphetamine," *Journal of Neuroscience*, volume 17, pp. 8491–8497, 1997. They reviewed this emerging field in "Structural plasticity associated with exposure to drugs of abuse," *Neuropharmacology*, volume 47, pp. 33–46, 2004. See also Claire Advokat, "Literature review: Update on amphetamine neurotoxicity and its relevance to the treatment of ADHD," *Journal of Attention Disorders*, volume 11, pp. 8–16, 2007.

Other relevant articles include (in alphabetical order): Esther Gramage and colleagues, "Periadolescent amphetamine treatment causes transient cognitive disruptions and long-term changes in hippocampal LTP," *Addiction Biology*, volume 18, pp. 19–29, 2013; Rochellys D. Heijtz, Bryan Kolb, and Hans Forssberg, "Can a therapeutic dose of amphetamine during pre-adolescence modify the pattern of synaptic organization in the brain?" *European Journal of Neuroscience*, volume 18, pp. 3394–3399, 2003; Yong Li and Julie Kauer, "Repeated exposure to amphetamine disrupts dopaminergic modulation of excitatory synaptic plasticity and neurotransmission in nucleus accumbens," *Synapse*, volume 51, pp. 1–10, 2004; Manuel Mameli and Christian Lüscher, "Synaptic plasticity and addiction: Learning mechanisms gone awry," *Neuropharmacology*, volume 61, pp. 1052–1059, 2011; Shao-Pii Onn and Anthony Grace, "Amphetamine withdrawal alters bistable states and cellular coupling in rat prefrontal cortex and nucleus accumbens neurons recorded in vivo," *Journal of Neuroscience*, volume 20, pp. 2332–2345, 2000; Margery Pardey and colleagues, "Long-term effects of chronic oral Ritalin administration on cognitive and neural development in adolescent Wistar Kyoto Rats," *Brain Sciences*, volume 2, pp. 375–404, 2012; Scott Russo and colleagues, "The addicted synapse: Mechanisms of synaptic and structural plasticity in the nucleus accumbens," *Trends in*

Neuroscience, volume 33, pp. 267–276, 2010; and Louk J. Vander-schuren and colleagues, "A single exposure to amphetamine is suffi-cient to induce long-term behavioral, neuroendocrine, and neurochemical sensitization in rats," *Journal of Neuroscience*, volume 19, pp. 9579–9586, 1999.

Most of the studies above are based on research in laboratory ani-mals, not in humans. But researchers have recently documented that stimulant medications prescribed for ADHD actually shrink the nu-cleus accumbens and related structures in the human brain, although these changes may be transient; see Elseline Hoekzema and col-leagues, "Stimulant drugs trigger transient volumetric changes in the human ventral striatum," *Brain Structure and Function*, volume 219, pp. 23–34, 2013. Other researchers have found that even occasional use of these medications by college students results in changes in the structure of the brain; see Scott Mackey and colleagues, "A voxel-based morphometry study of young occasional users of amphetamine-type stimulants and cocaine," *Drug and Alcohol Dependence*, volume 135, pp. 104–111, 2014. For a thoughtful review of the underlying neurochemistry, the similarities between prescription stimulant med-ications and cocaine, and an assessment of the long-term risks for people who take these medications, see the review by Heinz Steiner and Vincent Van Waes, "Addiction-related gene regulation: Risks of exposure to cognitive enhancers vs. other psychostimulants," *Progress in Neurobiology*, volume 100, pp. 60–80, 2013.

Studies like these strongly suggest that even short-term exposure to amphetamine or methylphenidate, particularly in the juvenile brain, may induce long-lasting changes both structurally (particu-larly in the nucleus accumbens and related limbic structures) and behaviorally. Iva Mathews and colleagues found effects that were dramatic in the adolescent animal but absent in the adult; see Iva Mathews and colleagues, "Low doses of amphetamine lead to imme-diate and lasting locomotor sensitization in adolescent, not adult, male rats," *Pharmacology, Biochemistry and Behavior*, volume 97, pp. 640–646, 2011. As mentioned in Chapter 1, the prepubertal or pubertal brain is plastic in a way that the adult brain is not. At least in laboratory animals, these changes may have profound consequences—for example, a lasting impairment in social bonding; see Yan Liu and colleagues, "Nucleus accumbens dopamine mediates amphetamine-induced impairment of social bonding in a monogamous rodent species," *Proceedings of the National Academy of Sciences*, volume 107, pp. 1217–1222, 2010.

29. I made this same point previously in my commentary for the *New York Times* "Room for Debate" feature; see my article titled "A.D.H.D. drugs have long-term risks," *New York Times*, June 9, 2012, http://nyti.ms/1dr390L.

30. These figures derive from Table 4 in Christian Bachmann and colleagues, "Antipsychotic prescription in children and adolescents," *Deutsches Ärzteblatt International*, volume 111, pp. 25–34, 2014. The German data showed a prevalence of 3.2 children per 1,000 per year, mostly adolescents. In addition, I refer to three other studies cited by Bachmann and colleagues in Table 4:

United States: Olfson and colleagues, "National trends in the office-based treatment of children" (2012), reported a prevalence of 37.6 adolescents per 1,000 and 18.3 children per 1,000 taking atypical antipsychotics, averaging to 27.9 individuals age 0 to 19 per 1,000 [(37.6 + 18.3) / 2 = 27.9], as of 2009. The American figure of 27.9 divided by the German figure of 3.2 yields 8.7. In Norway (see below) the figure is 0.5 per 1,000, so the American figure is 56 times higher (27.9 / 0.5); in Italy (see below) the latest figure was 0.3, so the American figure is 93 times higher (27.9 / 0.3).

Norway: Svein Kjosavik, Sabine Ruths, and Steinar Hunskaar, "Psychotropic drug use in the Norwegian general population in 2005: Data from the Norwegian Prescription Database," *Pharmacoepidemiology and Drug Safety*, volume 18, pp. 572–578, 2009.

Italy: Clavenna and colleagues, "Antidepressant and antipsychotic use in an Italian pediatric population."

31. For a review of the relation between these antipsychotic medications and weight gain, see Dr. James Roerig and colleagues,

"Atypical antipsychotic-induced weight gain," CNS Drugs, volume 25, pp. 1035–1059, 2011. See also José María Martínez-Ortega and colleagues, "Weight gain and increase of body mass index among children and adolescents treated with antipsychotics: A critical review," *European Child & Adolescent Psychiatry*, volume 22, pp. 457–479, 2013. For a review of the relation between these medications and diabetes, specifically in children, see William Bobo and colleagues, "Antipsychotics and the risk of type 2 diabetes mellitus in children and youth," *JAMA Psychiatry*, volume 70, pp. 1067–1075, 2013.

32. Martínez-Ortega and colleagues, "Weight gain and increase of body mass index among children and adolescents treated with antipsychotics."

33. In Bobo and colleagues, "Antipsychotics and the risk of type 2 diabetes mellitus in children and youth," the risk remained elevated for one year following discontinuation of the antipsychotic; longer follow-up is not yet available. At one year after discontinuation, there was no statistically significant difference in risk of diabetes between those who had discontinued the antipsychotic medication and those who remained on it.

34. Frank Elgar, Wendy Craig, and Stephen Trites, "Family dinners, communication, and mental health in Canadian adolescents," *Journal of Adolescent Health*, volume 52, pp. 433–438, 2013.

35. Jerica Berge and colleagues, "The protective role of family meals for youth obesity: 10-year longitudinal associations," *Journal of Pediatrics*, volume 166, pp. 296–301, 2015.

36. Rebecca Davidson and Anne Gauthier, "A cross-national multi-level study of family meals," *International Journal of Comparative Sociology*, volume 51, pp. 349–365, 2010.

37. Daniel Miller, Jane Waldfogel, and Wen-Jui Han, "Family meals and child academic and behavioral outcomes," *Child Development*, volume 83, pp. 2104–2120, 2012.

38. Incidentally, the lead investigator on the Boston University study that purported to show the unimportance of family dinners

per se gave a somewhat different message in his interview with the *Wall Street Journal*. Professor Daniel Miller told columnist Carl Bialik, "I have a family, I have kids. We still try to eat meals together and I would encourage other families to do so." See Carl Bialik, "What family dinners can and can't do for teens," *Wall Street Journal*, November 29, 2013, http://blogs.wsj.com/numbersguy/what -family-dinners-can-and-cant-do-for-teens-1302.

Chapter 4: Why Are American Students Falling Behind?

1. When I share this story, some Americans will describe a similar experience—a respectful student thanking a teacher for a great lesson—from their own school days in 1977 or 1987. But not in 2017.

2. Eamonn Fingleton, "America the Innovative?" *New York Times*, March 30, 2013, www.nytimes.com/2013/03/31/sunday-review /america-the-innovative.html.

3. The 4 American companies to make the top 20 were Qualcomm, Intel, Microsoft, and United Technologies Corporation. In case you were wondering, Google was #22 and Apple was #38. For the complete list, go to the WIPO listing at www.wipo.int/export/sites/www /pressroom/en/documents/pr_2015_774_annexes.pdf#page=1.

4. The evidence in these two paragraphs comes from Fingleton, "America the Innovative?"

5. To obtain rankings of international patent filings per capita, I first obtained the most recent figures for international patent filings per country, from the World Intellectual Property Organization (WIPO), www.wipo.int/export/sites/www/pressroom/en/documents /pr_2015_774_annexes.pdf#page=2. I then divided the number of patents per country by the total population of the country. The results are shown in the table at the top of page 239.

6. Here I am alluding to President Richard Nixon's speech in which he appealed to "the great silent majority of my fellow Americans." The full text of Nixon's speech, delivered on November 3, 1969, is online at "Address to the Nation on the War in Vietnam," Richard Nixon

Rankings of International Patent Filings Per Capita.

Country	Patents	Population in Millions	Patents Per Capita x 10^{-6}
China	25,539	1,357	18.8
Denmark	1,301	5.6	232
Finland	1,815	5.4	336
Germany	18,008	80	225
Israel	1,596	8.0	199
Japan	42,459	127	334
Luxembourg	392	0.54	726
Netherlands	4,218	17	248
Norway	690	5.1	135
Singapore	944	5.4	174
South Korea	13,151	50	263
Sweden	3,925	9.6	409
Switzerland	4,115	8.1	508
USA	61,492	319	192

Presidential Library and Museum, www.nixonlibrary.gov/forkids /speechesforkids/silentmajority/silentmajority_transcript.pdf.

7. The Torrance Tests of Creative Thinking are among the few well-validated tests of creativity. The tests have been normed for different age groups, from first grade through adulthood, and have also been validated across cultures. More information is available at Scholastic Testing Service, "Gifted Education," www.ststesting.com /ngifted.html.

8. I first encountered the work of Kyung-Hee Kim in Hanna Rosin's article, "The Overprotected Kid," *The Atlantic*, March 19, 2014, www.theatlantic.com/features/archive/2014/03/hey-parents-leave -those-kids-alone/358631. The quote is taken from this article. You can read Professor Kim's presentation of her own work, with links to the full text of her scholarly papers, at K. H. Kim, "Yes, There IS a

Creativity Crisis!" *The Creativity Post*, July 10, 2012, www.creativity
post.com/education/yes_there_is_a_creativity_crisis.

9. To be precise, the PISA examination is administered to students
who are between age 15 years, 3 months, and 16 years, 2 months, at
the time of the test; see "PISA FAQ," Organisation for Economic
Co-operation and Development, www.oecd.org/pisa/aboutpisa
/pisafaq.htm.

10. I have chosen not to include any Asian nations in this ranking.
In my presentations to parents and school administrators and teachers, I have found that the inclusion of scores from Asian nations often
leads to tangential and distracting discussions. After I shared PISA
rankings showing South Korea near the top, one parent said, "Maybe
South Korea does better than we do on the rankings, but I don't like
the conformism and pressure of the South Korean system. Even the
Koreans don't like their system." Perhaps that's true, but it's not relevant to our consideration of why the United States has declined relative to most European nations. I have found that it's more helpful to
focus on our status relative to Poland and Germany. More Americans
trace their ancestry to Poland and Germany than to Korea. In 2000,
American students outranked Poland and Germany on the PISA. In
2012, Polish and German students outranked American students. The
numbers I present from the 2000 administration of the PISA are taken
from Figure 10, "Mathematics and science literacy average scores of
15-year-olds, by country," in *Outcomes of Learning: Results from the
2000 Program for International Student Assessment of 15-Year-Olds in
Reading, Mathematics, and Science Literacy* (Washington, DC: National Center for Education Statistics, December 2001).

11. These data are taken from Figure 1.2.13, "Comparing countries' and economies' performance in mathematics," in OECD, *PISA
2012 Results: What Students Know and Can Do*, vol. 1: *Student Performance in Mathematics, Reading and Science*, revised edition (Paris:
OECD, 2014), http://dx.doi.org/10.1787/9789264208780-en.

12. Amanda Ripley, *The Smartest Kids in the World: And How They
Got That Way* (New York: Simon and Schuster, 2013), p. 136.

Analyzing PISA data, Ripley calculates that as of 2007, Poland was spending about $39,964 to educate one student from age 6 to 15, the age at which students take the PISA examination. The United States spends about $105,752 to educate one student from age 6 to age 15. Figures are in US dollars, "converted using purchasing power parity." See the note in Ripley, *The Smartest Kids in the World*, p. 281.

13. The "utilitarian and spare" quote is from Ripley, *The Smartest Kids in the World*, p. 52.

14. Ripley, *The Smartest Kids in the World*, p. 214. Ripley quotes Andreas Schleicher, the key person behind the PISA exam from its inception through the present day, who observes, "In most of the highest-performing systems, technology is remarkably absent from classrooms . . . it does seem that those systems place their efforts primarily on pedagogical practice rather than digital gadgets" (p. 214).

15. Ripley makes the case against American sports throughout her book. This quote actually comes from her article "The case against high school sports," *The Atlantic*, October 2013, www.theatlantic .com/magazine/archive/2013/10/the-case-against-high-school -sports/309447.

16. Ripley, *The Smartest Kids in the World*, p. 85.

17. Ripley, *The Smartest Kids in the World*, p. 93. She is citing a National Council on Teacher Quality report titled "It's easier to get into an education school than to become a college football player," ISSUU, http://issuu.com/nctq/docs/teachers_and_football_players. The report is a modified PowerPoint presentation.

18. Ripley, *The Smartest Kids in the World*, p. 59.

19. The numbers in this paragraph are drawn from John Cookson's essay, "How US graduation rates compare with the rest of the world," *Global Public Square* (blog), CNN, November 3, 2011, http:// globalpublicsquare.blogs.cnn.com/2011/11/03/how-u-s-graduation -rates-compare-with-the-rest-of-the-world.

20. The following OECD countries now have higher university completion rates than the United States: Iceland, Poland, United Kingdom, Denmark, Australia, Slovak Republic, Finland, New

Zealand, Ireland, Netherlands, Norway, Japan, and Portugal; see Table A3.2 in the OECD report, *Education at a Glance 2012: Highlights*, www.oecd.org/edu/highlights.pdf (accessed May 7, 2015).

21. Richard Arum and Josipa Roksa, *Aspiring Adults Adrift: Tentative Transitions of College Graduates* (Chicago: University of Chicago Press, 2014), p. 38.

22. See Arum and Roksa, *Aspiring Adults Adrift*, pp. 29–32, under the heading "The Necessity of the Social."

23. Here I follow Arum and Roksa's summary of the work of Philip Babcock and Mindy Marks in *Aspiring Adults Adrift*, p. 35.

24. Arum and Roksa, *Aspiring Adults Adrift*, p. 35.

25. Kevin Carey, "Americans think we have the world's best colleges. We don't," *New York Times*, June 28, 2014, www.nytimes .com/2014/06/29/upshot/americans-think-we-have-the-worlds-best -colleges-we-dont.html.

26. Carey, "Americans think we have the world's best colleges."

27. A reader of Carey's article posted this comment. To read the full comment, go to Carey's article (the link is in note 25 above), click on Comments, then click on "Reader Picks." This comment, by "OSS Architect," was #2 under Reader Picks when I checked in February 2015.

28. See, for example, the report by John Bound, Michael Lovenheim, and Sarah Turner, "Understanding the decrease in college completion rates and the increased time to the baccalaureate degree," University of Michigan, Institute for Social Research, 2007, www.psc .isr.umich.edu/pubs/pdf/rr07–626.pdf.

Chapter 5: Why Are So Many Kids So Fragile?

1. Jean Twenge, "Generational differences in mental health: Are children and adolescents suffering more, or less?" *American Journal of Orthopsychiatry*, volume 81, pp. 469–472, 2011.

2. Twenge, "Generational differences."

3. The census does not assess this distinction. The American census asks where you live and who else lives with you. If you are an adult living alone, then the fact that your parents support you is not readily apparent in the data published by the census.

4. For the raw data on which these lists are based, go to "ALFS summary tables," OECD.StatExtracts, June 25, 2015, http://stats .oecd.org/Index.aspx?DatasetCode=ALFS_SUMTAB. For a general commentary on this finding, see David Leonhardt, "The idled young americans," *New York Times*, May 5, 2013, www.nytimes.com/2013 /05/05/sunday-review/the-idled-young-americans.html?hp&_r=0.

5. Leonhardt, "The idled young americans."

6. For the study itself, see Ian Hathaway and Robert Litan, "Declining business dynamism in the United States: A look at states and metros," Brookings Institution, May 5, 2014, www.brookings.edu /research/papers/2014/05/declining-business-dynamism-litan. This quote comes from Thomas Edsall's column commenting on the Hathaway and Litan report; see Thomas Edsall, "America out of whack," *New York Times*, September 23, 2014, www.nytimes.com/2014/09/24 /opinion/america-out-of-whack.html.

7. Hathaway and Litan, "Declining business dynamism in the United States."

8. The rise in the prevalence of anxiety and depression among American teenagers has been more pronounced for girls than for boys. For a consideration of the several factors underlying that girl/ boy difference, please see Chapters 1 through 4 of my *Girls on the Edge: The Four Factors Driving the New Crisis for Girls. Sexual Identity, the Cyberbubble, Obsessions, Environmental Toxins* (New York: Basic Books, 2010).

9. Reif Larsen, "How doing nothing became the ultimate family vacation," *New York Times*, May 1, 2015, www.nytimes.com/2015 /05/03/travel/how-doing-nothing-became-the-ultimate-family -vacation.html?src=xps.

10. Canada is a special case. On each of the parameters we have considered, the United States represents the worst case among

affluent nations; Western European countries such as Switzerland are doing much better. On most of these parameters, Canada falls somewhere in between. Over the past 40 years, Canada has drifted away from the United Kingdom and toward the United States. Canadians have told me that back in 1970, much of Canadian culture—including television and radio—came from the United Kingdom, specifically the BBC. Today, when I visit Canada, from Halifax to Vancouver, the media are overwhelmingly American (i.e., the programming originates in the United States). The BBC is still there, but it's a small niche market.

Earlier I mentioned Dr. Gordon Neufeld, lead author with Gabor Maté of *Hold On to Your Kids: Why Parents Need to Matter More Than Peers*, second edition (Toronto: Vintage Canada, 2013). Dr. Neufeld is Canadian. The fact that he observed a decline in parental authority over four decades of practice in Canada is evidence that Canadians are struggling with many of the same challenges that face American parents. But as one who has met with parents in dozens of venues across Canada and in hundreds of venues across the United States, I believe that the problem of parental abdication of authority is generally worse in the United States than in Canada.

Dr. Neufeld was kind enough to meet with me face-to-face in 2014 when I was writing this book. We had breakfast together at a restaurant near his home in Vancouver. He believes that a central challenge for Canadians is to keep their country from becoming more and more American—to stay more connected with the rest of the world outside North America generally and with the Commonwealth specifically. "It's not easy," he acknowledges.

11. I am not the first to suggest the cheerleader/coach analogy for different parenting styles. See, for example, Dan Griffin, "Motivating teenagers: How do you do it?" *Slate*, February 14, 2014, www.slate.com/articles/life/family/2014/02/motivating_teenagers_how_do_you_do_it.html.

12. Nicola Clark, "France rethinks its no-school-on-Wednesdays week," *International Herald Tribune*, February 12, 2013, http://

rendezvous.blogs.nytimes.com/2013/02/12/france-rethinks-its-no-school-on-wednesdays-week.

13. Personal communications in January 2014 from Dr. Eva Shimaoka, my medical school classmate now living in Switzerland.

14. I attended Lomond Elementary School in Shaker Heights, Ohio, for kindergarten through 6th grade. I ate lunch at home every day, with rare exceptions such as school picnics. My junior high school, Byron Junior High School, was the first school I attended that had a cafeteria.

15. Neufeld and Maté, *Hold On to Your Kids*, p. 140.

16. Here I am paraphrasing the aphorism "Success means moving from one failure to the next with no loss of enthusiasm." There is no consensus regarding the source of this maxim. Although it is often attributed to Winston Churchill, scholars of Churchill's life insist that he never said it. It may have originated with Abraham Lincoln.

Chapter 6: What Matters?

1. An especially poignant illustration of this principle—that intelligence is distinct from personality—comes from accounts of people struggling with Alzheimer's. As intelligence declines and cognitive function slips away, the core of personality may remain largely intact almost until the very end. Journalist Robin Marantz Henig describes this interaction between the late Professor Sandy Bem and her husband, Daryl, when Dr. Bem was declining due to Alzheimer's.

> "I still feel as though I'm me," she told him on one ride. "Do you agree?" He did, sort of. In fact, he was surprised by how much herself Sandy could still be, even as she became less and less the formidable thinker he had always known. He was surprised, too, to discover that it didn't matter to him. "I realized how little of the fact that she was an intellectual played into my feelings for her," he said. "They were feelings for *her*, not her intelligence. And they were still all there."

Source: Robin Marantz Henig, "The Last Day of Her Life," *New York Times*, May 14, 2015, www.nytimes.com/2015/05/17/magazine/the-last-day-of-her-life.html.

2. For me, the most useful exposition of the Big Five theory of personality begins with the history of the theory, showing how it evolved from the 1960s through the 1990s as the result of many researchers working independently and in collaboration. This story is told by Oliver John and his colleagues Laura Naumann and Christopher Soto, "Paradigm shift to the integrative Big Five trait taxonomy: History, measurement, and conceptual issues," in *Handbook of Personality: Theory and Research*, third edition, edited by Oliver John and colleagues (New York: Guilford Press, 2008).

3. Angela Duckworth and colleagues, "Who does well in life? Conscientious adults excel in both objective and subjective success," *Frontiers in Psychology*, volume 3, September 2012, article 356, http://journal.frontiersin.org/Journal/10.3389/fpsyg.2012.00356/full.

4. See, for example, Margaret Kern and Howard Friedman, "Do Conscientious individuals live longer? A quantitative review," *Health Psychology*, volume 27, pp. 505–512, 2008. See also Tim Bogg and Brent Roberts, "The case for Conscientiousness: Evidence and implications for a personality trait marker of health and longevity," *Annals of Behavioral Medicine*, volume 45, pp. 278–288, 2013. Specifically regarding the finding that childhood Conscientiousness as measured at age 10 predicts a lower risk of obesity at age 51, see Sarah Hampson and colleagues, "Childhood Conscientiousness relates to objectively measured adult physical health four decades later," *Health Psychology*, volume 32, pp. 925–928, 2013.

5. See Helen Cheng and Adrian Furnham, "Personality traits, education, physical exercise, and childhood neurological function as independent predictors of adult obesity," *PLOS One*, November 8, 2013, http://journals.plos.org/plosone/article?id=10.1371/journal.pone.0079586. The abstract of this paper is confusing: it says that Conscientiousness was "significantly associated with adult obesity." That's true, but the correlation was *negative*: the more Conscientious

the child was, the less likely that child was to become obese as an adult. See also Hampson and colleagues, "Childhood Conscientiousness relates to objectively measured adult physical health four decades later."

6. See Robert Wilson and colleagues, "Conscientiousness and the incidence of Alzheimer disease and mild cognitive impairment," *Archives of General Psychiatry*, volume 64, pp. 1204–1212, 2007. See also Paul Duberstein, "Personality and risk for Alzheimer's disease in adults 72 years of age and older," *Psychology and Aging*, volume 26, pp. 351–362, 2011.

7. Bogg and Roberts, "The case for Conscientiousness." See also Terrie Moffitt, Richie Poulton, and Avshalom Caspi, "Lifelong impact of early self-control: Childhood self-discipline predicts adult quality of life," *American Scientist*, volume 101, pp. 352–359, 2013. See also Jose Causadias, Jessica Salvatore, and Alan Sroufe, "Early patterns of self-regulation as risk and promotive factors in development: A longitudinal study from childhood to adulthood in a high-risk sample," *International Journal of Behavioral Development*, volume 36, pp. 293–302, 2012, www.ncbi.nlm.nih.gov/pmc/articles/PMC3496279. In a careful study of data from seven different cohort studies—from the United Kingdom, Germany, Australia, and the United States—researchers found that after adjusting for health behavior, marital status, age, sex, and ethnicity, *only* Conscientiousness, and no other Big Five personality trait, predicted longer life. See Markus Jokela and colleagues, "Personality and all-cause mortality: Individual-participant meta-analysis of 3,947 deaths in 76,150 adults," *American Journal of Epidemiology*, volume 178, pp. 667–675, 2013.

8. In "Who does well in life?," Duckworth and colleagues found that although Conscientiousness is positively associated with life satisfaction, Emotional Stability and Extraversion are more strongly positively associated with life satisfaction. However, Emotional Stability has no association, positive or negative, with wealth, whereas Conscientiousness is positively associated with wealth. Extraversion demonstrates a small to medium association with wealth, but no

association with income and no positive association with health. Conscientiousness is positively associated with wealth, with income, and with health, as well as with life satisfaction.

9. Silvia Mendolia and Ian Walker, "The effect of non-cognitive traits on health behaviours in adolescence," *Health Economics*, volume 23, pp. 1146–1158, 2014.

10. Brent Roberts and colleagues, "The power of personality: The comparative validity of personality traits, socioeconomic status, and cognitive ability for predicting important life outcomes," *Perspectives on Psychological Science*, volume 2, pp. 313–345, 2007.

11. These findings are drawn from Figure 2 in Terrie Moffitt and colleagues, "A gradient of childhood self-control predicts health, wealth, and public safety," *Proceedings of the National Academy of Sciences*, volume 108, pp. 2693–2698, 2011.

12. Unfortunately we do not yet have a scholarly and comprehensive biography of Jim Morrison. The closest is the biography by James Riordan and Jerry Prochnicky, *Break on Through: The Life and Death of Jim Morrison* (New York: William Morrow, 2006).

13. Moffitt and colleagues, "A gradient of childhood self-control predicts health, wealth, and public safety."

14. These findings are from Moffitt, Poulton, and Caspi, "Lifelong impact of early self-control." The figures are from p. 355.

15. Moffitt, Poulton, and Caspi, "Lifelong impact of early self-control," p. 353.

16. For a survey of interventions to boost self-control in young children, see Alex Piquero and colleagues, "Self-control interventions for children under age 10 for improving self-control and delinquency and problem behaviors," *Campbell Systematic Reviews*, no. 2, 2010. Piquero and colleagues accept Michael Gottfredson and Travis Hirschi's assertion that interventions to boost self-control are not effective for children over 10 to 12 years of age. I don't accept that assertion. Gottfredson and Hirschi base their assessment on their experience (pre-1990) with teenage juvenile delinquents. I concede that there is evidence that the criminal justice system is not effective

in boosting self-control in incarcerated teenagers; see, for example, Ojmarrh Mitchell and Doris Mackenzie, "The stability and resiliency of self-control in a sample of incarcerated offenders," *Crime and Delinquency*, volume 52, pp. 432–449, 2006. But data based on incarcerated juvenile offenders may not be valid for parents like you and me, assuming that your child has not been convicted of a felony. More to the point, I have personally seen numerous cases in my own practice where kids over age 10 have reformed and become more Conscientious because parents implemented some of the strategies described in this book. Even very simple interventions, such as repeatedly telling a child, "Stop and Think! Before you act," can have profound and lasting beneficial consequences, even in kids who have been diagnosed with ADHD; see, for example, Molly Reid and John Borkowski, "Causal attributions of hyperactive children: Implications for teaching strategies and self-control," *Journal of Educational Psychology*, volume 79, pp. 296–307, 1987.

The more general premises here are that *personality can change at any age* and that *increased Conscientiousness is beneficial*. For evidence supporting these premises, see Christopher Boyce and colleagues, "Is personality fixed? Personality changes as much as 'variable' economic factors and more strongly predicts changes to life satisfaction," *Social Indicators Research*, volume 111, pp. 287–305, 2013; see also Brent Roberts and Daniel Mroczek, "Personality trait change in adulthood," *Current Directions in Psychological Science*, volume 17, pp. 31–35, 2008; Christopher Magee and colleagues, "Personality trait change and life satisfaction in adults: The roles of age and hedonic balance," *Personality and Individual Differences*, volume 55, pp. 694–698, 2013. Magee and colleagues find, not surprisingly, that the older you are, the less likely your personality is to change. I am not asserting that it is easy for a 65-year-old to become more Conscientious. But I have seen 15-year-olds who have become more Conscientious.

17. This is the British cohort study. For an overview, see Tyas Prevoo and Bas ter Weel, "The importance of early Conscientiousness for

socio-economic outcomes: Evidence from the British Cohort Study," IZA Discussion Paper 7537, Institute for the Study of Labor, 2013, http://ftp.iza.org/dp7537.pdf.

18. James J. Heckman and Yona Rubinstein, "The importance of noncognitive skills: Lessons from the GED testing program," *AEA Papers and Proceedings*, May 2001, p. 145, www.econ-pol.unisi.it /bowles/Institutions%20of%20capitalism/heckman%20on%20ged .pdf.

19. These quotes come from Dr. Heckman's essay "Lacking character, American education fails the test," http://heckmanequation.org /content/resource/lacking-character-american-education-fails-test.

20. Carol Dweck, "The secret to raising smart kids," *Scientific American Mind*, volume 18, pp. 36–43, 2008.

21. You can read Dr. Dweck's description of her classic study and many more studies like it in her book *Mindset: The New Psychology of Success* (New York: Ballantine, 2007).

22. Christopher Bryan, Gabrielle Adams, and Benoit Monin, "When cheating would make you a cheater: Implicating the self prevents unethical behavior," *Journal of Experimental Psychology*, volume 142, pp. 1001–1005, 2013.

23. Many of the points in this section were made by Adam Grant in his essay "Raising a moral child," *New York Times*, April 13, 2014, www.nytimes.com/2014/04/12/opinion/sunday/raising-a-moral -child.html.

24. Christopher Bryan, unpublished study of 3- to 6-year-olds, cited in Grant, "Raising a moral child."

25. I first encountered this statistic in the article by Richard Pérez-Peña, "Studies find more students cheating, with high achievers no exception," *New York Times*, September 7, 2012, www.nytimes .com/2012/09/08/education/studies-show-more-students-cheat -even-high-achievers.html? Mr. Pérez-Peña cites a survey of 40,000 American youth conducted by the Josephson Institute, available online at "The Ethics of American Youth: 2010," Character Counts!,

February 10, 2011, http://charactercounts.org/programs/reportcard/2010/installment02_report-card_honesty-integrity.html.

26. Pérez-Peña, "Studies find more students cheating, with high achievers no exception."

27. Quoted in Pérez-Peña, "Studies find more students cheating, with high achievers no exception."

28. William James, *Principles of Psychology* (Notre Dame, IN: University of Notre Dame Press, originally published in 1892, republished in 1985), volume 2, pp. 449–450.

29. Proverbs 22:6, New King James Version. For an introduction to the scholarship regarding the provenance of the book of Proverbs, see Robert Alter's *The Wisdom Books: Job, Proverbs, and Ecclesiastes* (New York: W. W. Norton, 2011), pp. 183–192.

30. The research I am thinking of here includes the cohort studies cited earlier in this chapter showing that increased self-control in childhood predicts better outcomes in adulthood. See, for example, Moffitt and colleagues, "A gradient of childhood self-control predicts health, wealth, and public safety."

31. See, for example, Eric Owens and colleagues, "The impact of Internet pornography on adolescents: A review of the research," *Sexual Addiction and Compulsivity*, volume 19, pp. 99–122, 2012. For an insightful perspective on how the normalization of pornography is changing the lived experiences of American teenage girls and boys, see Nancy Jo Sales, "Friends without benefits," *Vanity Fair*, September 2013, www.vanityfair.com/culture/2013/09/social-media-internet-porn-teenage-girls.

32. Will Durant, *The Story of Philosophy: The Lives and Opinions of the World's Greatest Philosophers* (New York: Pocket Books reprint edition, 1991), p. 98.

33. See, for example, Dov Peretz Elkins, *The Bible's Top Fifty Ideas: The Essential Concepts Everyone Should Know* (New York: SPI Books, 2006), p. 229.

34. Grant, "Raising a moral child."

35. C. S. Lewis, *Mere Christianity*, Book IV, chapter 7, "Let's Pretend," (San Francisco: Harper San Francisco, 2009), p. 188.

36. William Deresiewicz, *Excellent Sheep: The Miseducation of the American Elite and the Way to a Meaningful Life* (New York: Free Press, 2014).

37. Jennifer Finney Boylan, "A Common Core for all of us," *New York Times*, March 23 2014, Sunday Review, p. 4. Boylan's column illustrates a profound confusion. After disparaging the notion that parents should hand down "shared values of the community to the next generation," she concludes by recommending that "mothers and fathers, sons and daughters, [should] all read the same book, and sit down at the table to talk about it." But if she does not believe that parents should hand down shared values of the community to the next generation, by what authority can parents command their child to read any particular book, let alone discuss it at the dinner table? Like many of those who condemn the notion that parents should pass their values on to their children, Boylan seems not to have carefully considered the implications of her recommendation. Her closing recommendation, that children and parents should read and discuss the same book, is based on an assumption that children should read and discuss books recommended by their parents—but on what grounds, if not to learn the "shared values of the community"? How would Boylan advise parents to answer if the children say, *"I have no interest in reading any book recommended by you. I have discovered my own uncensored truth, in pornography and in social media, and you have nothing to teach me"*?

38. Roger Scruton, "The End of the University," *First Things*, April 2015, pp. 25–30. The quote about "a rite of passage into cultural nothingness" is on p. 28.

Chapter 7: Misconceptions

1. Among researchers, this study—the National Longitudinal Study of Adolescent to Adult Health—is known as the "Add Health" study. "Add" is spelled with a capital *A* and two lowercase *d*'s. I find

this jargon confusing. Many of us might assume that "Add" in this context has something to do with ADHD, or Attention Deficit / Hyperactivity Disorder, formerly known as ADD. But the Add Health study has nothing directly to do with ADHD and was not developed with ADHD in mind.

2. Two separate analyses of the same database have come to the same conclusion in this regard. See Matthew Johnson, "Parent-child relationship quality directly and indirectly influences hooking up behavior reported in young adulthood through alcohol use in adolescence," *Archives of Sexual Behavior*, volume 42, pp. 1463–1472, 2013; see also Kathleen Roche and colleagues, "Enduring consequences of parenting for risk behaviors from adolescence into early adulthood," *Social Science and Medicine*, volume 66, pp. 2023–2034, 2008.

3. Matthew Johnson and Nancy Galambos, "Paths to intimate relationship quality from parent-adolescent relations and mental health," *Journal of Marriage and Family*, volume 76, pp. 145–160, 2014.

4. Emily Harville and colleagues, "Parent-child relationships, parental attitudes toward sex, and birth outcomes among adolescents," *Journal of Pediatric and Adolescent Gynecology*, volume 27, pp. 287–293, 2014.

5. Baumrind herself used the terms "authoritarian," "permissive," and "authoritative," where I use the terms "Too Hard," "Too Soft," and "Just Right." As I pointed out in my book *Girls on the Edge*, I have always found it confusing that Baumrind used two similar-sounding words—authoritarian" and "authoritative"—to describe two very different parenting styles. My use of the terms "Too Hard," "Too Soft," and "Just Right" in place of "authoritarian," "permissive," and "authoritative" is not original. As I acknowledged in *Girls on the Edge*, I am borrowing that usage from Judith Rich Harris, *The Nurture Assumption: Why Children Turn Out the Way They Do*, revised and updated (New York: Free Press, 2009), p. 44. I disagree with Harris on almost every point of substance, but I do like her simpler formulation of Baumrind's categories. For a recent review of

Baumrind's program of research by Baumrind herself, see her chapter "Authoritative parenting revisited: History and current status," in *Authoritative Parenting: Synthesizing Nurturance and Discipline for Optimal Child Development*, edited by Robert Larzelere, Amanda Sheffield, and Amanda Harrist (Washington, DC: American Psychological Association, 2013), pp. 11–34.

6. Among "Too Soft" parents, researchers now distinguish two subtypes: the Indulgent parent and the Neglectful parent. Neglectful parents don't buy parenting books, as a rule. It's unlikely that you are a Neglectful parent. Neither am I. That is not our temptation. If you are interested in learning more about the distinction between the Indulgent parent and the Neglectful parent, you might start with the article by Susie Lamborn and colleagues, "Patterns of competence and adjustment among adolescents from authoritative, authoritarian, indulgent, and neglectful families," *Child Development*, volume 62, pp. 1045–1065, 1991.

7. See Baumrind, "Authoritative parenting revisited."

8. See Baumrind, "Authoritative parenting revisited." The comment about "definitional drift" is on p. 12. The article Baumrind is criticizing, in which the scholars included "easy-going" as a characteristic of authoritative parenting but neglected to include any measure of strictness, is Clyde Robinson and colleagues, "Authoritative, authoritarian, and permissive parenting practices: Development of a new measure," *Psychological Reports*, volume 77, pp. 819–830, 1995.

9. See, for example, Diana Baumrind, "The impact of parenting style on adolescent competence and substance use," *Journal of Early Adolescence*, volume 11, pp. 56–95, 1991. Although these findings are not well known to American parents, this article has been influential among scholars in the field of parenting; as of February 2017, it had been cited in more than 3,200 other scholarly articles.

10. Sarah-Jayne Blakemore and Kathryn Mills, "Is adolescence a sensitive period for sociocultural processing?," *Annual Review of Psychology*, volume 65, pp. 187–207, 2014, provides a useful review of

the mechanisms by which brain development in adolescence influences socialization, delay of gratification, and so forth.

11. See, for example, Douglas Gentile and colleagues, "Mediators and moderators of long-term effects of violent video games on aggressive behavior," *JAMA Pediatrics*, volume 168, pp. 450–457, 2014.

12. See Jan Hoffman, "Cool at 13, adrift at 23," *Well* (blog), *New York Times*, June 23, 2014, http://well.blogs.nytimes.com/2014/06/23/cool-at -13-adrift-at-23. Hoffman reports on a study by Joseph Allen and colleagues which was subsequently published as "What ever happened to the 'cool' kids? Long-term sequelae of early adolescent pseudomature behavior," *Child Development*, volume 85, pp. 1866–1880, 2014.

13. In the scholarly literature, the confusion between *happiness* and *pleasure* is often couched in terms of "eudaimonic well-being," that's real happiness, and "hedonic well-being," that's mere pleasure. Incidentally, some scholars believe that *gratitude* is key to becoming truly happy, and they observe that this premise is fundamental to Judaism, Christianity, and Islam. See Robert Emmons and Cheryl Crumpler, "Gratitude as a human strength: Appraising the evidence," *Journal of Social and Clinical Psychology*, volume 19, pp. 56–69, 2000.

14. David Brooks, "Baseball or Soccer?" *New York Times*, July 10, 2014, www.nytimes.com/2014/07/11/opinion/david-brooks-baseball -or-soccer.html.

15. Arthur C. Brooks, "Love people, not pleasure," *New York Times*, July 18, 2014, www.nytimes.com/2014/07/20/opinion/sunday /arthur-c-brooks-love-people-not-pleasure.html?src=xps.

16. This teacher spoke during a presentation I gave to parents at Hillview Middle School in Menlo Park, California, on October 22, 2013. The school where this particular teacher works is not Hillview Middle School but is another school nearby.

Chapter 8: The First Thing: *Teach Humility*

1. "Life is what happens while you are making other plans" is a paraphrase of John Lennon's 1980 song "Beautiful Boy," which

contains this line: "Life is what happens to you while you're busy making other plans." In the song, Lennon is speaking to his son Sean Taro Ono Lennon, who was 4 years old at the time. Lennon was shot and killed on December 8, 1980, just three weeks after the record was released on November 17, 1980.

2. I am paraphrasing Alina Tugend's paraphrase of David McCullough Jr.'s notorious 2012 commencement speech: "Just because they've been told they're amazing doesn't mean that they are." Tugend's article is titled, "Redefining success and celebrating the ordinary," *New York Times*, June 29, 2012, www.nytimes.com/2012/06/30/your-money/redefining-success-and-celebrating-the-unremarkable.html.

3. See Alex Wood and colleagues, "Gratitude predicts psychological well-being above the Big Five facets," *Personality and Individual Differences*, volume 46, pp. 443–447, 2009. Robert Emmons and Michael McCullough found that simply telling people to "count their blessings" had significant and sustained benefits; see their paper "Counting blessings versus burdens: An experimental investigation of gratitude and subjective well-being in daily life," *Journal of Personality and Social Psychology*, volume 84, pp. 377–389, 2003; see also their follow-up paper, "Gratitude in intermediate affective terrain: Links of grateful moods to individual differences and daily emotional experience," *Journal of Personality and Social Psychology*, volume 86, pp. 295–309, 2004.

4. See Wood and colleagues, "Gratitude predicts psychological well-being above the Big Five facets," for a discussion of gratitude as a *cause* of well-being rather than a *result* of well-being.

5. This comment is taken from an interview that Washington did on Oprah Winfrey's talk show on October 31, 2006. The full transcript is available at Boys and Girls Clubs of the Mississippi Delta, www.bgcmsdelta.org/Boys_&_Girls_Clubs_of_the_Mississippi_Delta/Media_files/Denzel%20Transcript%20-%20Oprah.pdf.

6. For insight into how social media are undermining the family, I recommend Dr. Catherine Steiner-Adair's book, *The Big Disconnect*:

Protecting Childhood and Family Relationships in the Digital Age (New York: Harper, 2013). For an earlier overview of how social media undermine literacy and other social skills, I recommend Mark Bauerlein's book, *The Dumbest Generation: How the Digital Age Stupefies Young Americans and Jeopardizes Our Future (or, Don't Trust Anyone Under 30)* (New York: Tarcher, 2009).

Chapter 9: The Second Thing: *Enjoy*

1. Daniel Kahneman and colleagues, "Toward national well-being accounts," *AEA Papers and Proceedings*, May 2004, pp. 429–434, http://www2.hawaii.edu/~noy/300texts/nationalwellbeing.pdf.

2. Daniel Kahneman and colleagues, "The structure of well-being in two cities: Life satisfaction and experienced happiness in Columbus, Ohio; and Rennes, France," in *International Differences in Well-Being*, edited by Ed Diener, Daniel Kahneman, and John Helliwell (New York: Oxford University Press, 2010), p. 26.

3. All three quotes in this section come from Kahneman and colleagues, "The structure of well-being in two cities," p. 29.

4. Jennifer Senior, *All Joy and No Fun: The Paradox of Modern Parenthood* (New York: Ecco [HarperCollins], 2014), pp. 55–59.

5. Suzanne Bianchi and colleagues, "Housework: Who did, does or will do it, and how much does it matter?" *Social Forces*, volume 91, pp. 55–63, 2012.

6. Senior, *All Joy and No Fun*, p. 57.

7. Senior, *All Joy and No Fun*, p. 59.

8. At my request, Bruneau provided me with a list of his awards (contact me if you would like to see the full list). Some of the awards reflect academic or athletic achievement; others reflect community services; still others, such as being elected to the Homecoming Court, are simply a measure of popularity. Bruneau demonstrates that it is still possible to be popular in the United States without being disrespectful to parents. It helps to be a champion athlete.

9. This is my paraphrase of Friedrich Nietzsche's aphorism in *Also sprach Zarathustra*, "Wenig macht die Art des besten Glücks" (a little makes for the best kind of happiness).

10. For two decades now, we have had good evidence that Americans work more hours per week, on average, than workers in any other developed country. See, for example, Jerry Jacobs and Kathleen Green, "Who are the overworked Americans?" *Review of Social Economy*, volume 56, pp. 442–459, 1998. For a more anecdotal account of the cultural contrast on this parameter between the United States and Europe, see John de Graaf's cover story for *The Progressive*, "Wake up Americans: It's time to get off the work treadmill. We need to come up with a different approach to work," *Progressive*, September 2010, pp. 22–24. While it's fairly easy to find documentation that Americans work more hours per week, on average, than workers in other developed countries, it's harder to find any documentation that Americans *boast* of being busier than people in other countries. That's my personal observation. It's also an observation shared by Tim Kreider in "The 'Busy' Trap," *Opinionator* (blog), *New York Times*, July 1, 2012, http://opinionator.blogs.nytimes.com/2012/06/30/the-busy-trap.

11. Kreider, "The 'Busy' Trap."

Chapter 10: The Third Thing: *The Meaning of Life*

1. See, for example, Jennifer Lee, "Generation Limbo," *New York Times*, August 31, 2011, www.nytimes.com/2011/09/01/fashion/recent-college-graduates-wait-for-their-real-careers-to-begin.html, profiling graduates of Harvard, Dartmouth, and Yale who are now working odd jobs to make ends meet. Of course, these anecdotes are merely anecdotes, not data. For quantitative evidence that a large proportion of graduates of selective colleges are failing to make a successful transition to the workplace, see Richard Arum and Josipa Roksa, *Aspiring Adults Adrift: Tentative Transitions of College Graduates* (Chicago: University of Chicago Press, 2014).

The fixation with getting into a "top" college or university is not only unjustified by the data on long-term outcomes; it is also downright harmful to adolescents, narrowing their focus and limiting their horizons. For a poignant account of the damage done by this obsession, see Frank Bruni, *Where You Go Is Not Who You'll Be: An Antidote to the College Admissions Mania* (New York: Hachette, 2015).

2. One of Maslow's core ideas was the hierarchy of needs. Everyone needs to fulfill basic human needs, such as the need for food, clothing, and shelter. Most human beings also have a need for love and belonging. Once those needs are fulfilled, Maslow believed, people will seek the respect and esteem of their peers. At the top of Maslow's hierarchy is the need for self-actualization, to fulfill one's deepest purpose. Maslow believed that a narrow focus on achieving wealth would not satisfy, because ultimately human beings need more than to satisfy their appetites. In Maslow's perspective, all people must discover on their own what they need to become "self-actualized." See, for example, Abraham Maslow, *The Farther Reaches of Human Nature,* reprint edition (New York: Penguin, 1993).

I am aware of the criticisms of Maslow's theories; see, for example, Mahmoud Wahba and Lawrence Bridwell, "Maslow reconsidered: A review of research on the need hierarchy theory," *Organizational Behavior and Human Performance*, volume 15, pp. 212–240, 1976. I am not asking you to swallow Maslow's theories whole. I am merely pointing out that figuring out what you want out of life, what will truly make you happy, is not a trivial task. On the contrary, it is a substantial undertaking because the answer differs for each person.

My other point here is that the contemporary American answer is lacking. The unspoken assumption in contemporary American culture is that material success—earning lots of money—will provide a satisfying life. Arthur C. Brooks recently observed that this basic assumption of 21st-century American life is not compatible with research findings on this issue. If you have read Chapter 6 of this book, this will not come as a surprise. As you will recall from that chapter, Conscientiousness predicts life satisfaction more strongly than income. And a life devoted to the pursuit of money *for its own sake* may not be a life characterized by high levels of Conscientiousness. See Arthur C. Brooks, "Love people, not pleasure," *New York Times*, July 18, 2014.

3. By one estimate, the average worker in the 21st century can expect to have 19 different jobs during his or her working life; see Sarah Womack, "19 jobs for workers of the future," *Daily Telegraph*, February 25, 2004, www.telegraph.co.uk/news/uknews/1455254/19-jobs -for-workers-of-the-future.html. *Forbes* magazine has reported that 60 percent of young American workers now switch jobs every three years or less: Kate Taylor, "Why Millennials are ending the 9 to 5," August 23, 2013, www.forbes.com/fdc/welcome_mjx.shtml.

4. For the full text of Steve Jobs's 2005 commencement address, see "'You've got to find what you love,' Jobs says," Stanford University, June 14, 2005, http://news.stanford.edu/news/2005/june15/jobs-06 1505.html.

5. David Brooks, "The ambition explosion," *New York Times*, November 28, 2014, www.nytimes.com/2014/11/28/opinion/david -brooks-the-ambition-explosion.html.

6. Mark Shiffman, "Majoring in fear," *First Things*, November 2014, pp. 19–20.

7. "Tiger Mom" is a reference to Amy Chua, *Battle Hymn of the Tiger Mother* (New York: Penguin, 2011). "Irish Setter Dad" is a reference to P. J. O'Rourke's article "Irish Setter dad," *Weekly Standard*, April 4, 2011, www.weeklystandard.com/articles/irish-setter-dad_55 5534.html.

8. These details about Theron "Terry" Smith come from the Associated Press, "Ted Stevens plane crash: NTSB issues report on cause of crash that killed Alaska senator," *Huffington Post*, May 25, 2011, www.huffingtonpost.com/2011/05/24/ted-stevens-plane-crash-n _n_866585.html.

9. According to the published reports that appeared within hours of the plane crash—before any of the four survivors had been interviewed—the plane had taken off at around 3 p.m. that afternoon.

However, Willy and his mother, Janet, have told me that the plane took off around 11 a.m. that morning. More than six hours passed before anyone knew that they were missing.

10. The pilot who thought that no one could have survived the crash was Eric Shade, owner of Shannon's Air Taxi, as reported by Mark Thiessen and Becky Bohrer for the Associated Press, "Rescuers saw a waving hand," Boston.com, August 12, 2010, www.boston.com/news /nation/articles/2010/08/12/rescuers_saw_a_waving_hand. The description of the crash scene is taken from the remarks of Jonathan Davis, an officer with the Alaska Air National Guard, as reported by Jim Kavanagh, "Rescuers battled weather, terrain at Alaska crash site," CNN, August 11, 2010, www.cnn.com/2010/US/08/11/alaska.crash .conditions.

11. This description is taken from Thiessen and Bohrer, "Rescuers saw a waving hand."

12. This sentence is a paraphrase of Brooks, "Love people, not pleasure."

Conclusion

1. My call to "reevaluate our values" is an allusion to Friedrich Nietzsche's call for *Umwertung aller Werte*, a reevaluation of all values. Nietzsche's point is that in the traditional European world before the Enlightenment, most people looked to religion as the foundation of their values. In the contemporary world, many people no longer accept religious doctrine or the Bible as the foundation of their moral perspective. Nietzsche was arguably the first to recognize that in such a world, *nothing* about morality can be taken for granted. He made this point emphatically in one of his last books, *Twilight of the Idols*:

> Christianity is a system, a whole view of things thought out together. By breaking out of it a fundamental concept [*einen Hauptbegriff*], the faith in God, one destroys [*zerbricht*] the whole: nothing necessary remains between your fingers. . . . Christian morality is a command; its origin is

transcendent; it is beyond all criticism, all right to criticism; it has truth only if God is the truth, it stands and falls with faith in God. When the English actually believe that they know "intuitively" what is good and evil, when they subsequently suppose that it is no longer necessary to have Christianity as the guarantee of morality, that is merely the effects of the dominion of the Christian value judgment and an expression of the strength and depth of this dominion: such that the origin of English morality has been forgotten, such that the very conditionality [*das Sehr-Bedingte*] of its right to existence is not perceived. For the English, morality is not yet a problem.

The translation is my own. Where my translation departs from the usual English translations, I have shown the German original in brackets. Nietzsche uses the word "English" to mean "those who speak English." He had no interest in the distinctions between English, Scottish, Irish, Australian, and American. For more of my writing on Nietzsche, see my article "What was the cause of Nietzsche's dementia?" in the *Journal of Medical Biography*, volume 11, pp. 47–54, 2003, www.leonardsax.com/Nietzsche.pdf. Nietzsche's *conclusions* about values are very different from mine. But he and I start from the same *premise*: namely, that in a post-Christian era, nothing can be taken for granted. All values must be reevaluated. We now live in the world that Nietzsche prophesied in 1888, a world in which all moralities are in question. All values must therefore be reevaluated. My point is that if you do not undertake this task explicitly and seriously, and you happen to live in the United States today, then it is likely that your children will adopt the values of American popular culture, in which what matters most is the pursuit of fame, wealth, and good looks, or "whatever floats your boat."

2. Quoted in Alina Tugend, "Redefining success and celebrating the ordinary," *New York Times*, June 29, 2012, www.nytimes.com/2012/06/30/your-money/redefining-success-and-celebrating-the-unremarkable.html.

3. Here I am referring to Jennifer Finney Boylan, whom I cited at the close of Chapter 6. See her article "A Common Core for all of us," *New York Times*, March 23, 2014, Sunday Review, p. 4.

4. In Chapter 8, I described Beth Fayard and Jeff Jones as "Just Right" parents. In my conversations with Beth, more than once she has told me that she strives to teach her children that "every choice you make has immediate, far-reaching, and unforeseen consequences."

5. Here I am paraphrasing C. S. Lewis's comment about duties that are "not a sort of special exercise for the top class" but are mandatory. Lewis observes that when faced "with an optional question in an examination paper, one considers whether or not one can do it or not; faced with a compulsory question, one must do the best one can." See C. S. Lewis, *Mere Christianity* (San Francisco: Harper-Collins, 2009), pp. 195, 100–101.

Credits and Permissions

Index

promotes transfer of allegiance to same-age peers, 113

provides alternative culture, 108

Socialization in schools, 17–18

Sonya (fictitious name), 142–143

South Korea, 85

Spain, 84

Speed. *See* Amphetamines

Sports
overemphasis on, 85
teenagers' interests overcome by video games, 55, 108
time with family should be valued more, 72, 105–106

Stanford University 2005 commencement speech (Jobs), 191

Statusunsicherheit. See Role confusion of parents

Steve (fictitious name), 93–95

Stirling, Scotland, 25–27

Strattera, 65

Strictness
essential for authoritative parenting, 141, 168
and love for Just Right parenting, 142, 147–148, 169, 180–181

Strong Fathers, Strong Daughters (Meeker), 144

Strong Mothers, Strong Sons (Meeker), 144

Success in life, 125–126, 191–192, 193, 198

Sulking, 30

Suppertime. *See* Meals eaten as family

Swiss child and Japanese child, cultural differences, 14

Switzerland, 25, 71, 80, 83, 87
culture described, 14–15
kids eat lunch at home with parents, 111
no stigma attached to blue collar work, 188

Tantrums, 30
medications now used for control, 66
misdiagnosed as psychiatric illnesses, 53
as mood swings, bad behavior, 31, 49–50, 68

Tara McMaster (fictitious name), 3–4

Teacher training in Finland, 86

Teachers
bitten by defiant second-grader, 66–67, 68
low selectivity in training, 86
no longer allied with parents about student discipline, 155
some mistakenly encourage inflated self-esteem, 161–162

About the Author

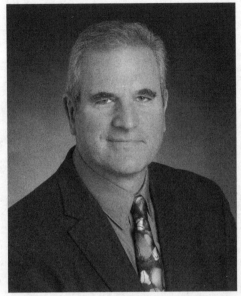

Leonard Sax, MD, PhD, is a practicing physician, a psychologist, and a speaker for community groups and for schools. The author of *Why Gender Matters*, *Boys Adrift*, and *Girls on the Edge*, Sax lives with his family in suburban Philadelphia, Pennsylvania.